W9-DII-407

WITHDRAWN

What's the Matter with the Internet?

Electronic Mediations

Katherine Hayles, Mark Poster, and Samuel Weber, series editors

VOLUME 3   *What's the Matter with the Internet?*
Mark Poster

VOLUME 2   *High Technē: Art and Technology from the Machine
Aesthetic to the Posthuman*
R. L. Rutsky

VOLUME 1   *Digital Sensations: Space, Identity, and Embodiment in
Virtual Reality*
Ken Hillis

What's the Matter with the Internet?

Mark Poster

Electronic Mediations

Volume 3

University of Minnesota Press

Minneapolis

London

Copyright 2001 by the Regents of the University of Minnesota

Chapter 1 was published in part in *Handbook for New Media,* edited by Sonia Livingstone and Leah Lievrouw (London: Sage Publications, forthcoming), and also in part in *New Media and Society* 1, no. 1 (April 1999): 12–18. Chapter 6 was originally published in *Philosophical Designs for a Socio-Cultural Transformation,* edited by Tetsuji Yamamoto (Tokyo: Rowman & Littlefield, 1998), 261–76; part of chapter 6 also appeared in *The Information Society* 15, no. 4 (October–December 1999): 235–40. An earlier version of chapter 7 appeared in *Cyberspace Textuality,* edited by Marie-Laure Ryan (Bloomington: Indiana University Press, 1999), 42–60. A modified form of chapter 8 originally appeared in *CyberSociety 2.0,* edited by Steve Jones (London: Sage Publications, 1998), 184–211. A different version of chapter 9 originally appeared in *Lusitania* 8 (December 1996): 67–78.

Published by the University of Minnesota Press
111 Third Avenue South, Suite 290
Minneapolis, MN 55401-2520
http://www.upress.umn.edu

Library of Congress Cataloging-in-Publication Data

Poster, Mark, 1944–
    What's the matter with the Internet? / Mark Poster.
       p.   cm. — (Electronic mediations ; v. 3)
    Includes bibliographical references and index.
    ISBN 0-8166-3834-9 (HC : alk. paper) — ISBN 0-8166-3835-7 (PB : alk. paper)
       1. Internet—Social aspects.   2. Culture.   I. Title.   II. Series.
    HM851 .P67   2001
    306.4'6—dc21   00-012951

Printed in the United States of America on acid-free paper

The University of Minnesota is an equal-opportunity educator and employer.

12 11 10 09 08 07 06 05 04 03 02 01   10 9 8 7 6 5 4 3 2 1

For Ketan and Natasha and their world

Contents

Acknowledgments   ix

ONE
The Culture of Underdetermination   1

TWO
The Being of Technologies   21

THREE
Capitalism's Linguistic Turn   39

FOUR
The Digital Subject and Cultural Theory   60

FIVE
Authors Analogue and Digital   78

SIX
Nations, Identities, and Global Technologies   101

SEVEN
Theorizing the Virtual: Baudrillard and Derrida   129

EIGHT
Virtual Ethnicity   148

NINE
CyberDemocracy: Internet as a Public Sphere?   171

Notes   189

References   197

Index   211

Acknowledgments

Although books appear under their authors' names, they represent in good part collaboration with numerous scholars in the field. I have benefited from responses to these chapters from very many people, from those who have listened to my presentations and posed questions; from colleagues at the University of California, Irvine, especially in the Critical Theory Institute and Emphasis, where my work has been scrutinized in an unusually collegial atmosphere; from the seminar "Media and Nations" in 1997 at the University of California Humanities Research Institute; from Katherine Hayles, who gave me numerous, often trenchant, suggestions for revision, some of which saved me from egregious errors; from my editor Douglas Armato; from Samuel Weber; from my friend Jon Wiener, who generously read and commented on my work; and finally from Annette Schlichter, who read these pages with a relentless critical eye and a warm heart.

In a new configuration of the virtual, an orthodox Jew at the sacred site of the Wailing Wall holds a cell phone so that a distant friend can pray. Photograph by Rina Castelnuovo/*New York Times Pictures*; reprinted by permission.

CHAPTER ONE

The Culture of Underdetermination

Electronic beams blow through the Iron Curtain as though it were lace.

—Ronald Reagan, speech in London, 1989

Culture and New Media

Culture has become a problem for everyone. What was once a safe ground of inquiry has shifted as if by some earthquake whose effects long went unmeasured on academic Richter scales. Culture is now an unstable terrain marked by the scars of two decades of discursive rumbles. Where you stand on the culture question immediately places you, a bit too precisely for the comfort of many, on the map of scholarly and even political dispute. The humanities, the arts, and the social sciences are now fractured into contentious subgroupings that run across disciplinary boundaries all by dint of that little word *culture*. Everyone wants to claim the term, yet when they do so *culture* receives new, unexpected meanings. Historians now practice empirical cultural history but find themselves slammed in the face of literary criticism and theory. Sociologists want to quantify culture, only to provoke the complaints of humanists who set in opposition number and subtlety, magnitude and meaning. Aestheticians decry the application of the term to popular culture. Anthropologists deconstruct culture and practice ethnography in the "advanced" societies. Adepts of cultural studies wonder if their discourse can survive departmentalization.

Minorities and subcultures of great variety raise the banner of culture and insist on recognition. Conservatives defend what they see as culture as if it were under attack by communism, terrorism, and Arabs. National cultures collapse into multiplicity. Avant-garde cultures are considered modern and therefore retrograde. Youth cultures are not simply rebellious but trickle up the social ladder, so to speak, to influence adult styles and habits. Genders are not biological but cultural, multiplying with the preferences and styles of their claimants. The most unstable groupings lay their claims to privileged cultural status: border cultures and even refugee camp cultures (Malkki 1995) become models for the rest.

Culture has lost its boundary. The high and low are mixed together. The finest creative sensibilities design packaging for commodities. The separation of culture from nature is in question. Scientists create animals in the laboratory. The air, the water, and the skies are polluted by the social activities of high-tech nations. Nothing stands outside the cultivatable, and so culture itself must be regarded as constructed rather than as given, historically contingent rather than timeless and certain. Skeptics say, If everything is constructed, then perhaps nothing is constructed. If everything emerges from a cultural process, the word *culture* has lost its specificity and coherence.

Despite this conflicted cacophony, the term *culture* remains useful, even essential, for studying new media. The paradox is this: without a concept of culture, the study of new media incorporates by default the culture of the dominant institutions in society. The state wishes, among other objectives, to perfect its system of control over the population so as to secure its territorial boundaries. Corporations and entrepreneurs want nothing more than to glean greater profits. These are the cultures of the state and the economy; these are their characteristic gestures and motivations. Imposing these aims upon new media, the state and the economy regard them as tools for a more convenient implementation. In short, they colonize new media with the culture of instrumentality. In their approach to the Internet, the state and the economy frame it as something that is useful to them, something that may improve their preexisting practices, make things go faster or more smoothly. Or not. These institutions are also concerned that the Internet might disrupt or hamper their ongoing activities: the state might be threatened by terrorists using the Net,[1] or banks and other financial institutions might be vulnerable to hackers. In either case, the question for them is instrumental: How will the Net benefit or harm their existing goals? Even when the state and the corporations look to the Internet for new ways of doing things, they do not put into question their foundations.

As long as we remain within an instrumental framework we cannot question it, define its limits, or look to new media in relation to how it might generate new cultures. In this way, the culture of instrumentality obstructs research on the Internet, research that might open up the question of culture.

The state and the economy are not the only institutions or groups that approach the Net in terms of their own culture: some of the democratizing political tendencies within the academy often exhibit similar impulses. The problem in this case is not exactly the culture of instrumentality, although at times it may be: it is rather the question of the subject, the self. In a collaborative volume on "race, class and gender on the Internet," the editor, Bosah Ebo, frames the work with the following question: "Will the Internet create a cybertopia or will it exacerbate class divisions by creating a cyberghetto?" (1998, 9). If the state and the corporations look to the Internet to perpetuate their positions of domination, scholars like Ebo look to it for signs of change among groups in positions of subordination. He asks if groups determined by race, class, and gender will, as a consequence of the Internet, improve their standing or recede further from positions of power. Here again the Internet serves as a tool for determining the fate of groups *as they are currently constituted.* Although this question is certainly legitimate, it is not critical of current cultural forms. Ebo and the authors in his book do not ask, in this regard, another question: How may the Internet mediate the transformation of existing cultural figures, or how may new cultural forms emerge that do not necessarily improve the position of existing groups as they are currently constituted but change them in unforeseeable ways? The question of culture in relation to the Internet involves a risk, a step into the unfamiliar precisely with respect to the figure of the self. If this question is foreclosed, one cannot examine critically the political culture of new media. One can merely put forward existing cultural figures of the self—race, class, and gender, or citizen, manager, and worker—to test the role of new media in furthering their positions as they see themselves and as they are. Such a framework is instrumental and overlooks systematically the constitutive character of media not in some form of technological determinism but as a space that encourages practices that, in turn, serve to construct new types of subjects.

There is a perhaps more subtle way in which critical studies refuses the cultural question of the Internet. In this case scholars do not so much presuppose existing forms of race, class, and gender. The uniqueness of the Internet is here fully recognized. But it is configured as a threat, not to specific groups but to general types of practice that are characterized as "human." Margaret Morse (1998), for instance, argues, "There is a basic human need for reciprocity and the reversibility of 'I' and 'you' in discourse—seeing and being seen, recognizing others and being recognized, speaking, listening and being listened to." And again: "There is a human need for and pleasure in being recognized as a partner in discourse, even when the relation is based on a simulation that is mediated by or exchanged with machines" (10, 14). The virtual quality of the Internet, Morse continues, undermines these human needs by its machinic mediation. She continues the lament noted above that the Internet promotes patriarchy and capitalism, but she is especially concerned that it erodes the "sociality" of "a well-functioning society" (35). For this cultural critic the Internet destabilizes community and undermines the felicity of face-to-face relations. As an aside one must ask, If humans are so needful of bodily presence, why do they so regularly turn away from each other and bury their heads in books and newspapers, stare vacantly at television, move somnambulistically with portable music players blaring in their ears, or gaze with fascination at a networked computer screen? If one assumes, as a cultural critic, that whatever intercedes between relations of presence detracts from the human condition, then one cannot investigate potentials for rendering cyberspace inhabitable, one cannot ask the political question of what to do about the Internet. Cultural critics are better served by acknowledging the innovation of the Internet and examining how democratic groups might explore it and act politically so as to assure its most beneficent configuration (McRobbie 1994).

To approach the cultural question of the Internet is no easy task. It so fundamentally shifts the registers of human experience as we have known them in modern society and even as they have been known through the ages. Time and space, body and mind, subject and object, human and machine are each drastically transformed by practices carried out on networked computers (Clough 2000). Even if one is aware of this and consciously acts in cyberspace as they do in territorial space, reproducing the motivations of the world of bodily presence, the effects of machinic mediation work just as surely to alter the human experience. What, then, can be the culture or cultures of cyberspace?

It is important not to pose this question in terms too stark. Cyberspace is surely no total departure from all previous history. Historians are right to remind us that the Internet does not mark the first reshuffling of the basic conditions of cultural formation as enumerated in the couplets above. From cave painting and smoke signals to writing and the alphabet, decisive shifts in the system of signification have accompanied humans throughout the past. In *Information Ages: Literacy, Numeracy, and the Computer Revolution*, Michael Hobart and Zachary Schiffman (1998) point out the long heritage of computer-generated information. What occurs with networked computing, they argue, began at least as far back as writing: the commutation of signification into information. "Information," they contend, "is . . . wedded to writing insofar as writing gives stability to the mental objects abstracted from the flow of experience, such that one can access them readily and repeatedly" (30). Writing thus changes the time and space of signification, making it endure and shifting it from resonating air to papyrus or paper. It changes the relation of signification to the body and mind, abstracting it from living beings and securing it in bound volumes. It alters the relation of subject and object, confirming signification as a practice of the subject but also affirming that signification subsists in the world of objects. Finally, writing shifts the relation of human to machine when printing began: signification would now require elaborate crafts, masses of capital, and collective labor.

If Hobart and Schiffman are wise to connect the Internet to earlier practices of signification, their insights need not deter us from formulating a problematic of the cultural novelty of cyberspace. We must turn to history for guidance in this project so as to acknowledge the constructedness of the Internet and to recognize its relations with earlier forms. Historical understanding alone enables the scholar to estimate the contours of the object under investigation as contingent and unfounded. But we must also turn to those deviant and most controversial historians of culture, Friedrich Nietzsche and Michel Foucault, who corrected the surreptitious reintroduction of foundationalism of historians seeing only the continuity of the present object with the past. The problem they raise for historians is to connect the present with the past in a way that undercuts the unreflective legitimacy of the present, that acknowledges lineage while allowing for innovation, that traces the links of rationality while holding open the emergence of the unexpected.

The study of the culture of the Internet, then, must seek in the analytics of man/machine, subject/object, body/mind, and time/space a new configuration of the construction of the subject. In the chapters that follow this is what I have sought to accomplish, if not in a final form, at least in a preliminary formulation. But more needs first to be said about the question of the subject. For it may be that this term is no longer useful in examining the Internet cultures.

Subject and Identity

We need to distinguish between the terms *individual, self, identity,* and *subject.* The term *individual* may be taken as an empirical given, an empty term that requires elaboration to specify its parameters in a given time and place. Similarly the term *self* refers in an undefined way to the mind, personality, soul, psyche of the individual. By contrast, the terms *identity* and *subject* are currently deployed in cultural analysis with much heavier meaning, much more theoretical and political weight than the former terms. *Subject* is used as the modern configuration of the self, best expressed in Descartes as ontological separateness from material objects, as the profound center of the individual, affording a distance from the world that enables the exercise of reason, reason that may grasp reality as certain truth. The figure of such an individual provides the legitimacy for most modern institutions—representative democracy, law, capitalist economics, science, education. Only if there is a prior and general sense that such a figure of the individual is viable does any argument for citizenship, the rational economic man, or long years of education in reading and writing make any sense. Of course all of this is determined in discourse at the ideological level. The "subject" then is the cultural basis for modern society.

Identity comes into discursive play when the coherence of the individual as a cultural figure begins to collapse. *Identity* was used seriously as an analytic term first in the 1950s by Erik Erikson (1968) precisely to step back from the Freudian subject and take an easier attitude toward the self. Instead of an autonomous agent who might control his or her destiny, instead of the subject of the progressive, humanist vision, Erikson presents an individual who is deeply confused about who he or she is. Erikson's self, far from a heroic bourgeois subject, goes through life as a series of crises, forming an ego that has a tentative stability, always under threat of defusion. This continually negotiated, fragile ego is what Erikson means by the term *identity*. Identity, then, is a renegotiated figure of subject that accounts for the failure of modernity to realize the metanarrative of progress. We need to keep in mind this massive cultural shift when we examine identity in relation to new media. The term *identity* is the recognition of the failure of Western culture, a failure inscribed in the massive disasters of the twentieth century. It is an ideological compromise that saves and masks traditional individualism, and adjusts it to such changes in culture as the disappearance of the proletariat, the emergence of consumer culture, the diffusion of electronic media, and the demise of Europe from world hegemony. When the term is carried over into the new social movements of women, minorities, sexual preference, and postcolonialism it carries the burdens of its past. Individuals defined as their identity are hardly agents in the sense of the figure of the subject.

The difficulty in using the term *identity* in the study of new media becomes clear in Manuel Castells's magnum opus, *The Information Age: Economy, Society, and Culture,* a heroic, three-volume effort to outline a general theory of information society from a critical perspective, a work that includes brilliant case studies of Japan and especially of Russia, as well as others. I cannot here even begin to present the arguments of *The Information Age*[2] and can only focus on the question of how to conceptualize the subject in relation to information. Castells recognizes the special need for understanding the cultural level when considering information as a leading aspect of society. In fact volume 2 of the work is entitled *The Power of Identity.*

Castells (1997) defines identity as follows:

> By identity...I understand the process of construction of meaning on the basis of a cultural attribute...that is...given priority over other sources of meaning. For a given individual, or for a collective actor, there may be a plurality of identities. Identities are sources of meaning for the actors themselves, and by themselves, constructed through a process of individuation.... they may become identities only when and if social actors internalize them, and construct their meaning around this

internalization.... identities are stronger sources of meaning than roles, because of the process of self-construction and individuation that they involve. In simple terms, identities organize the meaning while roles organize the functions. I define meaning as the symbolic identification by a social actor of the purpose of her/his action.... *in the network society*... for most social actors, meaning is organized around a primary identity... that is self-sustaining across time and space.... this approach is close to Erikson's formulation of identity.... the social construction of identity always takes place in a context marked by power relationships. (6–7)

One can agree with Castells on the difference between identities and roles. But his notion of identity relies heavily upon a model of consciousness, and this model works badly if one wishes to understand the role of the media in constituting the self. The problem becomes clear when Castells turns to that question. The media become instruments for the "projects" of groups resisting forces of domination. He writes:

Project identities emerge out of resistant identities such as ecological criticism which may end in plans for reorganizing society to be more compatible with natural limits, to integrating humankind with nature....

The same is true of the women's movement (feminism and sexual identity movements) and the resistance to patriarchy ending in more flexible identities around sex and family, affirm control of the immediate body over their disembodiment in the space of flows. (357, 358)

Nowhere in some fifteen hundred pages does he explore the relation of the self to the media in general or to particular configurations of self and media. The focus on identities impels the analysis, in a premature manner, toward resistant political questions. The issue is not the validity of these questions or even their urgency. Instead the problem is that such a focus loses sight of the important question of the way selves are formed in relation to different media. If one wants to highlight political resistance, one turns to a model, like that of identity, that grasps the moves of consciousness; if one wants to grasp how new configurations of the self are in formation, one must shift away from consciousness toward a model of language/media assemblages. The closest Castells comes to this problematic is a general parallel he makes between networking and new identities: "A *networking, decentered form of organization and intervention, characteristic of the new social movements,* mirroring, and counteracting, the networking logic of domination in the informational society. . . . [these networks] *are actual producers, and distributors, of cultural codes.* Not only over the Net, but in their multiple forms of exchange and interaction" (362). Castells is unable to say how the networks structure selves that act in organizations mirroring the Net. His level of analysis does not attain the micrological level of media practices.

The difference between the individual as subject and the individual as identity becomes exigent in relation to new media. Individuals are constituted as subjects or identities (as cultural selves) in linguistic practices. In repeated enunciations individuals become interpellated and recognized as coherent selves who function in a social world. Increasingly the process of interpellation occurs through mediations of information machines in addition to face-to-face interactions. First printed pages, then broadcast media, and now networked computing shift the scene in which the individual becomes and continues to practice selfhood. I use the term *postmodernity,* however contested it has become, to designate the shift in incidence from a combination of face-to-face and print arenas of interpellation to one that includes to an important degree broadcast media and networked computing.

The term *postmodern* designated for Lyotard (1984) the collapse of modern culture's metanarrative of progress and for Jameson (1991) a change in the culture of capitalism. In both instances *postmodernity* registered not an institutional transformation or an alteration of practices so much as a new figure of the self. *Postmodernity* certainly referred to social phenomena like the collapse of the distinction between high and low culture, or even a more general blurring of boundaries in all areas of everyday life. But the weight of the category bore most heavily on the process of subjectivation or the constitution of the self. For Lyotard the self was disengaged from historicity and for Jameson in addition it was fragmented, dispersed, low in affect, and one-dimensional. These theorists discerned a new figure of the self only through the backdrop of the older modern subject, the heroic bourgeois/proletarian agent. In both cases the trope for the change was tragedy, a fall from a higher place. In the study of the culture of new media that follows I keep this theoretical heritage in mind but also recognize the importance of framing the change to postmodernity in a way that opens the analysis to political possibilities, rather than closing the discussion with a large sigh of regret.

Those who would further the critical cultural study of the media have begun to recognize the need for a deployment of the term *postmodern* in a manner that makes it suitable for analysis without either a celebratory fanfare or sarcastic smirk. In the study of broadcast media, for instance, Lynne Joyrich (1996) argues persuasively that television brings consumer desires to the individual with an immediacy that undermines the separation of subject and object, the basic condition for the constitution of the self as subject (63). If this is the case, the cultural study of new media has no choice but to register this transformation with some term. Like Joyrich, I use *postmodernity* for this purpose.

The danger of the term, as she recognizes, it that it illicitly incorporates a certain universalism. Lyotard and Jameson certainly suffer from this tendency. Since the category of the subject was discursively inscribed as universal, even though it betrayed its conditions of birth in white, Western male culture, the suggestion that it has collapsed incorporated the same universalist gesture. The problem rests not with the aspiration for the universal as such but rather with the fact that the universal can only escape clandestine hierarchical resonances if it is enunciated universally, a condition that has never been possible in human history. Lacking such a condition, the universal must be approached with great caution. Until the enunciative conditions exist for the articulation of the universal, we must always stress the contingent quality of discursive claims, the situatedness of knowledge, as Donna Haraway (1991) says. The issue is not really who speaks but how they speak, how they recognize themselves and inscribe themselves in their discourse in relation to the Western pattern of the all-knowing, unconditioned subject. As a corrective to the universalist inscription of the term *postmodern* I suggest a focus on the specificity of the media in the process of self-construction.

Joyrich deploys the category of gender to much the same end. Gender operates to render specific and contingent the epistemological position of enunciation. But gender—along with race, class, sexual preference, and age—are not enough to deflect enunciation from reinscribing foundational identity. We can escape better, if never completely, this danger if we include the machinic and the space/time configuration specific to the scene of interpellation. If we are to study the culture of new media we need to take into account the information machines that increasingly mediate our symbolic practices. And these machines (be they print, broadcast, or networked computing) extract us from territorial spaces and phenomenological time, repositioning us in strange new ways. These media, of course, are not themselves born innocent but arise from existing patterns of hierarchy in relation to class, race, and gender. But they enable practices that fit badly with earlier complexes of domination, putting them into question and thereby opening the field—if we are not too defensive about and beholden to these older patterns—to new spaces of politics. This book will look at some of these spaces—ethnicity, the nation-state, democracy, capitalism—keeping these prospects in mind.

Joyrich (1996) recognizes the destabilizing effects of the multiple, fragmented self of postmodernity. She proposes a most promising stance toward the phenomenon: "I am trying neither to celebrate nor to lament postmodern fragmentation. Instead I hope to reveal the ways in which the sexed and cyborg body have been linked in both the televised and the critical imagination" (132). In her analysis she applauds television shows like *Peewee's Playhouse, Max Headroom,* and *Moonlighting* for their transgressive potential, although she reminds readers of their commercial and discursive limitations, even of their recuperating closures. What she pays less attention to, however, is the machinic level, that is, television as an information machine of the broadcast model that sets into play practices of self-constitution whose specificity and difference from other such devices, in particular books and networked computing, require elaboration. If television, like consumption, is associated in critical writing with the feminine, as she argues, those discourses also deal poorly with the machinic quality of this visual medium, either ignoring it or instrumentalizing it. It is to this crucial mediation that I want now to turn.

Underdetermination

Some social scientists tell us that media machines are different from mechanical machines in the crucial sense that we take them, consciously or unconsciously, as humans. Our brains, they say, formed and congealed in a time before information machines. Any machine that speaks to us, responds to our symbolized actions, frames pictures, and so forth, we assimilate, in our perceptions, as humans. Byron Reeves and Clifford Nass (1996) term this phenomenon "the media equation." After an extensive series of carefully controlled studies of interactions between human beings and machines, they conclude, "We have found that individuals' interactions with computers, television, and new media are *fundamentally social and natural,* just like interactions in real life" (5). In one study, at the conclusion of a test taken by computer, subjects were asked to evaluate the test first on the computer on which the test was taken and then on another computer. Just as when speaking about friends, the subjects responded far more favorably about the test when it was asked by the computer upon which the test was taken and gave more critical responses when the question was posed by another computer. The subjects of the experiment were not aware they were relating to media machines as humans and tended to deny outright that they were doing so when confronted by this fact. Nonetheless, this is, the authors argue convincingly, what occurs. "Mediated life," they assert flatly, "equals real life."[3]

There are numerous problems with the Reeves-Nass thesis. Certainly mediated life is not identical with real life. One can fall in love with a television personality, treat people on sitcoms as friends, speak to one's computer, and respond to it as one does to another person. But there are limits to the media equation. TV friends are not the same as actual friends: one cannot go shopping with them or play baseball with them. The computer may be a source of consolations and aggravations, but one cannot have a glass of wine with it. We may indeed respond to new media in ways very similar to our responses to friends, family, and associates, but the machines have characteristics and limits that are quite distinct from those of human beings. A body is not like a machine, however much our biological scientists may reduce it to a computer program or language.

Granting the basic, even ontological, differences between new media and humans, one must however acknowledge an important consequence of even the relative merit of the media equation. It is now imperative to study a new region of experience, the domain of the mediated, a domain that is imbricated with everyday life in a manner that is different from industrial society's man-machine relation. The first step is to recognize that new media and humans constitute relations that are different from those of human relations with natural objects and mechanical machines, on the one hand, and from human-to-human relations, on the other hand (Turkle 1995). So there is something new in the world, and we are called upon to account for it.

The question of the new requires a historical problematic, a temporal and stadial framework in which there are risks of setting up the new as a culmination, telos, or fulfillment of the old, or as the onset of utopia or dystopia. The conceptual problem is to enable a historical differentiation of old and new without initiating a totalizing narrative. Foucault's proposal of a genealogy, taken over from Nietzsche, offers the most satisfactory resolution of the problem because it attempts to see each emergence in relation to a field of forces and because it configures each in relation to its own systematicity. In this way the new emerges out of the past but also in a disruptive relation to it. And the new is thereby simultaneously legitimized as a historical construction and also delegitimized as less than a fulfillment of the past. The new is "just like" the old in the sense of its relative or historical construction with its own coherence but is also different from old in the sense that it contains different potentials for freedom and domination. If we look at the Internet from a genealogical point of view we might avoid technophobic demonization and naive celebration, and we might avoid overlooking what is genuinely different about it as well as greeting it as an impossible, absolute novelty.

What is new about the medium of the Internet—which I distinguish from print and broadcast media—is that as a machine, a thing in the world, an object extended in space, in short, as simply one more technological device, it is nonetheless *underdetermined*. Let me explain.

In the early part of the modern period, until perhaps the 1920s, print was the dominant symbolic medium. For the most part print sustained the figure of the subject, the agent, the free individual, over against the world of objects, as Descartes said, *res cogitans* against *res extensa*, constituting objects as malleable, as a world to be shaped to the ends of the subject though constrained by laws of nature. Although print, as Bible, sermon, and tract, furthered certain forms of religion or, as novel, incited the imagination of readers, it supported the construction and dissemination of the autonomous, rational individual. Newspapers, journals, and discourses, in their extensive distribution, were possible for the first time through print, through the mechanical reproduction of the cultural object. The citizen, the intellectual, the democratic subject of the nation-state—these characters who fill the landscape of modernity were inconceivable without print. The material character of print as disembodied signs, stable on the page, open to visual reception, and generally received in isolated circumstances all nurtured the growth of critical, cognitive functions and a cultural identity priding itself on these traits. The question is not whether this Cartesian subject is possible without print, is "real" in a transcendental sense. The historical fact is that with print that figure was born, grew, and came to dominate modernity, excluding numerous groups from its position, groups that, since then, too often dream of nothing else but attaining its seemingly ineluctable, glowing status. Print objects then were open to a relation with an other, a human, as a subject. Print objects were (and are) determinate, allowing/promoting/enabling/encouraging a relation of opposition in the shape of a subject. In Baudrillard's sense, we are in the domain of the real, of agents constituted as and thinking of themselves as capable of resisting the world around them.

With the coming of radio, film, and television, the subject/object relation of the modern period is in part extended and broadened. These media enable the disembodied distribution of identical cultural objects to much greater numbers and with much greater rapidity than print. Like books, cultural objects produced for broadcast media are received by large numbers of individuals remotely both in time and space from their authors, producers, and distributors. Since these media are electronic in form (in the case of film, quasi-electronic), they obey a different regime of space and time from paper. To some extent, radio, film, and television permit the flow of information from centers to peripheries more quickly and with greater spatial reach than do books, thereby sustaining the opposition malleable object/autonomous subject.

Yet, again as Baudrillard has shown, the electronic media, in their material form and their space/time regime, construct a hyperreal or simulacral world. In this technocultural landscape the subject/object relation changes. Instead of supporting a stable, centered identity, subjects are constituted as diffuse, fragmentary, multiple. The searing, angry critiques of broadcast media, from Adorno to Postman, register a perceived threat to the autonomous individual, either in their tyrannical monologues according to the former or their banality according to the latter (Postman 1985). But such jeremiads get us nowhere. In their nostalgia, they only deflect attention from the important task of understanding. Nor will it do to take the opposite approach of many in cultural studies who discover in the act of the reception of broadcast a transformed, original creativity and independence that bears too much resemblance to the subject of modernity. It is important to learn from cultural studies that the couch potato is also capable of writing zines, that novel, subcultural creations emerge in relation to mass cultural objects. But these efforts remain marginal until a means emerges of disseminating the reworked mass object, of producing and distributing it cheaply and widely. In the age of radio, film, and television such capabilities did not exist, so the broadcast model of few to many maintained its sway over culture and subject formation.

Faced with a simulacral object, the subject does not sustain its modern characteristics. A book or newspaper article invites a cognitive response, encourages an independent act of critique; a television advertisement invites an identification with the object in question, whether that television advertisement is about soap or a presidential candidate. This is surely not an absolute distinction. Print also elicits credulity. One says as if to nail down an argument, "I saw it in the newspaper," just as one says, "I saw it on TV" to achieve the same rhetorical end. The difference, however, is more compelling: the broadcast media structure objects that are both different from their originals and so deep in their own mediation that the referential function of language is reduced. Printed discourses and newspapers, at least in the modern period, appeared as representations of an outside world, nurturing the reader to reflect upon the representation as correspondence or contradiction. To some extent broadcast media perform the same operation but to a greater degree they undermine the relation of representation to an outside and foreground a relation of representation to themselves. Broadcast cultural objects are, in the first instance, their own representation. The question of their veracity measured against the real world may be asked, of course, but it appears less pertinent, less exigent. When great political events are broadcast, such as the 1991 Gulf War, one returns to the logic of representation (one thinks one is seeing the war) and one is sadly disappointed. Patriot missiles were not 80 percent effective, as televised in 1991, but 20 percent effective, as determined or revealed several years later. For the purposes of political mobilization in the United States, the controlled television broadcast of the Gulf War effectively produced consensus through the simulation of effective yet bloodless warfare. The Gulf War in the sense of actual battles of participants with deaths and casualties did not take place for TV viewers in the United States. Instead a simulation was aired and received, decisively shaping the domestic political situation. And the domestic political complexion had a good part to do with the ability of the U.S. government to continue the killing in the Gulf.

Broadcast media, then, shift and mix up the cultural registers of modernity, consisting in a technology of power, in Foucault's sense, that constitutes individuals as subjects in a way quite distinct from that of the world of print. This postmodern subject, who remains in part a modern subject, tends not to totalize him- or herself in a metanarrative of progress, as an agent who shapes, controls, and transforms the world of objects. The object (the cultural objects of broadcast media) has become too mobile, too self-representing, too enticing to sustain the subject in its older form. But even here in the world of broadcast media, subjects and objects retain their separation and distinction. Perhaps the objects have "fatal strategies," as Baudrillard maintains, or subjects are multiple, as the postmodernists contend. The hyperreal, though, remains tied to the real, and simulacra sustain their character by their difference from copies with originals. When the question turns to the new media, and, in particular, to the Internet, it is no longer clear if this is the case. The simulacral culture of broadcast media, then, in part strengthens the modern subject, in part constructs new objects without originals, and in part constructs new subjects as multiple and diffuse.

With the Internet, by contrast, we find objects before us whose determination is to a very considerable extent underdetermined. The Internet carries forward the modern subject/object relation by vastly increasing the efficiency of producing mass cultural objects and distributing them around the globe. The Internet carries forward the late modern broadcast subject/object by incorporating radio, film, and television and distributing them through "push" technology. But the Internet transgresses the limits of the print and broadcast models by (1) enabling many-to-many communications; (2) enabling the simultaneous reception, alteration, and redistribution of cultural objects; (3) dislocating communicative action from the posts of the nation, from the territorialized spatial relations of modernity; (4) providing instantaneous global contact; and (5) inserting the modern/late modern subject into an information machine apparatus that is networked. The result is a more completely postmodern subject or, better, a self that is no longer a subject since it no longer subtends the world as if from outside but operates within a machine apparatus as a point in a circuit.

Allow me to generate a concept of underdetermination to designate the machinic character of the Internet in contrast to the concept of overdetermination.

Louis Althusser (1970), with some reluctance, adapted the psychoanalytic term *overdetermination* to the context of social theory (87–128). In Freud, overdetermination designated the multiple causes of the onset of neurotic symptoms. A patient suffered because immediate traumas combined with older ones to produce symptoms. The "cause" of illness was not singular but wrapped up in the patient's long psychic history. For Althusser the term served to help differentiate Marx from Hegel. The question concerned the unity of phenomena in their contradictions. Althusser argued that the Hegelian dialectic was too unified to allow for contradiction. The process of negation was sublated into the center of consciousness, whereas in Marx determinations of an object could not be so homogenized. Superstructural or ideological determinations, for example, were distinct from those of the base, yet combined with them and related to them to form a conjuncture. Ideologies "reactivated" older elements that merge with new class conflicts, as the republicanism of ancient Rome was overlaid upon the French Revolution of 1789 or Pauline theology was invoked in Luther's break from Rome. A historical object, then, was a complex of distinct aspects, all combining, through the engine of contradiction, to "overdetermine" an outcome. Although this outcome may, for Althusser, be either a blockage of political change or an eruption of revolution, the term *overdetermination* has paradoxically come to suggest the contingency of events. Since social objects consisted of many discrete determinations, causality is not unilinear and history is governed by a law of complexity. Discourse cannot pin an event to a cause, and in this sense events are to an extent contingent or indeterminate. Event as outcome is fated but not singularly directed.

With the term *underdetermination,* I contend that certain social objects that I call virtual (hypertexts, for example) are overdetermined in such a way that their level of complexity or indeterminateness goes one step further. Not only are these objects formed by distinct practices, discourses, and institutional frames, each of which participates in and exemplifies the contradictions of capitalism and the nation-state, but they are also open to practice; they do not direct agents into clear paths; they solicit instead social construction and cultural creation. In a museum one contemplates a painting or even enters into an installation. In the former case one is moved by the sublime, the unpresentable in the work of art. In the latter case one forms the work of art while observing it, since by moving within it one may instigate changes in lighting or sound that are part of the installation. Downloading an image of a painting on the Internet, one may find the image within a program (such as Lview) that allows the viewer to alter any aspect of the image, not just to signal a light or sound as in the programmed structure of the installation, but to reconstruct the image from inside out, displacing it into a text, and with an HTML composer, adding sound to it or combining it with other images. The image on the Internet is virtual in the sense that it only becomes actual through the countless transformations it undergoes as people copy it and change it. A type of object thus emerges into social space that is overdetermined in the sense of being structured through multiple contradictory practices but is also underdetermined in the sense that it remains an invitation to a new imaginary.

One may argue that this is always the case, that "virtualization" is the normal, not the new, state of things, that books are as indeterminate as hypertexts, for instance. Lévy considers this question and argues, as a philosopher, for the transcendental possibility of the always already, that what may be conceived now, may be conceived at any time. While in principle one cannot disagree with the philosopher, as a historian I would rather assert that the transcendental is a condition of thought, not a condition of history. I prefer to acknowledge the logic of the transcendental but defend against projecting it as a conceptual tool for historical analysis, in short ontologizing it. Thus in the realm of the actual and the real, the structure of objects and subjects, while never absolutely fixed but always open to resymbolization, maintains a consistency of presence in space and time. In modern society, for example, objects and subjects appear never as a full presence but as a presence whose absence is rendered difficult by its material root in space and time. The phenomenon of virtualization, what I call "a mode of information," enables subjects and objects increasingly to appear in configurations of space and time, mind and body, human and machine that disaggregate the real/actual into constellations of indeterminate—not amorphous—complexity. What is above all necessary is to specify the parameters of these "virtual" configurations. What are objects like in electronic communities? What are they like in helmet-and-glove virtual reality technologies? What are they like on e-mail, computerized databases, World Wide Web pages, Internet Relay Chat channels? How are identities associated with the body, such as gender and ethnicity, configured in these virtual "places"? How are these genders and ethnicities different from and similar to those of television shows, telephone conversations, synchronous meetings, serendipitous urban encounters, massed refugee camps, and rural dwellings?

In this sense one may theorize and study the Internet as an underdetermined object that constitutes the self in configurations that are outside those of the modern and late modern subject. A word of caution is in order, however. The Internet is changing rapidly so that statements about it and studies of it must be received as tentative. For example, scholars routinely argued that the Internet was male-dominated, but in 1998 more women than men went on-line for the first time. Not only is the demography of the Net changing, but its material infrastructure is also in a continual flux. Non-U.S. hosts now equal U.S. hosts; intranets are spreading rapidly; text is less and less the dominant format as sound and graphics increase; the sales function of the Net is increasing; but games and pornography are still prevalent. Cable modems challenge telephone modems, but telephone service is expanded to wider bandwidths. Telecommunications corporations are rapidly replacing copper with fiber-optic cable, promising speedier transmissions. Complaints about the corporate takeover of the Net must be modified to recognize that without the resources of private enterprise, truly wide bandwidth communications—fast enough for real-time transmission of moving images with sound—would not be possible. At the level of the provider, AOL dominates today, but media conglomerates, software manufacturers (such as Microsoft), and hardware producers (IBM, Sun) all eagerly seek the market of the Internet. The outcome of the convergence of computing, telephones, and television is impossible to forecast. Because of these and other ongoing transformations, students of new media must be modest in their claims and hypothetical in their voices. This book is presented very much in that spirit.

My study is organized in a pattern of theoretical elaboration followed by exploration of domains of the Internet. The theoretical texts and concepts attempt to clarify the issues at stake in investigating the culture of new media. Chapter 2 looks at Heidegger's provocative work on technology and being. Chapter 4 poses the issue of the subject in relation to new media by way of Foucault's theory of the author and the feminist critique. Chapter 7 examines the question of virtuality through a critical discussion of the work of Baudrillard and Derrida.

The other chapters apply the conceptual work of the earlier chapters to the interplay of cultural domains and cyberspace. Chapter 3 looks at digital commodities. Chapter 5 discusses the emergence of digital authorship. Chapter 6 speculates about national identities and global citizenship. Chapter 8 raises the issue of the fate of ethnicity and race in electronic space. Chapter 9 brings a critical stance to discussions of the democratizing effects of the Internet.

Throughout this study I have attempted to sustain a framework that keeps open the possibility that the Internet affords an opportunity for a contribution to a new politics, that it may play a significant role in diminishing the hierarchies prevalent in modern society and in clearing a path for new directions of cultural practice. It is all too obvious that existing institutions have availed themselves of new media, expanding their reach and control and increasing their powers. Yet I believe that an exclusive focus on these dangers, however well intentioned, incurs the rhetorical effect of paralysis and closes off chances of critique and new political moves. I am by no means optimistic about these chances, but such a perspective is, I think, in the finest tradition of critical theory.

CHAPTER TWO

The Being of Technologies

Terms and Confusions

The term *technology* is particularly difficult to define and to translate. In one sense there is no problem: the English *technology* is uniformly translated in French as *la technique* and in German as *die Technik* or *Technologie.* The root of the term in all three languages is the Greek *technikos,* "pertaining to art." But here the difficulties begin. *Technology,* in the *Oxford English Dictionary,* is defined as discourse about the arts, whereas *technique* is defined as simply the arts or skills used in crafting something. In French, *la technique* is closer to the English term *technique* than to *technology,* and there is a term in French *la technologie,* even though it is seldom used in translating its English homonym. What is worse, the English term *technology* refers in the first instance in common parlance not to discourse about technique, not to skill in craftsmanship, and certainly not to the arts, but rather to machinery, to the apparatus of tools. In addition, the term *machinery* is understood as a valid general category, indicating that all machines have something in common. I will argue that this usage of the term *technology* is particularly misleading in the age of "smart machines." The only modifier for *technology,* "high technology," refers to advanced assemblages of machines but does not distinguish clearly between particular types such as mechanical or electrical, or machines that generate energy versus machines that manufacture objects, or, what is decisive now, machines that work upon natural materials versus machines that work upon information or cultural objects. The term *technology* is thus fraught with semantic difficulties, an issue that must be kept in mind in what follows.

Intellectuals in France, and in the West more generally, have two opposing responses to technology. One view sees technology as beneficial to the humanist project of diminishing toil, eliminating disease, and pacifying the earth. In this spirit Denis Diderot assiduously studied the techniques of his day, visiting centers of production and arranging for drawings to be included in *L'encyclopédie*, the great monument of the Enlightenment, depicting the most advanced methods of production. Diderot endeavored to further human progress by disseminating as widely as possible knowledge about the practical sciences, knowledge that earlier remained the secret province of guilds. Diderot (1965) defined the purpose of *L'encyclopédie* and predicted its future influence with these words: "Discoveries in the arts will no longer run the danger of being forgotten; facts will become known to the philosophers, and reflection will be able to simplify and enlighten blind practice" (159). The perfection of tools went hand in hand with human perfectibility, which Condorcet, a generation after Diderot, predicted would continue indefinitely into the future. Against these optimists have stood those finding grave dangers in technology. From Blaise Pascal's skepticism toward progress in the seventeenth century to Jacques Ellul's horror in the face of advanced industrial society, these thinkers have warned against the seductions of the machine, its potential to corrupt humanity. In general the first group are instrumentalists, understanding technology as a neutral tool that only becomes objectionable by the uses to which it is put. The second group, termed *substantialists* by Andrew Feenberg (1991), discern significant effects to any implementation of technology, whatever their moral outcomes.

What both groups share in common, however, is a comprehension of technology as machines for acting upon natural materials. From the hammer to the robot, technology remains an instrument to shape and reshape matter. By the late twentieth century a new order of machines increasingly populate human societies, machines that have their effects not upon matter but upon symbols. These information machines, or smart machines, as Shoshana Zuboff (1988) calls them, generate, transmit, and store text, images and sound. The most compelling and fecund questions about technologies concern these smart machines, of which the computer is the emblem. Earlier discussions of technology are often misleading or inadequate when applied to information machines. The instrumentalist position fails to recognize the transformative powers of information machines, whereas the substantialist position gears its critique of technology to processes that have little play when acting upon matter is not at issue. The terms of the debate over technology must be reconceived in relation to the emergence of qualitatively new kinds of machines. The relation of information machines to society, culture, and politics must be assessed with respect to its own problematics.

The failure to distinguish between machines that act upon matter and those that act upon symbols mars the humanist critique. Ellul (1964) defines technology *(la technique)* not as machinery but as instrumental-rational practice. "In our technological society," he writes, "*technique* is the *totality of methods rationally arrived at and having absolute efficiency* (for a given stage of development) in *every* field of human activity" (xxv; italics in original). His purpose in *The Technological Society* is to gauge the effects of technology thus understood upon economics, politics, and society in general. In each case the effects he discerns are baleful. But can the same complaint be raised against information machines? On this question Ellul is silent. The issue is particularly grave because information machines upset the position from which the critique of mechanical machines was raised, the view of humans as agents or subjects distinct from and in a stance of opposition to a world of objects. Information machines put into question humanity as instrumental agent and thereby disqualify the critique of technology as "dehumanizing."

Theorists of information machines reproduce the bifurcation of the discussion of earlier technological regimes but with differences connected to the specific features of this system of techniques. One salient change characterizes the new discussion: everyone agrees that information technologies are substantive, that, to embellish the celebrated words of Marshall McLuhan, the medium *shapes and transforms* the message. Information machines transform the humans that use them. For McLuhan they alter the ratio of the senses from one of ocular priority, during the age of mechanical machines and print, to one of tactile primacy during the age of electronic machines. In France, Jean Baudrillard and Paul Virilio have most fruitfully carried forward the critique of technology in relation to the question of how the subject is reconfigured in relation to information machines. Here the focus has been not so much on the sense ratio of McLuhan but on language, in the case of Baudrillard, and space, in the case of Virilio.

Baudrillard's early work concerned not technology but consumption. Instead of attending to the question of the forces of production, he launched a critique of Marxism by arguing for the importance, even the priority, of the domain of consumption. With the aid of semiology, Lacanian psychoanalysis, and anthropological theory, Baudrillard articulated a shift in social importance from production to consumption. In 1981 with *Simulacra and Simulation,* however, he began to explore the effects of communication technologies in terms of a basic change in the construction of reality: the media produced hyperreality, undermining the credibility of representational discourse to capture "the real." The culture of print, with its newspapers and books, gave way to the electronic cultural construction of the television screen. Here signs are constructed in a new way, one that eludes the logic of a discourse that depends on originals that it can symbolically reproduce. Electronic media construct and present a world of symbols and images that exists only on the screen. They broadcast simulacra that bear no clear relation to a prior reality. Television reproduces and expands the semiotic logic of advertising: it uncouples the signifier from the signified and the sign from the referent, opening a new space of cultural production.

Baudrillard's exploration of the hyperreal extended generally throughout advanced industrial society: from Disneyland to malls, from the deserts of California to the postmodern architecture of Beaubourg. He never restricted his analysis to a particular technology and never defined his cultural critique in relation to technology. Yet it appeared that television was the engine of the hyperreal. Before the television monitor, the individual participates in a new cultural space in which the definition of truth is altered. No longer a correspondence to reality, no longer posing the critical question ("What relation does what I see bear to what I know?"), televisual epistemology asks rather, "Does what I see hold my attention or urge me to switch channels?" The truth of television is the Nielsen rating system: being in front of the screen and tuned into a show is the only criterion for judging the validity of the show. Without a ground in a real "behind" the simulacra, truth becomes WYSIWYG, "What you see is what you get." The implications of information technology are revolutionary: liberal and Marxist positions dissolve in favor of a postmodern logic of the hyperreal.

Baudrillard's broad reception hinged on his acute portrayal of the culture of the simulacra. Infuriating to many but intriguing to most, Baudrillard's essays outlined a world in which the humanist discourse of enlightenment seemed ineffective or even irrelevant. The mere presentation of hyperreality offended and threatened liberals and Marxists alike. When he wrote in *Libération* that "the Gulf War did not take place," the Left and Right alike shook their heads in disbelief (Baudrillard 1995b). Yet Baudrillard's own relation to simulacral culture was always deeply mixed with anxiety and disgust. His writings oozed with the spleen of the very humanist culture that found him outrageous. Indeed the limits of Baudrillard's perception of emerging postmodernity are drawn by his reluctance to take seriously the technological component in the new structuration of culture. His continued adherence to the humanist scorn of *la technique* prevented a deeper exploration of an emergent mode of information. His categories of simulacra and hyperreal, disjunct from their technological imbrication, retain a relation of opposition to the true and the real, failing to go the next step to a perception of the virtual as a new combination of real and imaginary.

The revulsion toward the postmodern evident in Baudrillard's writing was even more pronounced in Virilio's. If Baudrillard addressed mainly consumer culture and the television media, Virilio focused on war and the media of cinema. More than Baudrillard, Virilio knew about and was attuned to technological innovations of the twentieth century. His early books linked warfare and cinema through their technical connections. Virilio crossed the boundaries of political analysis, architectural engineering, and cultural studies with novel and fascinating explorations of their interconnections. In his hands the study of technology spread into the arts and the domain of culture seeped back into the sciences and their applications in society. Martin Heidegger's noteworthy phrase "The essence of technology is nothing technological" achieved in Virilio's work empirical validation. In *Speed and Politics* (1977) and *War and Cinema* (1984), Virilio opened new paths to the understanding of the present by shamelessly mixing and recombining the cultural and the technological. If Heidegger achieved a philosophical critique of technology as culture, Virilio accomplished a detailed and convincing analysis of technology as culture and the culture of technology.

For Virilio speed was the key to understanding the twentieth century, and this required a mixture of technological and cultural analysis that forever changed both terms. "Dromology," his term for a new science of speed, combined the study of the perception of the passage through space with the vehicles, the technology, by which space was transgressed. He provided stunning examples of the cross-fertilization of technocultural fields: the influence of war on cinema and the reverse, the impact of aerial photography on the cultural experience of space, and so forth. In later works, such as *La vitesse de libération* (1995), Virilio turned his attention to the virtual spaces created in computer networks and the speed associated with electronic communications. Here the darker side of technology seems to grow in importance. The simultaneity of e-mail and chat modes on the Internet completely erases spatial factors and implodes time. The vectors of space and time are drastically reconfigured in the new technologies. They allow and even promote, he warns, forms of eroticism that threaten to destroy basic social institutions. Like Baudrillard, Virilio's awareness of and fascination with technologies of information induce in him high anxiety levels and evoke "alarms" about the future of civilization. Yet Virilio's work, in a different but parallel way from Baudrillard's, pioneers a heuristic combination of technological and cultural analysis in relation to specific machinic formations.

A continuing problem in the work of both is a residual dread of the machinic that derives not from a proper cautionary sense about innovations but from humanist assumptions about the relations of machines to people. Neither is prepared to recognize a new planetary relation of humans to machines based on the emergence of new kinds of information machines as well as a continuing, rapid dissemination of both industrial and postindustrial machines. By the late twentieth century machines populate the earth in considerable numbers and variety. Two basic questions that need to be posed about technology at this point are, Synchronically, how do we understand the combinations of humans and machines? And diachronically, do we dare ask if humans are a stage in a development of which machines are the inheritors of the planet? Initiatives in these directions were begun by Pierre Lévy and Félix Guattari.

Pierre Lévy opens a new level in understanding information machines as a new kind of object and as evoking a new kind of human subject. In works such as *Collective Intelligence* (1994) and *What Is the Virtual?* (1995), Lévy focuses on such objects as the Internet and hypertext, characterizing them as a domain of complexity in which humans are transformed, indeed transported into a new kind of community. The virtual world of the Internet connects human intelligence from around the globe, installing in principle a new structure of interaction. Here space and time, body and mind, and subject and object are all reshaped by the parameters of the communication technology. Not Baudrillard's hyperreal but Lévy's virtual begins to render intelligible the ontology of the Internet. Modern philosophy understands objects as resulting from a process in which a potential is realized or a virtual possibility becomes actual. With phenomena like a computerized hypertext or a networked real-time community or a helmet-and-glove virtual reality (VR) system, we are confronted by objects whose structure is so indefinite that they must be characterized as virtual, not actual. These objects, through their interfaces, open to the human subject in such a manner that the subject is immersed within them and reconstituted as an element of the object. In VR systems participants are part of the computer-generated world and experience themselves as such. Object and subject combine and reshape each other in new paradigms of existence, into the realm of the virtual.

These new technologies are objects like none before them also in the sense that, especially in the case of the Internet, they are thoroughly decentralized. Whereas mechanical machines are inserted into hierarchically organized social systems, obeying and enhancing this type of structure, the Internet is ruled by no one and is open to expansion or addition at anyone's whim as long as its communication protocols are followed. This contrast was anticipated theoretically by Gilles Deleuze and Félix Guattari especially in *A Thousand Plateaus* (1980), in which they distinguished between arboreal and rhizomic cultural forms. The former is stable, centered, hierarchical; the latter is nomadic, multiple, decentered— a fitting depiction of the difference between a hydroelectric plant and the Internet. In *Chaosmosis* (1992), Guattari, in a critique of Heidegger's machinic synecdoche of the hydroelectric plant in "The Question concerning Technology" (1955), elaborated this opposition into an ontology of the "heterogenesis" of machines, the most rigorous effort thus far to comprehend the being of machines outside a humanist framework. Guattari attempts an ontology of machines outside all subject-based perspectives, such as psychoanalysis. He develops a category of the assemblage to suggest combinations of machines and humans in surprising and unanticipated configurations. The question concerning technology, then, is no mere exercise about the destruction of nature by the irresponsible deployment of machines or the loss of human reality into machines or even the cultural "misshaping" of the human by its descent into the instrumental, the bringing forth or challenging or enframing of the human by the technological. Instead the conservative, "sensible" question of technology is now one of the nature of the cyborg, of the new order of humachines. And the rigorous or outrageous question of technology must be the possible inheritance of the globe by a species we call "machines" but whose nature we can barely foresee.

The Question concerning Heidegger

These are profound, even overwhelming, questions, and no one has posed them more acutely and suggestively than Heidegger. At first glance a resort to Heidegger may seem inappropriate in this context, since he is known for attributing to modern technology "the spiritual decline of the earth." Yet his antipathy to technology is matched by his sensitivity to its importance, as in the following:

> At a time when the farthermost corner of the globe has been conquered by technology and opened to economic exploitation; when any incident whatever, regardless of where or when it occurs, can be communicated to the rest of the world at any desired speed; when the assassination of a king in France and a symphony concert in Tokyo can be "experienced" simultaneously; when time has ceased to be anything other than velocity, instantaneousness, and simultaneity, and time as history has vanished from the lives of all peoples; when a boxer is regarded as a nation's great man; when mass meetings attended by millions are looked on as a triumph—then, yes then, through all this turmoil a question still haunts us like a specter: What for?—Whither?—And what then? (Heidegger 1959, 31)

So Heidegger is no simple technophobe.

To the end of carrying forward and clarifying further the theoretical issues of the matter of technology a scrupulous reexamination of his position is required. I undertake such an interrogation with no interest in an overall evaluation of Heidegger's work and certainly not of his life or his lamentable political commitments.[1] I wish to hold in suspense or better to bypass the effects of "the author function," as Foucault calls it, whereby evaluations of discourse are placed in reference to a name, an author's name as the final level of consideration (1984, 101–20). I turn to Heidegger's essay "The Question concerning Technology" with the single concern of delimiting its discursive accomplishments and confusions and with the hope, still flickering in its Enlightenment lamp, that this will contribute to allaying some anxiety in those who so greet the topic. I pose the following question to the text: To what extent can Heidegger's discussion be applied to information technologies? And I reply: Not very much.[2]

Heidegger's argument may be summarized, however inadequately, as follows. The question of technology is not about technology per se but about modern humanity's way of being. Technology is fundamental to modern "culture," a term I will use for Heidegger's *Dasein*. This relation of technology to culture is always important since humanity brings itself forth in part through its way of using things, its arts and crafts. The peculiar aspect about humanity is that it brings itself forth in order to be and must recognize this process as it is happening in order to have a free relation to itself. But modern technology is a way of using things and bringing humanity into appearance that conceals this process, does violence to nature ("challenges" it), and finally ends in treating humanity with the same violence that it treats nature. Heidegger calls this way of being or culture of technology "enframing." If mankind can recognize the process of enframing for what it is, joggle its consciousness to understand the grave stakes in its deployment of technology, then it may establish a different relation to itself and to technology, one that is free in the sense that it recognizes and accepts its own cultural form, its own being. Heidegger's solution is not to abandon technology in some return to nature but to offer a spiritual shift in which technology would become entirely different from what it is.

One may approach "The Question concerning Technology" from a rhetorical point of view. In this case, Heidegger tells the reader a story: there is "an extreme danger" facing humanity. His tale, he says somewhat coyly, is "almost harmless" (1977, 20), but as a result of listening to the tale we may be saved and be free. Within this charming and alarming tale there is an argument. And within this argument Heidegger reflects on his own writing and is surprised to discover that the topic, technology, is actually important, if not apocalyptic (30). In narrative form we have an American Gothic tale or horror movie with a possible happy ending. As a consequence of hearing the story one must be frightened by the imminent and horrible danger facing us all; yet thanks to Heidegger, there is a way out. The escape is not high-tech, as in James Bond movies, but is achieved through thinking, through becoming a philosopher (what else would one expect a philosopher to propose?). The narrative also partakes of the suspense genre. The danger to the characters ("man") is hidden from them, though the narrator, an omniscient voice if ever there was one, lets the audience know about it. The narrator himself is in a dangerous position: he is revealing a danger to the reader but one that might backfire. If the story is not effective, the audience might feel manipulated and get angry at the narrator, not believing there is any danger at all. So Heidegger protects himself by insinuating that what he has to say is after all harmless. If one does not become exhilarated at the prospect of being saved, one may still forget the harmless story and go on with one's life.

The effectiveness of the horror story depends on convincing the audience that there is a terrible danger. The audience must be scared. This is particularly difficult since Heidegger thinks that the danger is dangerous because it is concealed and hidden. If it is concealed the audience cannot know about it beforehand but must learn of it from Heidegger's tale. Heidegger must somehow present technology as a danger, reveal it, bring it out into openness in such a way that everyone will come to see the horror of it. Since everyone already is quite familiar with technology, Heidegger is confronted by a difficult rhetorical task. To accomplish it he turns to a tried-and-true method, the flashback. The flashback is able to shake up the audience, take it out of its normal consciousness, like a Brechtian alienation effect, by moving to another point in time. Heidegger moves to ancient Greece, a time, he thinks, when the danger did not exist. In Greece technology was different, was not hidden but part of the openness to Being of that culture. After glimpsing a different imbrication of technology in culture through the flashback, the reader can appreciate the horror of his or her own circumstance.

I shall present my evaluation of "The Question concerning Technology" in terms of five theses. The first thesis is that culture is invisible to its members or, in relation to technology, that the instrumental attitude commonly attributed to technology obscures its cultural aspect. Outside of the academic disciplines of the humanities, technology is treated as a neutral tool for the accomplishment of pregiven ends and is judged by an economic criterion of efficiency. This understanding of technology places it within a social world composed of rational, autonomous agents and passive objects. Heidegger brilliantly and convincingly shows how one must step back from such a social world and see how technology is no mere object or set of objects within it but rather is the way this world is set up or brought forth. And the setup includes human beings within it so that the traits one normally ascribes to technologies also apply to human beings.

The essence of technology is then a way of being in the world, a manner of appearing to oneself and others such that everything emerges as ready at hand for use or as a "standing reserve," or as prefigured for instrumental action. Such making things ready for use involves a drastic reduction of other possible ways of being in the world, so drastic that Heidegger terms it a "challenging." To transform the Rhine into an energy source by means of the technology of the hydroelectric plant is for Heidegger a severe, unlikely form of acting upon things. And yet we moderns are within this frame in such a manner as to be unaware of its cultural form. As a result of the unconscious quality of our relation to our framing of things, we do not perceive the setting up of the scene in which we act and take our own cultural shapes. The problem Heidegger raises concerning technology is not simply that it rudely transforms nature and our relation to others but that our own being in the world is invisible to us.

The second thesis is that one can dispel this invisibility by studying ancient Greek philosophy. Heidegger goes back to another culture (the Greek) as a point of difference, in order to distance himself from today's culture and thereby to see it as from outside and thereby also to depict it, to define its limits, to critique it. Greek artisanal culture is a different framing, a different setup, one that in qualitative terms is just as much a determining of being, just as serious a form of bringing forth both objects and subjects. But it is so in a manner, he thinks, that draws attention to the process itself, letting it emerge as a realization of Being. Precisely because humans are not prefigured as agents counterposed to an object world that is other to them they paradoxically are able to perceive their agency within Being. The modern, privileged agent is for him less of an agent, a diminished agent, because it is cut off from its relation to Being, conceiving itself as transcendent to objects rather than within Being and as a being whose being can only exist as a bringing forth or an appearing.

The third thesis is that the return to Greece is taken as a discovery of "the truth." The Greek way of bringing forth is at some level *the* way. It establishes human beings in a relation to Being that Heidegger once termed "authentic" and continues in "The Question concerning Technology" to treat in a similar fashion. From the Greeks Heidegger learns that bringing forth entails revealing, for example. From this he concludes that the main understanding of technology in the modern West—as a tool—is simply wrong. In no uncertain terms he pronounces, "Technology is therefore no mere means. Technology is a way of revealing" (12). Heidegger is aware that he may be accused of universalizing the local conditions of Greek technology, that technology may have been a revealing for the Greek but remains a means for "modern machine-powered technology." Heidegger insists that modern technology is a revealing but agrees that it differs from the Greek in that the latter was a revealing as poiesis, whereas the former is a revealing as "a challenging, which puts to nature the unreasonable demand that it supply energy that can be extracted and stored as such" (13–14). As a result modern revealing is a concealing that blocks human beings from entering into a free relation to technology. In italics Heidegger states flatly: *"In truth . . . precisely nowhere does man today any longer encounter himself, i.e., in his essence"* (27). The important words here are "any longer," as if man once did so encounter himself *[sic]*. It was of course in the time of the ancient Greeks that this encountering occurred.[3] The Greek way of revealing in technology provides Heidegger with a basis to critique the modern but in a manner that places the Greeks as the limit case. Heidegger frames his departure to the Greeks as "the truth," elevating his critique into universality and losing its specificity and power to the disciplined gesture of the philosopher—as in *the* human essence.[4]

The fourth thesis is that the philosopher's transcendentalism still affords an understanding of technology as culture. He does give us a beginning point in the theorization of the relation of technology to culture by allowing us to see technology as a culture, what he calls a revealing. In the current conjuncture it is essential to insist upon this point and to underline it.

The fifth thesis is that this understanding is flawed by its inability to discern different technologies, different technocultures, different modes of revealing.[5] In his Greek-dominated insistence on the question of the essence Heidegger underplays the search for difference. All technologies are, in essence, modes of revealing, but all modern technology reveals as enframing. The limits of this position are that it captures the revealing of modern technology only, not postmodern technology—of technology in its debt to physics and in its "unreasonable" action upon nature, not technology as information processing, storage, and dissemination. Heidegger considers the question of the multiplicity of technologies: "Is then the essence of technology, Enframing, the common genus for everything technological? If that were the case then the steam turbine, the radio transmitter, and the cyclotron would each be an Enframing" (29). He complains that he does not mean essence as a genus, a category that includes like singulars. Instead, in its form as revealing, the essence of technology, its inner cultural form, is what he calls "challenging," in which both the turbine and the transmitter are included. I contend that some information technologies, in their complex assemblages, partake not only of enframing but also of forms of revealing that do not conceal but solicit participants to a relation to Being as freedom.[6] And these do so not as a return to the Greeks but as a departure, as a new imbricated configuration of human and machine, ensconced with a new space-time continuum eliciting new combinations of body and mind, object and subject.

The very strength of Heidegger's treatment of technology as culture is also its weakness. Technology is one thing for him, a unified field, a homogeneous domain that he connects so brilliantly to the deepest issues of human life. To the extent that technology is not so unified his analysis loses its force, or so I will argue.

Technology is often treated as unitary both from the favorable perspective of toolmaking and progress and from the negative standpoint of degradation and loss. Heidegger has no sympathy for the former position, but in many places he betrays an affinity with the critics of technology. In these places he presents the commonplace jeremiad of technology as the loss of high culture, the descent into mass society. In *An Introduction to Metaphysics* from 1953 he writes, "From a metaphysical point of view [one that is not necessarily his own], Russia and America are the same; the same dreary technological frenzy, the same unrestricted organization of the average man" (1959, 31). In nationalist terms, Germany may provide the antidote to the twin superpowers surrounding it to the extent that it resists technology. But Heidegger also goes beyond this critique of technology as mass culture when he perceives this critique as itself part of the phenomenon it depicts. In "The Turning" (1949) he warns, "All attempts to reckon existing reality morphologically, psychologically, in terms of decline and loss, in terms of fate, catastrophe, and destruction, are merely technological behavior" (1977, 48). Although there are many traces in Heidegger of a disdain for mass society and a Black Forest peasant's distrust of modern society, Hubert Dreyfus (1995) is surely correct when he dismisses these misunderstandings of Heidegger as a simple technophobe (97–107).

The homogeneity of technology in Heidegger is the key to the limits of his critique. He is able to recognize and mention some different forms of technology: ancient Greek artisanal culture, medieval European windmills, industrial hydroelectric plants, tourism, and mass media.

The chief question is this: what does the understanding of technology as enframing enable in the study of information machines? One may argue that information technologies are no different from other modern technologies with respect to enframing.[7] Computerization transforms analogue text, images, and sound into a digital code that may be considered a bringing forth that is a challenging, an enframing. Here the sequence of bits of ones and zeros does violence to the alphabet, the visual play of light, or the aural movement of air in waves. Once in its digital form, information may be stored, transmitted, edited, and reproduced in ways that are at best much more difficult and often impossible in analogue form. In this way, computer processing of information might be regarded as enframing. And Heidegger says as much: "Today, the computer calculates thousands of relationships in one second. Despite their technical uses they are inessential" (Heidegger 1969, 41).

But the question of the appropriateness of the category of enframing for information technologies is not rightly posed at this level. Heidegger does not coherently raise the issue of enframing by an analysis of technologies. Quite the contrary: he argues that enframing is not a property of technology but of the manner in which humans bring forth technology and themselves. It is a relation of being, not of the object per se. What makes the hydroelectric dam different from a Roman aqueduct is not any quality of the technologies but of the "setup," the way the technique is placed in the world and the related meaning it has for those who encounter it. It might appear otherwise, that Heidegger is speaking about qualities of machines. He complains, for instance, that the hydroelectric plant is "monstrous" since it dams up the river for the sake of a power plant (16). What renders the machine "challenging" is not so much the mechanical engineering of the dam but the instrumental stance that places nature as object; that is where the "setup" resides. Only because the setup is crucial can Heidegger claim that a free relation to technology is possible, that we may be saved from it without literally destroying it.

I want to argue the opposite: that there is a being of technology and that it varies depending upon the material constraints of the technology. Surely the engineering of information technologies may partake of enframing, but it originates in the same "setup" as the hydroelectric plant. If Norbert Wiener (1950) is our guide to information technologies, they are indeed framed in the physicist's standpoint of a ratio of signal to noise. Who is to deny the advantages in efficiency gained by the use of computerized word processing over the typewriter or the pen? Yet careful attention to the way some information technologies position their human agents, or better, an analysis of the assemblages of humans and information machines, suggests a different possible interpretation.

An alternative understanding of information technologies may be approached through raising the question of technological determinism and doing so in relation to Heidegger's concept of destining, of sending, of starting upon a path. The enframing of technology starts humanity upon a path of concealment, of the hiding of our relation to being. But for Heidegger destining is not technological determinism: "Always the destining of revealing holds complete sway over man. But that destining is never a fate that compels" (25). We are under the influence of technology as enframing only insofar as it is concealed from us. The notion of technological determinism on the contrary is itself part of enframing, part of the culture of technology. Thus for Heidegger enframing sets up mankind as determined by technology in the mode of a "standing reserve." While Heidegger counters the problem of technological determinism, his notion of destining also sidesteps the role of the specificity of technology. He avoids the trap of technological determinism by lifting the question of technology so far from the technological that he loses the capacity to make distinctions among technologies. The windmill no less than the hydroelectric plant may fall within the enframing of technology. As paradoxical as this may sound, Heidegger remains within a humanist frame insofar as he does not allow the inscription of meaning through the machinic.

Machinic Epistemology

The materiality of technology may be recovered without returning to technological determinism by going further than Heidegger away from the humanist position. Technological determinism is the mirror opposite of Heidegger's culturalist understanding of technology as bringing forth. His critique of the Cartesian dualism of subject/object, *res cogitans/ res extensa,* as an unconscious articulation of enframing retains the privilege of the subject except in a form different from that of Descartes. The other way around the problem of the essence of technology is through the specificity of the machinic. In this regard Félix Guattari's *Chaosmosis* (1995) attempts to grasp the being of technologies not as an emanation of *Dasein,* but by a sort of phenomenology of technics, a very different project from Heidegger's. Guattari announces his aim: "For each type of machine, we will pose a question... about its singular power of enunciation: what I call its specific enunciative consistency" (34). The machine itself inscribes meaning, enunciates, but it does so within its own register, not as a human subject would. It is a form of presencing, to use Heidegger's term, of the object.

To refute the Heideggerian position on technology, Guattari turns to the example of the airplane on the runway. For Heidegger this is a pure case of a "standing reserve." The being of the vehicle is contained by its enframing, its being set up as a useful object for travel. For Guattari, on the contrary, the realm of the machinic incorporates intersections of widely diverse domains, constituting an assemblage of enunciation in that "the machine speaks to the machine before speaking to man" (47). Instead of the Heideggerian subject gazing at the airplane on the runway, inscribing its meaning for the singular philosopher, Guattari proposes to delve beyond the appearance for the individual to the heterogeneous domains that interpellate the object. With this in mind we may grasp that the airplane, say it is a Concorde, may not be ready at hand at all. Guattari writes: "The Concorde object moves effectively between Paris and New York but remains nailed to the economic ground. This lack of consistency of one of its components [the economic] has decisively fragilised its global ontological consistency. Concorde only exists within the limited reproducibility of twelve examples and at the root of a possibilist phylum of future supersonics" (48). Economic constraints prevent the use of the airplane, reconfiguring its significance from use for travel to economic waste, a reconfiguration that may only be discerned by examining the full array of heterogeneous machinic domains of the object.

These domains are not equally subject to the cultural logic of enframing. Information machines in particular resist instrumental enframing, especially those that are embedded within complex congeries of technologies, and they do so particularly in their interface with humans (Laurel 1991). Take, for example, the Internet. The telephone network was in part appropriated by the Defense Department for advanced research projects by connecting computers to it with protocols that assured a decentralized structure. Any individual or group could communicate through text to any other individual or group. Individuals who happened to be graduate students reappropriated this apparatus adding Usenet and multiuser domains (MUDs). Physicists in Switzerland added graphics and later sound and moving images. These enhancements enabled the further dimensions of hypertext, hypermedia, and virtual reality. In addition real-time audio and video exchanges became possible. The network has become more and more complex as dimension has been overlaid upon dimension, progressing to the point that Cartesian configurations of space/time, body/mind, subject/object—patterns that are essential components of enframing—are each reconstituted in new, even unrepresentable forms. What began as a Cold War effort to speed up communications has become cyberspace, an electronic geography that reterritorializes preexisting geographies, opening new social and cultural worlds that are only beginning to be explored but that quite probably are already redefining what it means to be human (De Landa 1997).

To bring forth in an electronic café is a presencing that returns to the individual an insistence upon his or her absence and concealment. *Dasein* emerges or appears as an opening/concealing in which neither term cancels the other. Ancient Greek *Alethea* becomes not a lever of critique of a modern falling away from being, but as just one possibility, somewhat quaint, perhaps, and certainly no Archimedean point of reference for humanity. In electronic cafés one cannot be authentic or be present in full presence since one's body is not there and one's identity is fabricated by design. Individuals may "feel" more real in cyberspace or more artificial, alienated, disjointed. Yet the machinic solicitation is to reveal to oneself that one is never oneself and that this is legitimate, a condition of the new human-machine interface, the being of technology that has seduced humanity into its own heterogenesis. And what is more, things have only begun to get interesting because the current state of the Internet is clearly a bare beginning of things to come.[8]

The gothic tale of technology as the being from the dark lagoon is perhaps then narrativized otherwise as a romance with an alien cyborg, a monster who is always already none other than ourselves.

CHAPTER THREE

Capitalism's Linguistic Turn

Capitalism burns off the nuance in a culture. Foreign investment, global markets, corporate acquisitions, the flow of information through transnational media, the attenuating influence of money that's electronic and sex that's cyberspaced, untouched money and computer-safe sex, the convergence of consumer desire—not that people want the same things, necessarily, but that they want the same range of choices.

—Don DeLillo, *Underworld*

A dreadful prospect is looming on the horizon. In the industrial era of the nineteenth century, capitalist relations of property were imposed on new sources of energy, work relations, and the resources of manufacturing. Steam energy, wage labor, and heavy machinery were organized under the aegis of private enterprise. In the twentieth century, industrial capital expanded to the realms of consumption, fantasy, and desire. The sale of the product was mediated by advertising that invoked images to incite unconscious libido, and the shopper as a valued social figure was constructed as a structural effect of promotion. Now it seems that language itself is falling under the domain of private property. As systematic knowledge becomes central to production, as consumer objects increasingly take the form of symbols, sounds, and images, and, most important for this discussion, as communications of all forms are increasingly digitized, capitalist relations of property are asserted to cover language. Information, we are told, is not free. What was previously celebrated as spirit, the highest human aspiration, is now for sale as "intellectual property." Culture is now the contested domain that is at stake and at risk in aggressive efforts to extend property laws to the region of digitized intellectual objects.[1] Capitalism is taking a linguistic turn. And as it does so I want to ask how this process is occurring and what forms of resistance may be raised against it.

But first I must explain my appropriation of the term *linguistic turn* from philosophy to social analysis. Richard Rorty (1967) coined the term to refer to the tendency within analytic philosophy to convert problems into terminological disputes and clarifications. He wrote, "I shall mean by 'linguistic philosophy' the view that philosophical problems are problems which may be solved (or dissolved) either by reforming language, or by understanding more about the language we presently use. This view is considered by many of its proponents to be the most important philosophical discovery of our time, and, indeed, of the ages" (3). Rorty was annoyed that philosophers of the linguistic turn reduced substantial difficulties to a mere question of accurate words.

With the advent of poststructuralism in the 1970s, the phrase *linguistic turn* was applied to a very different context. The shift to a focus on language was not seen as a reduction of theoretical depth but a recognition of the importance of language in questions of metaphysics, epistemology, ethics, and so forth (Jay 1982). In the context of what may be called American-Continental philosophy, the linguistic turn meant a rejection of philosophies of consciousness in favor of philosophies of language, meant that human nature was not to be understood in the Cartesian-Kantian-Hegelian tradition as consciousness or spirit but as constituting itself in and through, and being constituted by, language. The self was not a point of awareness over against a world but negotiating within symbolic systems, defined and defining itself through those systems. The linguistic turn then had the profound import of redefining the real or, as some would prefer, redefining the way the real is addressed. The priority accorded to language in these discourses signified a general reorientation of philosophy, what some have described as a move from a humanist to a posthumanist perspective.

I deploy the phrase *linguistic turn*, then, to signify an equally profound change in the way commodities are produced, distributed, and consumed. Since the 1930s, observers have attempted to understand changes in industrial capitalism: first "managerial capitalism" denoted a shift in control of the firm from owners of capital to executives, then "organizational capitalism" or "monopoly capitalism" pointed to a change from individuals and families to corporate bureaucrats in the 1950s, then to "postindustrial" capitalism in the 1960s, a "service economy" in the 1970s, "consumer capitalism" or "late capitalism" in the 1980s, "postmodern or post-Fordist capitalism" in the 1990s, and now "a digital" or even "a global economy." In each phase theorists endeavor to characterize a change from a nineteenth-century model of decentralized production units in which human labor guided machinery powered by natural energy forces to shape raw materials into useful goods. In these processes, a great deal of knowledge was required of both capitalists and workers, but the perceived accomplishment of the system of production was physical: the power of the machines and the artistry of labor. With the advent of the mass assembly line and Taylorist labor practices, knowledge in the design of production was increased. Manual and mental labor were perhaps made more separate (Noble 1977). But the central achievement of capitalism remained the efficient use of energy, the expeditious deployment of human and machine labor.

Since the 1920s, the center of the economy has shifted more and more away from the accomplishment of making objects by organizing efficiently men and machines. The productive act of course remains necessary and is the ultimate object of the economy. First, however, the success of capitalism in producing objects led to the question of consumption. The consumer became a problem: humans had to be trained to consume, to consume greater and greater quantities and new types of objects. The gravitational center of the economy, as John Kenneth Galbraith (1958) pointed out long ago, became not how to make objects but how to sell them. The consumer had to be produced, so to speak. And this was a matter of language, the language of advertising. The definition of economics changed from the efficient use of energy to the creation of effective demand.

If the construction of the consumer through the language of advertising was a major shift toward capitalism's linguistic turn, today observers characterize the change as a general transformation of the economy. Many now speak of a "knowledge economy" or even a "digital economy." They do so in relation to what they called "value added." Here is Don Tapscott's depiction of the linguistic turn:

We are at the dawn of an Age of Networked Intelligence—an age that is giving birth to a new economy, a new politics, and a new society. Businesses will be transformed, governments will be renewed, and individuals will be able to reinvent themselves—all with the help of the new information technology.... In the new economy, more and more of the economy's added value will be created by brain rather than brawn. Many agricultural and industrial jobs are becoming knowledge work. Already almost 60% of all American workers are knowledge workers and eight of ten new jobs are in information-intensive sectors of the economy. The factory of today is as different from the industrial factory of the old economy as the old factory from the craft production that preceded it. (1996, 2, 7)

If Tapscott's statistics are to be believed, the majority of the workforce now operates on symbols. Machines do the greater part of physical labor. Human beings manipulate data in computers and monitor computers, which in turn monitor and control machines. The value of the commodity derives increasingly, according to this argument, not from the efficient application of resources, but from the design of the product and the application of information tools to its creation.

Tapscott goes on to argue that the organization of the firm itself becomes increasingly knowledge-based or virtual. The product must be designed in a computer with suppliers of materials and parts dependent upon the model that is in the information machine. The product is first of all a virtual one, and this virtual product governs the rest of the production process. It follows, he contends, that knowledge workers who create the virtual product cannot be supervised in the hierarchical, top-down model of the nineteenth and early twentieth centuries. Production increasingly relies upon teams of experts who work best in informal associations rather than in institutions with rigidly delineated authority relations. In addition, the speedup resulting from computers networked globally requires flexibility in the design and production of the product, flexibility in relations with suppliers and distributors, and close attention to changes in consumer taste. Everything conspires to give value to knowledge that is recent rather than to know-how based on experience. Everything conspires, in Tapscott's digital economy, to give precedence to information and to people who have it or know how to get it. The problem of production is not how to make the product or even how to sell it: the problem is how to *invent* it.

It may be that Tapscott overemphasizes the extent to which the economy has become a knowledge-based or a digital one. And it may be that he overstates the benefits of the novelties he analyzes and foresees. He is attentive to the negative sides of the digital economy, such as the vast inequalities of wealth it creates, and this on a global scale. But in his eagerness to promote what he calls a platform model of production, which diminishes hierarchy in the workplace, and a general reorientation of management toward the imperatives of knowledge-based production, he overlooks one side of the question of the linguistic term: the digital commodity. For it is not only the production process that is becoming digitized and the organization that is becoming knowledge-based, but the products themselves, both those used in production and those purchased by consumers, are becoming digital. And digital commodities, though they will never replace material commodities, have a logic that confounds the principles of capitalism at a very basic level. It may be that the economic principles of scarcity, marginal utility, supply and demand, and production for a market are all in question in the realm of digital objects.

The extent of the contemporary problem in economics may be measured by the spread of software piracy, the unprecedented appropriation by users of commodities produced for a market. Recent studies indicate that in 1997 40 percent of business software applications installed worldwide were, in the view of software producers, stolen. In North America the figure is 28 percent, while in Vietnam and China piracy reached high points of over 95 percent (*USA Today*, August 14, 1998, 8A). One may estimate that in the nonbusiness sector the figures may be even higher. These startling statistics register a willingness to violate legal and ethical norms that are essential to the legitimacy of capitalism. Had Henry Ford's cars been stolen at this rate in the 1920s, we would no doubt never have seen the advent of the automobile industry. If these figures bear any relation to actual social practice, something is clearly and very deeply amiss and it is so on a global scale. Digital technology renders copying easy and cheap, if not cost free.[2] Could it be that, with the new technical conditions of reproduction, free enterprise norms are in crisis or at least seriously in question? If so, what are the merits of increasing the effort to impose them? Or perhaps the new circumstances open the question of new norms.

The Hegemony of Market Principles

While one underlying condition of the present is the commodity in the age of its electronic production and reproduction, the surface level of attention is the spread and dominance of market principles. The collapse of communism in the Soviet Union and Eastern Europe and the adoption of capitalist mechanisms in the People's Republic of China led easily to the conclusion that the market, not the state, is the best institution for allocating scarce resources. Capitalism conquered socialism. In North America and Europe, encouraged by these events, conservatives in the United States, liberals in England, and reformers in Russia all celebrated the market as the superior economic institution. Market principles were extended to areas in which it had been muted, such as medicine with the spread of health maintenance organizations and higher education in which funding by governments was reduced and criteria of economic competition were imposed. At the same time increasing globalization of the economy encouraged in the early 1990s the signing of treaties like GATT and NAFTA that extended and strengthened free trade principles. In every location the market became the shibboleth of progress and rationality.

This festival of free enterprise was the mood when the World Wide Web was started in 1993, enabling the easy exchange not only of text but of images and sound. Clumsy Unix command structures, which hitherto restricted Internet use to the more advanced computer adepts, gave way to browsers and menu-driven e-mail programs. The Net was ready for the masses. But it was also ready for trade and for the market, or so many businessmen thought. Beginning in 1994, economic institutions began to explore ways of adapting the Internet to economic transactions. At the same time the other media—newsprint, radio, and television—began to run articles that drew attention to the Net. A simultaneous celebration and demonization of the Internet by other media drew public attention to the Net, appealing to and manipulating the hopes and fears of the audience and readers. By 1995 even Bill Gates recognized the importance of the Internet to computing and communications. Microsoft developed Internet Explorer, its Web browser. The signs were clear that the Internet represented a vast new domain for capital investment, entrepreneurship, and moneymaking.

And when capitalism enters the domain of the Net it does so with a vengeance. Media and software companies are falling over one another to grab the new market in cyberspace (Hiltzik 1999). Cable, telephone, and wireless industries fall over each other in the race to become the conduits of the Net. The millions made by such firms as Yahoo.com have not gone unnoticed. Retailers and manufacturers in general ogle the Net and look with envy at the sales of companies like Amazon.com. Financial markets went simply berserk over any public corporation that had anything to do with the Internet. Take the example of Theglobe.com, a firm that assists in the construction of Web pages. In mid-November 1998 the first day of stock sales for the company broke the record for price gain, from nine dollars to more than sixty-three dollars per share (Hamilton 1998, C1). The company had reported no profits and no likelihood of them in the near future. Yet investors eagerly bought interests in the company. This case was multiplied over and over again in the late 1990s. Although the real economic basis of Internet stocks constituted but a tiny portion of the national economy, a mere 8 percent, its portion of growth was, in the years 1995 to 1998, considerable: more than one-third of the total ("Internet Stimulus" 1999).

Long-time Net afficionados were for the most part distressed at these developments. The Internet was designed for the free, fast exchange of ideas between researchers and the unconstrained communication between users more generally. Many felt that capitalist principles would destroy the Internet as they had known it, introducing censorship by the government and copyright law by the economy, transforming the free space of exchange and sharing into a nightmare of surveillance and greed. Fears and hopes were exaggerated on all sides. The hacker mentality of early users was strongly opposed to any inhibition or censorship of communication, and the basic architecture of the Internet materialized these preferences. The Net is highly decentralized: for a small fee and subject to no regulatory body, anyone using the proper protocols and having a telephone line can connect to it. This decentralization enables anyone connected to have a position of enunciation, sometimes to the chagrin of existing authorities. Disgruntled employees may now easily register their complaints against their bosses and their corporations for all the world to see (G. Miller 1999). Corporate executives are often outraged that their underlings can vent their grievances against them so publicly and with seeming impunity. The irreverent attitudes of users sometimes spill over to the streets, as happened when Linux users protested at Microsoft offices against its monopolistic practices (Harmon 1999).

Furthermore, data that is transmitted contains its own transport instructions, with routers simply following these directions. Instead of intelligent switching operations that direct the message to the next post, routers allow data to flow to its destination by any route that is available to it. The "intelligence" of the system is at the bottom rather than at the top, as it has been in analogue telephony. What is more, any user can connect with any number of other users, without needing permission from authorities or great resources. This structure, moreover, is designed to make it very difficult to calculate the cost of a single transmission as packet switching replaces line switching.

In addition, the communication system of the Internet, like other media, benefits and adds value by the increased number of users. The more people who are on-line, the more valuable is each person's connection. The more people who are connected, the more value one's connection has. This principle is at odds with capitalism's law of supply and demand, in which scarcity, not abundance, is the basis for the determination of value, although there are exceptions, like television advertising, in which value increases with audience size. Under market principles a commodity has greater value to the extent that it is rare in relation to demand. And a consumer may purchase a product more cheaply to the extent that there are fewer consumers in relation to the available supply of the product. With the Internet, as with other networked media, a counterposition is installed in which a communication has greater value the more individuals it reaches, the more it multiplies itself, the more common or universal it is. And digital technology renders the reproduction of information easy and cheap. So the logic of the Internet is the more the better, and more is no more costly than less, a logic that flies in the face of traditional free enterprise economics.

Consumer as Producer

Current legal and ethical codes, standards, and assumptions concerning economic relations between producers and consumers originated in the context of industrial capitalism. When an individual purchases a product of industrial capitalism, such as an automobile manufactured by the Chrysler Corporation, it does not arrive at the consumer's door, as did vinyl records, with the warning inscribed on the face of the object, "Unauthorized reproduction is a violation of law and will be prosecuted." Chrysler safely assumed that the consumer could not make a copy of the automobile. In industrial technology, reproduction of commodities was the exclusive privilege and capability of the producer. Producer and consumer stood apart and were differentiated precisely by this distinction. The consumer had no right to reproduce the commodity but, since he or she was incapable of doing so, the point was moot. The legal and ethical questions of the privilege of reproduction did not exist as an issue for the consumer. They were confined to the realm of competition between producers. Capitalism legitimized the exclusive privilege of producers to produce commodities on the grounds of adequate resources, in this way differing from precapitalist systems in which political authority prevailed over the market; for example, in Europe only the monarch or prince could authorize reproduction of commodities and, in the realm of nonagricultural commodities, only the guild could regulate the quantity of production.

But now all of that has changed. Information technologies place into the hands of the consumer the capacity to become a producer of cultural objects. The line dividing the two functions increasingly is blurred. In the 1970s, audiocassette technology enabled consumers to copy vinyl records onto cassettes that were often of higher quality than cassettes available at a cost from the recording companies, and could do so as many times as one wished. Record companies mass-produced tapes at speeds greater than real time—the time of listening to the music—thereby degrading the signal (losing information and smearing it). For the first time in my experience, consumers were able to build large music collections for a fraction of the market cost, little more than the cost of audiocassettes. This blurring of the boundary between producer and consumer continued with the development of videocassettes, enabling the consumer to reproduce films from their broadcast on TV or from prerecorded videocassettes. Photocopying also opened printed material to reproduction by consumers, although sheets of paper were not quite the same as bound volumes. Now writable CD and DVD technologies are available, extending considerably the power of consumers to make exact copies of all forms of information—text, audio, and video—with great speed and at little cost. The Internet also offers the consumer such a vast domain of information for easy and cheap reproduction that one no longer thinks of Web surfers as consumers. Digitized music available on the Web may be downloaded and played on one's computer or transferred in digital form to a cheap portable player. The distribution of music, like all cultural artifacts, may now flow directly from artist to consumer (Pareles 1998).

The Internet extends the figure of the producing consumer of earlier technologies and makes this the very principle, the automatic operation, of every communication. To click on a Web page, to send an e-mail, to transmit a message to a chat room is to copy information and distribute it. To be on-line is to appropriate the right to copy. Cyberspace means producing culture as you consume it.

What then happens to the legal and ethical prescriptions of the industrial age? What is the status of the ethical obligation to desist from reproducing music, film, images, and texts when the technical possibility of doing so is incredibly simple and embodied in the means of communication? What happens to the legal effectiveness of industrial age codes governing reproduction? Is it possible to enforce, let us say, copyright laws over software programs, music albums, films, and works of fiction under present conditions? Is it possible to sustain ethical imperatives against violating copyright when reproduction technology is so advanced? Ought one even to attempt such feats? What is the current value of legal and ethical codes of the age of mechanical reproduction? Is it even worth the effort to discover justifications for them in the present context? Ought we not instead to examine the new conditions and seek to elaborate codes and rules that are commensurate with the greatest benefit for all? Simply because the legal and ethical legacy of the industrial age helped to advance us to our present condition, ought we out of some nostalgia do nothing but insist on their inherent worth? The age of print, of mechanical reproduction, of industrial production are now folded within new practices, new technologies, and new spatial expanses. As a result the issues are now reversed: no longer do we need to ask how best to advance production, given the constraints of industrial capitalism. We need to ask instead, Can capitalism still justify itself in an age when the consumer is already a producer? Rather than asking how we can apply the law (of copyright) to the Internet, we need to ask, Is copyright the best law to apply to the Internet? We need to turn the question against the old productive system and compel it to justify itself.

Culture as Political

When capitalism takes a linguistic turn, when emergent areas of economic creation center on symbolic objects and when the most technically advanced production processes depend upon symbolic processes, then the domain of culture receives new energy and becomes a center of political attention. The initiative of questioning no longer gravitates toward production as it did in early phases of capitalism: instead culture becomes coherent as a separate sphere of the relations of production. The emergent domain is not, as it was for Marx, the reorganization of labor under the conditions of natural forces applied to the mechanical production of commodities. While these older relations remain in place, today culture is also in question, culture understood as information, as the practice of constructing subjects through the network of computerized communications. What laws and ethics, we need to ask, will promote the optimal development of the emergent domain of cyberspace?

Attention also shifts to the global level. True enough new media arose out of the West, reflecting its cultural and social traits. But they have spread quickly beyond its confines. First production was globalized with computers, for example, being composed of parts from around the world. Then software was globalized: Indian programmers, for instance, worked at home and sent their code through the Internet to the United States, an unusual application of assembly-line methods, to say the least. But increasingly the Internet is being extended to all parts of the planet and English is becoming a lingua franca and less dominant at the same time. George Yúdice (1992) refers to this process as "transculturation," which he defines as "a dynamic whereby different cultural matrices impact reciprocally—though not from equal positions—on each other, not to produce a single syncretic culture but rather a heterogeneous ensemble" (209). With its decentralized structure, the Internet enables non-Western culture to have presence on an equal footing with the West. It establishes for the first time the possibility of a meeting and exchange of cultures that is global in scope, albeit favoring the wealthy and the educated everywhere. This global system of communication raises at a practical level the question of how to coordinate, organize, and conduct global exchanges. Whose cultural preferences ought to prevail in a nonimperialist context of exchange of symbols? Ought there to be a plurality of rules, a new order of rules created for this explicit purpose, or a universalization of one existing set of rules, such as those of capitalism? These issues have never been faced before in so practical a context, never been so forcefully presented as issues to be addressed. One of the challenges confronting us in the age of the digital reproduction of commodities is to construct a framework in which these questions can be posed.

Digital Commodities

The commodity is a mysterious thing, Marx wrote, like a hieroglyph that resists easy interpretation. At the beginning of volume 1 of *Capital*, Marx spoke of a coat made of linen and found it enigmatic. But what if the commodity in question were a computer program, say a Web browser like Netscape? In this case the commodity is produced by labor, just like the coat. And the labor is paid and the laborer is him- or herself a commodity on a market. In these respects Netscape is identical to Marx's coat. But Netscape is given away for free and the coat must be paid for. What kind of economic logic is there in a commodity that is given away for free? In addition, Netscape, in 1997, made its underlying code public or open source, inviting those with the requisite skills to make revisions and improvements which the corporation would include in future releases. In principle the firm extended its reach to programmers all over the world, promising them no payment at all. One might think that Netscape was simply amplifying the old idea of a suggestion box. But the case now is different: nothing prevents someone with programming abilities to improve Netscape and compile it into his or her own program. In fact, digital programs encourage just this sort of economic principle. Freeware and shareware are terms designating postcapitalist principles of the mystery of commodities. Great programs such as Shawn Fanning's Napster, Qualcomm's Eudora, David Harris's Pegasus Mail, and even operating systems like Linux (written by Linus Torvalds of the University of Helsinki) are either shareware or freeware. Many of such programs are for use on the Internet, suggesting to some that a structural motive of giving away the product is to seduce the user to participate in the Web. RealAudio, QuickTime, Acrobat, and Shockwave are examples of programs that one downloads for free but that one needs to decode the contents of Web pages. Skeptics have the sense of wasting time endlessly downloading and installing programs, updates, and yet newer programs all in order to negotiate Web pages. True enough, the Internet promotes its own use, and a sordid relation of codependence entwines the user in endless upgrades. New versions of operating systems require more memory and more hardware purchases. New hardware purchases come with new versions of programs that require the consumer to buy updates for other programs. A self-perpetuating cycle of purchases and time-consuming installation procedures absorbs the potential Net user in coerced, time-consuming computer fiddling. But numerous programs have nothing to do with Web browsing or downloading pages. File managers, utilities, and other programs are plentiful. Also, it must be recognized that the Internet is not simply an appendage to computing or an aspect of it, like word processing or games. More and more computers are hooked into the Web as part of the structure of computing. In this sense, programs for the Web are not ancillary to computing but part of a new system of networked culture. We are in a phase of transition whose completion—if ever there is one—cannot be foreseen but that will in all likelihood entail the convergence of media and other technologies into a great domain of virtual space.

The Net was designed not for marketing and distributing commodities but for the cost-free sharing of cultural objects. Capitalism, since 1994, has moved into the space of the Net at first blind to its peculiar material traits, what I call its underdetermination. As capitalists place their objects into the space of the Web, it remains uncertain if its principles can remain intact or if the new spatial-temporal qualities of cyberspace will enable new principles of exchange that do not necessarily reproduce those of the past. It may be that commodities produced under capitalist principles cannot sustain their status as objects in the temporal-spatial domain of the Net.

If we shift attention from computer programs to cultural objects themselves, the issue of new economic principles may be clarified further. Take the example of audio music. It is no longer necessary to obtain a copy of a work of music by going to a retail store, looking in a catalog, even browsing the Web at sites like Amazon.com. The musical commodity no longer needs to take the shape of a cassette or CD and then move through space. It now may exist in digital form on the Web and be copied to one's hard disk by a simple click. If one records the music off the air, one depends on a broadcaster to beam it to one's receiver and even then, if the transmission is analogue, the copy will not be as good as the original. With the Web, one may download a small decoding file that takes only a few minutes and then download the music or have a bot or intelligent agent locate the piece and download it. The music may then be played on one's computer or stereo system, if the systems are interconnected. Or one may use a cheap headset player, download the music to it, and play it wherever one chooses (Bunn 1998, 17–18). Like the opposition to video recorders from the movie industry, the audio industry is attempting without much success to prevent the player from being sold. The music industry also attempted to prosecute sites that contained encoded music compressed in an MP3 format, also without success. The next move of the audio culture industry has been to appropriate the new format: Why can't Time Warner make MP3s available just as teenagers do? Except Time Warner wants to sell the MP3s for a price (Philips 1999). To that end, some Web sites will let you download a song for a price. But again the same problem reappears: the downloader may then upload the file to a site where anyone in the world can get a copy for nothing. So culture industry executives propose to introduce locks on the files, for example watermarks identifying the file's source as a defeat system that deletes the file after a certain number of plays or a certain number of days (Peraino 1999). This strategy failed miserably in the 1980s, when software companies like Lotus included copy protection devices. As quickly as copy protection was introduced, so quickly did copy protection cripplers appear on the Internet. Finally the software companies gave up the battle. The culture industry is simply repeating the mistakes of the past. These are the desperate measures of the music industry faced by its technological obsolescence (Vankin 1999). Here the culture industry works to hold back an advance in consumer electronics. One side of capitalism, the established part, is threatened by the side that extends new media to the public.

But the issue at stake is not only over the spread of new technologies to the consumer: capitalism is far more resistant to the ability of the Web to act as a source in which the consumer *produces* his or her own copy. The challenge to capitalists is to figure out a way to charge for cultural objects when the consumer has the ability to reproduce the commodity for a negligible cost. If I can download music from the Web for nothing, why should I pay Columbia Records to make a CD or tape for me? In fact I can make my own CD that will be exactly the same as the one the multi-billion-dollar company can make. One line that capitalists are taking is that they must not put the music on the Web in the first place. Of course, consumers can and are doing it for them, on a rapidly expanding scale. The scale of "illegal" copying is significant enough to worry the music industry. Young people with little disposable income but considerable spare time are the main market for music CDs, and these are the people who post the music and download it from the Web. The second line the industry takes is that the music should be available on the Web but that one can charge for downloading it. The question is how much to charge. The actual labor by the music company in making the file available is very small and the work of making the copy, as I indicated above, costs the company nothing. Perhaps the distributor should charge a very small fee and bill the amount to the user's credit card.

The only role left for the music industry is its editing function: its system of selecting musicians to produce. Today of course musicians are able to produce their own recordings, without the help of the industry's studios, and distribute them through the Internet. But the problem for the musicians remains how to get the attention of the audience. With thousands or even tens of thousands of musicians potentially making their work available on the Web for a small download fee (which might be approximately equal to their royalties from the industry), the issue shifts to the question of selection. How is a music listener able to find work that he or she likes? A new type of editor might be the answer but an editor who has no connection with production. Music portals, like MP3.com, are already at work, attempting to mediate between the artist and the listener. This process is in its infancy. At this point it is impossible to discern the shape that future "editors" will take.

What has happened in the music industry is now being reproduced in film. Young people attend a movie with a recording camera. Copy the film while viewing it; transfer the copy into a compressed data file; post it on the Web, and, voilà, the movie is available worldwide for free. Or someone gets a copy of the film during the production process, after it is complete but before it is released. This copy is transferred into digital format and uploaded to the Internet for anyone to copy. *The Matrix, 8mm,* and *Shakespeare in Love* were all available on the Net before release in theaters (Wallace 1999). The handwriting is on the wall: the culture industry is in trouble. As one industry executive said, "The party's over. People are tired of paying $8.50 to subsidize a $250-million budget for a story that—at its most basic level—is not told very well" (Huff-stutter 1999, A1). The bandwidth for the rapid distribution of moving images with sound is not yet available but one can predict its imminent appearance. After all, only a short time ago observers thought the distribution on the Net of four-megabyte MP3 files was not feasible.

At stake in these examples is the new principle that the producer and distributor have become unnecessary to the exchange of music and films between the composer or performer and the listener. The apparatus of production and reproduction has been so transformed by the advent of the Net that the mediations between artist and listener almost disappear. The role of the media in culture, in their capitalist form, is sharply in question. But this is a question that the culture industry wishes not to pose. Their question is how to make money distributing cultural objects on the Net, when it should be what role, if any, they ought to play in the new regime of cyberspace. Maintaining home pages for artists might be one. Above all, as I have said, there is a new role for editors, disc jockeys of all sorts, in finding music that the consumer likes and disseminating information about what is worth hearing. These are profound changes in comparison with the current roles of the media giants.

If the digital reproduction of commodities calls capitalism into question in the domain of cultural objects, it also raises difficulties in all areas of production where knowledge and computing, where the mode of information, inserts itself in an important way. When the material reproduction of the product becomes increasingly less significant as an aspect of production, traditional systems of economic calculation make less and less sense. What is the value of the labor time of a computer programmer at Microsoft in relation to the ninety dollars charged for Windows, for example? And what is the relationship of the cost of Windows to its cost of production? While cost accounting procedures may work for assembly line types of labor, they become less and less pertinent as the design of the product overtakes in importance and value its material production and distribution. One may say that all labor is subject to a market mechanism and it alone determines the value of a computer programmer's time. Yet it is not a simple task for labor markets to regulate salaries in the domain of knowledge work.

As political economy faces enormous difficulties coping with digital commodities, so does the critique of political economy. In general Marxists attempt to downplay the novelty of the digital commodity as a mechanism or articulation and highlight the conditions of labor that produce it. Robert Markley (1996), for example, performs a vanishing act with the entire technology of new media: "To ask what is on the other side of the computer screen is, in my mind, a crucial step. . . . Behind the screen of my laptop lie silicon chips, a battery, microprocessors, and even what seem to be a few old-fashioned screws. . . . The imaginary realm of cyberspace . . . is a fantasy based on the denial of ecology and labor, a dream that is also an apology for the socioeconomic power to bring together sophisticated technologies" (77). In this essay, entitled "The Metaphysics of Cyberspace," Markley dismisses the complexity of cyberspace as a medium and digital technology as a set of capacities, introducing instead a materialism that bolsters the concepts of nineteenth-century historical materialism: labor, socioeconomic power, and so on. We find here no effort to discern tendencies in the forces and relations of production, to use terms Markley is comfortable with, that might upset prevailing power arrangements or even open space for developing new options. Markley's metaphysical disappearing act surely is a peculiar deployment of dialectics.

A different strategy is taken by Jay Bolter and David Grusin in their concept of remediation. They introduce this very promising category to understand the history of the media as a complex set of rearticulations. They argue that media present themselves as mediations, as powerful innovations in cultural practice, but also attempt to naturalize themselves, make themselves transparent, in short, to erase their material effects as mediations. Bolter and Grusin wish to place this process which they term "remediation" into prominence. "*All* mediation," they claim, "is remediation. . . . at this historical moment all current media function as remediators and . . . remediation offers us a means of interpreting the work of earlier media as well" (Bolter and Grusin 1996, 345). The use of the term *remediation* serves, in their view, to draw attention to the force of the mediation and to render media intelligible in a new, historical manner. The heuristic value of the category of remediation rests with those aspects of the media that are somehow a repetition, and the weakness of the concept of remediation, I suggest, rests with depicting novelty, since all media are little more than their remediating function.

If Markley vaporizes digital media, Bolter and Grusin ventriloquize it: that is, they project into the structure of new media a motivation to deny mediation, a logocentric motivation of full presence. They write, "The digital medium wants to erase itself, so that the viewer stands in the same relationship to the content as she would if she were confronting the original medium" (340). Bolter and Grusin accuse digital media of a logic of "immediacy," that it strives to make nugatory the difference between normal reality and virtual reality. If Markley wants us to look behind the screen to the act of labor that he thinks is the basis of media such as virtual reality, Bolter and Grusin deplore the willful deception of the digital commodity in hiding or repressing its material basis.

Another type of Marxist criticism is more cognizant of the unique features of contemporary capitalism. Dan Schiller (1999) dubs the current economy "digital capitalism," and Philip Graham (2000) calls it "hyper-capitalism." In these analyses the significance of the economic linguistic turn is more fully recognized. Classic categories of historical material-ism, Graham argues, must be retired. He writes: "Terms such as material and non-material production; production and consumption; forces and relations of production; base and superstructure; social capital; and, perhaps even politics, society, and economy . . . are often used in a more obfuscatory than explanatory manner" (152). Because of the new and expanded role of information in the economy, the critique of political economy requires different categories. What is unique about the digital economy for this Marxist are the blurring of formerly distinct cate-gories such as production and consumption, the mental and the physi-cal, knowledge and labor. With the speed of new media, the rapid cir-culation of commodities in an abstract and ephemeral form, and the fact that information is not destroyed as it is consumed, a new social formation has emerged. Under hypercapitalism, "source of productivity" becomes problematic, as every idea, Graham continues echoing Castells, is arguably at the same time a production process in itself. The novelty of digital capitalism amounts to this: "[K]nowledge exchanges imme-diately produce new knowledge, as well as forming the foundations for the production of even more knowledge. Thus production, circulation and consumption become analytically inseparable" (138).

The new Marxist analysis must also account for drastic changes in the culture industry, Graham contends: "The point at which language, thought and technology converge in their mass and immediacy, at the same time being collectively deployed in controlling technological, physical *and* social systems, is also the point at which knowledge *about* these systems becomes the most valuable knowledge of all. In such conditions, an individual's *mind* takes on the qualities of the commodity-fetish" (150). Culture must now be considered fully part of what used to be called the base in an older Marxist lexicon. Although Graham goes a long way toward retrofitting historical materialism for the new digital age, he still fails to examine the internal logic of the digital commodity. His focus remains on the dangers of informational capitalism in amplifying the existing inequalities, solidifying the capitalist class in its hegemony, and extending throughout the globe the reach of capitalist relations. All of which cannot be gainsaid. But the other side of dialectical analysis, the side that points toward potentials for democratizing change, go unattended. And the analytic categories that would reveal these dimensions of capitalism's linguistic turn remain obscured.

Public Goods and Sharing

Some economists regard the Internet as a public good. By this they mean two things: that scarcity does not apply and that all individuals in principle have access to the good. Scarcity does not apply to the Internet because copying is internal to the technology. When a file is copied the original remains with its owner. And open access is equally the rule on the Net because it is difficult to exclude anyone from logging in. Public goods are like common lands in preindustrial society: they are abundant and available (Kollock 1999, 223). Yet the old commons is different in several important ways from the Internet. Common lands are natural resources designated by a community as public. The Internet by contrast is a collective creation. Its value lies not in its natural qualities (good location, the right combination of grasses, trees, and so forth) but in the cultural objects placed in it by countless users. On the Net, each user uploads a cultural object, thereby making it available to all other users. The Internet therefore is a socially constructed public good.

Others have argued that the Internet is a gift economy. Each user presents cultural objects to other users in an exchange without money. But again the Internet does not fit the model of a gift economy because gifts are exchanged between specific individuals. The purpose of a gift is to create an obligation in the recipient, fulfill a prior obligation from a donor, or achieve recognition by a community as a donor. On the

Internet the posting of cultural objects—texts, audio, or video—is by and large anonymous: the users who download the file do not, for the most part, know the user who uploaded it.

Instead of a gift economy or a public good, I prefer to think of the Internet as an economy of sharing. Uploading a file or posting a message on a Usenet group in answer to a query is best understood as a contribution to all users for no direct reward. The act of sharing is little recognized in economies characterized by commodity exchange but is unique to the Internet. Nor is sharing on the Internet an act of barter because there is no exchange of specific goods of agreed-upon equality. Sharing on the Internet returns humanity to a primordial social act that persists, outside the Internet, probably only among children, those who are presumed to be incapable of contracts.

It may appear paradoxical to speak of the Net as revivifying a prehistoric social principle of sharing at a time when private enterprise has entered the Net with a ferocity and intensity rarely seen. Shares of Internet-related companies, as we have seen, are hyperbolically inflated on the stock market. Every corporation now has a Web site, and those who can do business on the Web. The Internet has drastically transformed the financial markets, globalizing and disseminating financial transactions. In some cases, entire economies, such as Brazil in 1998, have been seriously affected by Web trading in currencies. The speed of Internet transactions alters the region of arbitrage. And Web gambling is now a planetary concern. Far from introducing a postcapitalist economy, the Web, to many observers, creates hypercapitalism.

Conclusion

The question raised by the new hieroglyph is this: is there a new economy of commodities in these examples? If so, what legal and ethical rules enable us to promote its expansion and development? If capitalism is the best system for allocating scarce resources, if it alone takes these resources and maximizes their efficiency in producing the maximum number of commodities at the lowest possible cost, what is the best system for promoting digital, networked commodities, what rules will enable a global, multicultural, multigendered proliferation and enhancement of these commodities?

If, as DeLillo says, "Capitalism burns off the nuance of culture," must we, like him, assume that global, networked communication is automatically capitalist and nationalist? We must develop a sense of what is possible, what is given out of the material characteristics of these media and out of their history. And then we must formulate these new possibilities as political options. In a recent book, Jacques Derrida called for a New International. The development of a legal and ethical framework for global communications is precisely a task that requires such a new movement.

CHAPTER FOUR

The Digital Subject and Cultural Theory

I argue for profound changes in the discourse of critical theory, and of academia in general, as a consequence of the digitization of writing. For, as Sandy Stone (1995) writes, "We no longer live in a world in which information conserves itself primarily in textual objects called books... but inescapably, at the threshold of a new and unsettling age [in which we must] reimagine the scholarly enterprise" (177–78). If what Stone argues is convincing, we must invent the Humanities in relation to digital texts. "Reimagining the scholarly enterprise" does not necessarily entail an improvement. Indeed David Noble envisions digital writing in academia as a decline into capitalist relations. Professors are now, he thinks, becoming automated just as workers have been since the introduction of Taylorism in the earlier part of the past century. With digital writing, the academy, Noble contends, becomes a "diploma mill," subject to the exploitative logic of capital. Distance learning is a euphemism, in his eyes, for speedup. Posting syllabi on home pages on the World Wide Web is theft of labor (Noble 1998; Weiss 1998). And e-mail enables students to intrude at all hours of the day and night upon the lives of teachers, rendering the workday equivalent to the twenty-four-hour day. The Internet also facilitates plagiarism, though Noble does not mention this complaint, by making term papers easily obtainable (Zack 1998).

Since the end of the Cold War public universities have increasingly turned to market principles. Administrators, strapped for funds, eagerly anticipate the economies of on-line courses, often paying little regard to its harmful effects. In noting these trends and connecting them with digital writing, Noble certainly makes valid arguments. But Noble does not acknowledge any benefits to digital technology. Access of disabled and rural people to higher education through distance learning, extended exchange of ideas among professors through sharing syllabi on the Web, and greater student contact with professors through e-mail are somehow nothing but capitalist incursions. I wonder who the capitalist is in Noble's scenario? Perhaps he, the professor, is the entrepreneur hoarding his great ideas in paper-based syllabi, maintaining his superior social status vis-à-vis students by restricting sharply his availability to them, delimiting his intellectual property to face-to-face classrooms that many cannot afford or access. The Marxist professor needs to remember that his master's lesson is not that capitalist technology is evil but that capitalist relations restrict its optimal deployment.

I hope in this essay to clarify some of the issues at stake in a technological change from print to digital texts. But I hope to do so without the defensive anxiety of David Noble and equally without the uncritical enthusiasm of prophets of progress who greet each new communication technology, from printing and photography to the telegraph, telephone, radio, film, and television, with a certainty of humanity's imminent perfection, global unification, and eternal peace.[1] And yet one cannot deny that the potential for change enabled by digital writing is vast. The point is not to predict utopia or dystopia but to understand what is happening and attempt to shape the outcome in the best way we can.

My attempt to clarify the issue of digital writing confronts a special difficulty because I deploy a predigital form of presentation: an oral, face-to-face format (in spoken version) and print. Although this essay was written on a computer, with the keyboard input mediated by binary code before becoming a graphic, alphabetic representation as pixels on a screen, then a series of ink marks on paper, the machine product has been appropriated by analogue apparatuses of authorship.[2] If you were reading this essay using a browser on your computer to access an Internet site where the work exists, let us say, in hypertext format, my arguments might be more convincing and my illustrations might hit home with greater effect. Instead I am like a reporter returning home from a foreign culture to relate exotic discoveries, except the foreign culture, digital authorship, is right here, to the extent that cyberspace is anywhere. I am not, then, a foreign correspondent but a local informant, and perhaps you the reader, if you have not already shared my experience, are becoming other, becoming distant, like all analogue authors, within your own discursive home.

Insisting on the Medium

The 1996 Geneva conference of the World Intellectual Property Organization (created in 1967) attempted to reform copyright law to reflect computer communications technologies (Samuelson 1997, 61 ff.). The problem for the group was daunting: to adjust laws originally formulated during the print age of the seventeenth century to the conditions of the digital age. How could the medium of the Internet be reconciled with the media of print and broadcast? Copyright law presumes what has become no longer necessarily true: that the reproduction of information requires costly material casings (books, audio records or tapes, celluloid films), that the dissemination of information entails expensive construction of channels and apparatuses of transmission, and that the audience of information is unable to alter it in the form in which it is received. In Geneva delegates contrived to ignore above all these momentous changes in technological form (Browning 1997, 185). This is the problem I want to address. With the digitization of print, film, radio, and television broadcasts and their insertion into a global network, the media in which intellectual property appears alters the message of its legal integument. Put otherwise, the commodity form of cultural objects and the authorial coherence of individual subjects are shaken by digitization.

A great deal is at stake in the current change of the media of cultural objects, with those most benefiting from the existing arrangements also most resistant to the change and generally least able to discern the significance of what is happening. In current debates, the figure of the author becomes one such rallying point for much ideological jockeying. The television industry, for example, cannot do without the author because without the author there is no copyright protection, a must for broadcasting. Even though, properly speaking, there is no author of television shows, the author stands behind the tube's success (Streeter 1996). In the guise of protecting authors, media moguls—those who have most exploited authors—raise the banner of copyright protection against what they see as the anarchic exchange of bytes on the Internet. A "Copyright Assembly," an extraordinary meeting of leaders of media industry, on

February 17, 2000, witnessed Jack Valenti, spokesman for Hollywood, defending "creative works" against "illegitimate intruders on the Internet who steal copyrighted works" (Snider 2000). Such self-righteous posturing poorly conceals the helplessness of the media industry in the face of the sharing of cultural objects on the Net. The meeting ended with no specific legislative proposals to tame the Internet, a sure sign that the great wealth of the cultural industry is not enough to alter the basic architecture of cyberspace.

If we set aside the tendentious positions of those who wish only to extend existing copyright provisions to include new media such as the Internet, we may then ask, What might actually be the fate of authorship when technology shifts from print to the Internet? Is the figure of the author in fact a good point of defense against alarming technical innovations? Is cyberspace an occasion of strengthening or of restructuring or of abandoning authorship?

This chapter brings together an analysis of the technical conditions of authorship in print and in cyberspace with the theoretical proposals for understanding the question of the construction of the author. In most cases the discussion of these two related issues fails adequately to connect them: either one is knowledgeable about technology or one is adept in social and cultural theory. Those who understand the technology are frequently hampered by an unexamined instrumentalist framework, while theorists who address questions of the media often have limited grasps of their technical characteristics. By bridging the gap between technology and culture I hope to illuminate the relations between them.

Benjamin's Legacy

An important precursor in the effort to comprehend the relation of authors to machines is Walter Benjamin, whose celebrated essay "The Work of Art in the Age of Mechanical Reproduction" ([1935] 1969) is a model of technocultural analysis. Benjamin theorized image and sound media (photography and film) in relation to their effects on audiences and authors. He was especially concerned with the extent to which film might construct critical audiences and thereby renew the project of emancipation, reinvigorate struggles against structures of domination by popular forces. He drew attention to the importance of the spatial dissemination of film, its multiple distribution for wide access to the scenes of viewing (collective, darkened spaces with large, projected images); to the mediation of the camera in the production of the art object and to the audience subjected to its point of view, its scopic regimen; to the mediation of film itself displacing actors from the stage by their recorded image; and to the technique of montage, the stitching together of photographs through an editing process and passing them by a projector so as to create a sense of what we now call real-time motion.

Benjamin's analysis ran counter to the prevailing view that media such as film and radio extended the grip of domination over the masses, distracting them from interior contemplation with identical monologues of image and sound. He criticized the underlying basis of this view by unveiling an aspect of domination in the author figure from earlier high-cultural forms, especially painting. In Western culture the author enjoyed a position of command in part by dint of the technical character of the work. As long as the work could not easily be reproduced, whether as manuscript, painting, or sculpture, it was adorned with an aura. The reader or viewer was put in a position of subordination by the placement of work in a museum or even by the mere existence of a manuscript in a library. The viewer traveled to the work and confronted it in its immobility in an act of contemplative respect. With mechanical reproduction, especially in film, where there exists no original, properly speaking, the aura surrounding the work vanishes, the control of the meaning of the work by the author diminishes, and new, reversible relations become possible between the audience and the author.

As suggestive as Benjamin's work has been, it contains a number of limitations; most noteworthy for my purpose is its focus on the image, whereas I wish to examine writing. Furthermore, he wrote before the birth of computer technology with its transformation of writing and more recently of film. Yet the promising perspective of Benjamin's work deserves attention: he was able to write about media without undue suspicion of popular culture, without technophobia, and at the same time with a sense of the mobility and constructedness of basic cultural forms such as author and audience, detaching these from a foundationalist view that ensconced them within the figure of the Cartesian subject. It is this enormously suggestive spirit of Benjamin's essay that I shall try to carry over into a discussion of writing media.

Above all, Benjamin opened a critique of the function and status of the author before mechanical reproduction, a critique that drew attention to the high authority enjoyed by authors when their names were attached to originals. This aura is a kind of analogue extension of the person of the author into the work. The spirit or aura of the author subsides in the work. The work derives its interest from its inscription of an analogue of the author's creative genius. That analogue is now in question. For those of us in universities and colleges, books are part of our second nature. With the onset of computer writing, linked to networks, we must rethink this basic component of our practice as teachers and researchers and begin to analyze the mediation of the book, what it enables and what it constrains.

Beyond the Author Function

The cultural figure of the modern author begins in the eighteenth century, emerging in a confluence of print technology, a book market, a legal status, and an ideology of individual as creator. Mark Rose (1993) has shown how the inception of the modern author required the preexistence of these elements as well as their convergence into a particular social form (142).[3] The legally defined rights of the author required a print technology that could reproduce large quantities of texts, a market system that could determine printed products as objects for sale, and distribution institutions that could make identical copies available in many places, a discursive regime in which individuals were understood as agents capable of inventing new things and as proprietors with interests in accumulating capital. The interlocking of each and every one of these elements alone affords authorship both cultural recognition and social place. Authorship also required, as I shall argue below, a technology of the analogue: a conviction that what was printed in the book was a direct representation of an author's intention, be it in the form of idea, style, or rhetoric; in short, that the book was an analogue reproduction of an original, authentic author.

Before turning to the possible fates of the author in a digital age, I shall explore the characteristics of what I call the analogue author by briefly reviewing Foucault's position. Foucault has presented the most complex and convincing conceptual articulation of the modern author. What is remarkable in his analysis is not only its rigor and comprehensiveness but also its anticipation of digital authorship. To grasp the full extent of the question of the author, I contend that Foucault's insights are essential.

In his influential and well-known essay "What Is an Author?" ([1969] 1984), Foucault delimits four perspectives on the modern author:

1. The humanist author who governs the meaning of the text. This author expresses, intends, and creates all the meanings that may be read in the text.

2. The structuralist rejection of the humanist author, most notably in Roland Barthes's essay "The Death of the Author." In this view, the meaning of the text has no connection with the author. It is a pure synchronic, semiotic object contained within the external materiality of the printed page. Foucault is here not interested in the shift Barthes enacts in the essay to the position of the reader.

3. A poststructuralist move in which Foucault rejects the structuralist annihilation of the author, returning to recognize the importance of the author but not as the humanist understood him or her. Foucault uses the term "the author function" as the discursive figure and institutional practice of modern society that inscribes the author as a source of meaning. Now the critic can acknowledge the importance of the figure of the author in modern society, but instead of translating his recognition into affirmation, legitimation, and celebration, can turn it rather into an analysis of the construction of the figure. This "genealogy" of the author, as Foucault calls it, would also serve as a basis for its critique.

4. The last perspective on the author Foucault offers is a most uncharacteristic one for him.[4] Foucault sets forth an alternative, future, utopian nonauthor whose position, presciently, bears remarkable resemblance to the position of authors in cyberspace, or what I call digital authors. I shall examine this discursive move in more detail.

Foucault's effort to delineate a post-author-function future reproduces a theoretical problem he did much to counter in the writings of others and in his own projects. As part of his critique of the modern subject, Foucault opposed as a conservative gesture the penchant of "the traditional intellectual" to compose metanarratives that totalized the historical field. In this discursive regime, the theorist produced a discursive closure either by legitimizing the present as the fulfillment of human essence or by predicting a future ("the tenth epoch" in Condorcet, communism in Marx, "the transvaluation of all values" in Nietzsche) that served the same purpose. It is most surprising, then, to find Foucault making a similar gesture, as when one reads the following in "What Is an Author?": "I think that, as our society changes, at the very moment when it is in the process of changing, the author function will disappear, and in such a manner that fiction and its polysemous texts will once again function according to another mode, but still with a system of constraint—one which will no longer be the author, but which will have to be determined or, perhaps, experienced" (1984a, 119). The passage is maddeningly brief, not indicating which processes are changing or why they will lead to the disappearance of the author function. Yet even in this prescriptive moment of his text, Foucault is careful to indicate that the inconveniences of authorship will be replaced by new constraints. In addition, one cannot, according to him, speculate about the new regime, by time traveling into the future, but must patiently await its appearance to "experience" it before attempting to name and to outline these impediments to freedom. With these caveats, Foucault offers his "tenth epoch" beyond the author function.

Foucault's future eviscerates the author's presence from the text, shifting interpretive focus on the relation of the reader to a discourse understood in its exteriority, without resort to a founding creator, without reference to the patriarchal insemination of text with meaning. His picture of writing beyond the author function would seem to contravene both Benjaminian aura and culture industry celebrity. Here in his own words is the Foucauldian heterotopia:

> All discourses . . . would then develop in the anonymity of a murmur. We would no longer hear the questions that have been rehashed for so long: Who really spoke? Is it really he and not someone else? With what authenticity or originality? And what part of his deepest self did he express in his discourse? Instead there would be other questions, like these: What are the modes of existence of this discourse? Where has it been used, how can it circulate, and who can appropriate it for himself? What are the places in it where there is room for possible subjects? Who can assume these various subject functions? And behind all these questions, we would hear hardly anything but the stirring of an indifference: What difference does it make who is speaking? (119–20)

If one can imagine the future according to Foucault, where so little interest rests with the author's relation to the text, the question of the transition, the hoary Marxist conundrum, raises its head. How would the author function disappear, especially considering that it has adapted itself so well to the change from print to broadcast media? What social process would work to strip the author from his or her reign over discourse? What conceivable transformation would undo the cultural operations through which the reader, listener, or viewer thinks of little else than "who is speaking"?

Foucault envisioned his post-author-function culture as a heterotopia, as a different sort of space that functions as a critique of established spatial forms. Heterotopias, in his words, "have the curious property of being in relation with all the other sites, but in such a way as to suspect, neutralize, or invert the set of relations that they happen to designate, mirror, or reflect" (1986, 24). How then would some new space be established that would serve this function of undoing the author? How would a discourse arise in a space that uncoupled the links between author and text, author and book, author and reader, author and press, author and government that had been so firmly stitched together in the course of the formation of modern society?

I contend that the practice of digital writing, linked to electronic networks, may be the mediation Foucault anticipated but did not recognize.[5] Digital writing in many of its forms separates the author from the text, as does print, but also mobilizes the text so that the reader transforms it, not simply in his or her mind or in his or her marginalia, but in the text itself so that it may be redistributed as another text. Digital writing may function to extract the author from the text, to remove from its obvious meaning his or her intentions, style, concepts, rhetoric, and mind—in short, to disrupt the analogue circuit through which the author makes the text his or her own, through which the mechanisms of property solidify a link between creator and object, a theological link that remains in its form even if its content changes from the age of God to the age of Man. Digital writing may produce the indifference to the question "Who speaks?" that Foucault dreamed of and may bring to the fore in its place preoccupations with links, associations, and dispersions of meaning throughout the Web of discourse. And this is so not simply for alphabetic text but for sounds and images, as well. The issue rests with the mediation, with the change from analogue to digital techniques.

Foucault's insistence on a "murmur of indifference" to the question "Who speaks?" echoes his critique of Cartesian-Hegelian individualism but also raises difficulties for his genealogical method. He produces in his writing, within the domains of the book and the author function, an alternative cultural position. Rather than simply delineating the genealogy of the author function and leaving to his readers the task of conceiving and building an other to it, he breaches the limit of theory, expanding its function to trace a direction for political action. Since Foucault did not, and could not, in the 1970s, recognize networked authorship as his future beyond the author function, one may object that he took on too much.[6] To some extent the direction he indicates is highly suggestive. Without the referent of the practice of digital writing in the world, however, his proposal flirts with inflating again the author function, his own, rendering his text an empty proponent of a new culture. Only by reference to the context of networked computing can the indifference to the question "Who speaks?" make a link with a line of practice in a contingent domain of relations of forces. Thereby the author function, in this case my own, is recognized but at the same time reduced and available for a critique.[7]

I introduce, then, the term *analogue author* in place of Foucault's *author function* and *digital author* in place of Foucault's *postauthor utopia*. The terms *analogue* and *digital* are taken from the world of technology and their use here suggests the centrality of the machinic mediation. So much I hope is already clear. But I do not mean the terms in an apodictic, transcendental sense by which certain media would necessarily produce certain figures of authorship. I am not making a philosophical argument but a historical one: that the figure of the author in the modern period is bound to print technology, while in the more recent, perhaps postmodern, perhaps future, computer-mediated, even networked form of writing produces, amid the contingent world of events, a digital author. The chief difference between the two, I contend, is the degree and shape of alterity in the relation of author to writing. Analogue authors configure a strong bond between the text and the self of the writer, a narcissistic, mirroring relation as the text is fundamentally an expression of the author—his or her style, mind, or feelings. The digital author connotes a greater alterity between the text and the author, due in part to the digital nature of the writing. I claim that digital writing is both a technological inscription of the author and a term to designate a new historical constellation of authorship, one that is emergent, but seemingly more and more predominant. So I borrow from the world of technology the terms *analogue* and *digital,* but I also reconfigure them to designate degrees of otherness in the relation of authors to texts.

Gendered Authors

The change from analogue to digital author systems disrupts the existing arrays of powers that supported and benefited from it. Necessarily this includes the ruling subject positions—from those who directly controlled analogue media (Hollywood tycoons, transnational corporations, and in rare cases canonical authors and artists) to the more generally established powers (men, Western Europeans, older adults). The disturbance of the author function shakes up positions of enunciation and subject formations generally. It correlates with those political movements that, from quite other perspectives, have also challenged the status quo. It may come as a surprise, then, to find some of these social and cultural critics not at all pleased with the utopia envisioned by Foucault; instead they see in it a threat to their perceived opportunities for justice. Before turning to examine the question of digital mediation, I shall pause to consider these objections.

The protest against "the death of the subject" is made eloquently by Nancy Hartsock (1990b):

> Somehow it seems highly suspicious that it is at this moment in history... that doubt arises in the academy about the nature of the "subject," about the possibilities for a general theory which can describe the world, about historical "progress." Why is it, exactly at the moment when so many of us who have been silenced begin to demand the right to name ourselves, to act as subjects rather than objects of history, that just then the concept of subjecthood becomes "problematic"? (206)

Hartsock elsewhere (1990a) even accuses Foucault of "getting rid of subjectivity or notions of the subject" (170), which is the opposite of his effort at a critique of the subject. Foucault does not wish somehow to erase the subject but to make the construction of the subject the center of a historical problematic.

Hartsock's complaint that theories of the death of the author disempower dominated groups was echoed again and again as a defense against the perception of depoliticization in works like Foucault's "What Is an Author?"[8] Here, for instance, is Nancy Miller (1982), who adds to the motif a particular gender allusion: "Only those who have it can play with not having it" (53). And again Anne McClintock (1995) echoes the concern: "As colonized countries wrestled their way into independence after World War II; and as women and men of color entered the universities in significant numbers, insisting on defining an alternative to the enshrined white male subjectivity; at just that moment, the requiem was rung on the subject. At the very moment that disenfranchised voices forcibly clamored for the privilege of defining their own identity and authority, 'the author' was declared dead" (304). Indeed the argument that the Foucauldian critique of the subject disempowers dominated groups might be, in Foucault's terms, the enunciative gesture that defines a certain form of feminist discourse.

Hartsock and McClintock complain about the timing of the critique of the subject. If it had happened at some other time, perhaps it would be permitted or even applauded. And there is some truth to this feminist critique of Foucault: he does not put into question gender (Diamond and Quinby 1988) or indeed race (Stoler 1995). Finally he does not contextualize his position in relation to the women's movement, decolonization, and antiracist movements more generally. But there is a context to his thought and it is pertinent to understanding his critique of the subject. Foucault wrote after the collapse of working-class movements in Western Europe, and his work reflects this historical juncture. The critique of the subject represents a repositioning of theory toward the question of the culture of modernity. It is an effort to explore its historical development and its remarkable success. In the context of the late 1960s and early 1970s, Foucault and others recognized the need to get behind the continued presentation, in critical theory, of the resisting agent and the Cartesian ego so that the cultural foundations of the West might be historicized and put into question. It is regrettable that thinkers such as Hartsock and McClintock, not finding the context of Foucault's thought identical with their own, chose not to explore his context and seek ways to deploy elements of his position that might enhance their own, but instead find in him only a challenge to their move, which actually goes back to and repeats the problems of identity that he had already opened to critique.

Some critics countered this defense of the subject by arguing that subordinated subject positions ought not to strive to occupy the place and take on the subject position of the ruling group. Pointing to the danger of such a move, Luce Irigaray and other feminists contend that "any theory of the subject will always have been appropriated by the masculine" (Irigaray 1985, 133). But Foucault makes it clear that in the first instance he neither defends the subject nor rejects the subject. He wishes rather to develop a method of analysis that elucidates how the subject is constructed so that we become capable of proposing new forms of the self.

I do not wish to engage at length this debate over the gendered character of Foucault's work at the general level of its implications for the critique of the subject but in particular to focus on the question of the effects of digitization on the construction of the author/subject. The shift from analogue to digital authorship is not primarily an effect of theory but a change in the material practices of writing. I do not denounce the author/subject in a theoretical gesture but note its reconfiguration in social space. The theoretical problem posed by digital authorship is the question of how to comprehend these changes so that the most beneficial political outcomes are recognized and seized.

One promising theoretical direction is offered by Judith Butler (1995), who directly confronts the charge raised by Hartsock. Butler writes, "There is the refrain that, just now, when women are beginning to assume the place of subjects, postmodern positions come along to announce that the subject is dead" (48). Butler goes on to argue that speech acts in modern society produced the sovereign agent as a false denial of the way language structures agency in the first place. Butler's important argument is worth citing at length:

> My presumption is that speech is always in some ways out of our control. . . . Untethering the speech act from the sovereign subject founds an alternative notion of agency and, ultimately, of responsibility, one that more fully acknowledges the way in which the subject is constituted in language, how what it creates is also what it derives from elsewhere. Whereas some critics mistake the critique of sovereignty for the demolition of agency, I propose that agency begins where sovereignty wanes. The one who acts (who is not the same as the sovereign subject) acts precisely to the extent that he or she is constituted as an actor and, hence, operating within a linguistic field of enabling constraints from the outset. (1997, 15–16)[9]

Language here is a material, structuring constraint on identity. A notion of agency that configures the subject as outside of language may offer certain political solace, but it occludes this constraining factor.[10] When the configuration of language undergoes fundamental change, as in the case of digitization, the failure to recognize the effects of its materiality becomes especially problematic.

Foucault himself had responded to similar complaints about his earlier but similar proclamation of "the death of man" in *The Order of Things* (1966). Lucien Goldmann, a noted Western Marxist theorist, objected to the antihumanism of Foucault's assertion. Foucault's important response makes precise the stakes of the question:

> The death of man is a theme that allows light to be shed on the way the concept of man has functioned in knowledge. It is not a matter of affirming that man is dead; it is a matter of seeing, based on the theme—which is not of my invention [and] has been repeated incessantly since the late nineteenth century—that man is dead (or that he is about to disappear, or that he will be replaced by the superman), in what manner and according to what rules the concept of man has been formed and has functioned. I have done the same thing with the notion of the author. Let us hold back our tears. (1983, 28–29)

Without tears, but also, one might add, without Foucault's ironic smile, we must comprehend the shift in subject construction attendant to the emergence of digital authorship.

The issue at stake in digitization of authorship may now be sharply posed: how is the subject reconfigured in this process? Butler's theory of the performative is useful in exploring the question. Speech acts not only represent things but do things. One thing they do is constitute the subject. But speech acts accomplish this ambiguously, partially, never with certainty, Butler contends (1997, 125). She argues for an analysis of the incompleteness of the performative in constituting the subject, not, as Derrida does, in relation to the formal characteristics of the trace (150) but in the fully social context of enunciation. Speech acts *perform in the world,* Butler reminds us, and therein lies political hope: "The possibility for the speech act to take on a non-ordinary meaning, to function in contexts where it has not belonged, is precisely the political promise of the performative" (161). And performatives are so imbricated in the social in part because they are "never fully separable from bodily force" (141). The body is fundamental, to Butler, in the performative speech act as both constituting and constituted. The role of body, she insists further, is at play in writing as well, although she allows for some difference in this regard.

To summarize then: In speech and writing, performatives incompletely but effectively constitute subjects in the world and on the body. Yet if Butler insists on the social and political nature of the process, she does not indicate how different body-text relations, in speech, in handwriting, in print, on the radio, in film, on television, and in cyberspace, each configure the performative process differently and produce, incompletely to be sure, different incarnations of the subject. In one analysis, the video of the Rodney King beating by police, Butler (1993) relates her theory of performativity to the medium of video. She points out the dangers in forgetting the medium and presuming that vision is apolitical: "To claim that King's victimization is *manifestly* true is to assume that one is presenting the case to a set of subjects who *know how to see*" (17). She objects to the use by the defense attorneys of the technique of freeze frame, which rips gestures from their "temporal place in the visual narrative" and eliminates the sound track (20). But these examples of Butler's sensitivity to the medium of the performative do not go far enough. Instead of a more extensive examination of the role of the medium in speech acts, she contextualizes them. She points out that "the field of the visible is racially contested terrain" so "that there is no simple recourse to the visible" (17). The deconstruction of the visible in this manner is, of course, necessary. Yet Butler deploys it against naïveté about the medium ("to think that the video 'speaks for itself' is, of course, for many of us, obviously true"; 17) when the medium itself requires sustained analysis in addition to the social context.

Sandy Stone (1995) makes the argument for the importance of the media and the body in performativity: "Most Western theories of the self, even feminist theories, stop just short of tinkering with the framework upon which the idea of gender itself is based—the framework of the individual's self-awareness in relation to a physical body" (85). As soon as we consider the relationship between bodies and selves, she continues, we must take into account communications technologies as these mediate social groups and speech acts (88). And in a further clarification Katherine Hayles (1999) writes, "Whereas in performative utterances *saying is doing* because the action performed is symbolic in nature and does not require physical action in the world, at the basic level of computation, *doing is saying* because physical actions also have a symbolic dimension that corresponds directly with computation" (275). How then does digital authorship differ from analogue authorship in the performative process of interpellation?

Let us take the example of on-line, synchronous communications in electronic communities where participation requires that one fashion one's own identity and gender. In these cases individuals type messages on computers at different locations, watching their own words and those of others on the screen as they are typed. Each individual is a character, and participation is successful to the extent that the character is believable by others. This is disembodied communication just like letters and print, where the enunciation is separate from the body of the sender. But the communication in on-line communities is also like speech in that it is simultaneous. The important question is the way identity is performed in these contexts. Participants are interpellated by each other, suturing identity in performatives, but the construction of the subject occurs entirely on the screen, determined entirely by the words entered on the keyboard. Participants are authors of themselves as characters, not simply by acts of consciousness, but by the interactions that take place on the screen. In these situations, the body, mediated by the interface of computers and the communications network, enters a new relation with the subject, a dissociated yet actual relation that opens identity to new degrees of flexible, unstable determination. The body no longer constrains the performativity of speech acts to the extent that it does in face-to-face relations. These digital authors enact an unprecedented type of performative self-constitution in which the process of interpellation becomes an explicit question in the communication. Instead of the policeman-teacher-parent-boss hailing the individual in a manner that conceals the performative nature of the communication, in on-line communities one invents oneself and one knows that others also invent themselves, while each interpellates the others through those inventions. Unlike earlier forms of mediated communication, digital authorship is about the performance of self-constitution.

In *The Domain-Matrix* Sue Ellen Case (1996) wrestles with the implications for politics of on-line communities, with their screen genders and volatile identities. She first attempts to privilege sexual orientation politics as a point of resistance to the virtual. She writes:

> Lesbian and gay politics, when theorized, raise the issue of the relation of the virtual to the flesh—the relation of desire to social relations. . . . As the book is challenged by the hypertext, writing by the transmission of digitized images, print culture, in its hermetic, colorless, linear form is intersected by the morphing, multi-spaced environments of new

technologies, money is abstracted through virtual banking procedures, and fleshly social relations transmit through MUDs, MOOs, bulletin boards, and email courtships, the representation of lesbian and gay relations, their political work, is offering up some of the critical strategies necessary to comprehend the new form of exchange. (64)

Case is determined to come to terms with the possibilities offered up for politics by cyberspace, to connect a lesbian agenda with globalized communications technologies. At one point she argues that "lesbian" is not an identity but a space, a collective space in which struggle is performed, a struggle against "the homogenizing effects of Integrated World Capitalism and tele-presences that register commodification and transcendence" (187). "Lesbian" politics would then attempt to confront the enemy on its newest electronic terrain and claim a space for revolt within it. Yet by the conclusion of the work, Case, in moving passages, confesses that the writing of *The Domain-Matrix* brought her to question the basis of her own political views: "I had a firmer notion of how the body and performance related to the screen and performativity when I began to write than when I finished. As I distributed issues around gender, sexuality, and ethnicity within the field, my critical control of their signification seemed to weaken. The field overcame its subdivisions, and I began to feel as if some form of globalism were overcoming my critique of it" (235). In this brutally honest passage, the radicality of the move to the networked computer screen is registered. The stability of earlier forms of critical agency waver when the body is hooked up, through the keyboard, mouse, and screen, to the Internet.[11] So exigent is the practice of self-constitution in communications in cyberspace, so strongly is agency here mediated by information machines, and so utterly dispersed is the space of interaction that oppositional practices of earlier decades no longer seem able to take hold of the situation. To insist upon agency politics in this context is to bury one's face in the sand of the bygone age of Man.

Digression on the Indeterminacy of Technology

Cultural theorists might raise immediately the objection that I am flirting dangerously with technological determinism by drawing direct conclusions about discourse and practice from the introduction of new techniques. To forestall these skeptics I maintain that technologies are no more monosemic than language or action, that the impact of technologies is never the linear result of the intention of their creators or of their internal, "material," capabilities. The Internet, for example, bears not a trace of the U.S. Department of Defense's purpose in developing it: to ensure computer communications in the event of nuclear attack from the Soviet Union. The Soviet Union falls now in the category of proper nouns designated by "formerly," and the Net seems more a threat to the Department of Defense than an instrument of its design. In my own experience with writing technologies, the same contingencies are evident. In junior high school in the mid-1950s in New York City I was required to take a series of courses introducing me to the practical arts. I took cooking, sewing, carpentry, and typewriting. The curricular intent was to train me in manual skills in the event that a middle-class occupation was not in my future. This training was also highly gendered, since women of my generation with a college degree were often hired in professional fields such as publishing with the reduced status of typists. Even with my academic career these basic skills—or at least some of them—have proven useful. In particular, typewriting, considered at the time a menial practice of secretaries, proved invaluable as this technology changed its social status, becoming acceptable first for academics, then, with the introduction of computing in business, even essential for managers and executives. The technology of the keyboard changed within my lifetime from a machine used by low-level clerks to an essential tool of scientists and leaders of industry. With the use of computers in communication, it mutated further into an instrument for sending messages, "chatting" in electronic meeting places, and such. It has also become the source of crippling diseases like carpal tunnel syndrome. This brief exploration of one technology suffices to indicate the complexity of the relation of machines to humans. And we must now move on to consider the question of digital writing.

CHAPTER FIVE

Authors Analogue and Digital

Analogue and Digital

The change from print to computer writing requires a material change in the trace, in the way writing enters the world, circuits through it, and is stored in it. This alteration in the material structure of the trace is not given much importance by most scholars in the human sciences,[1] yet it is fundamental to the reconfiguration of authors and readers, of subjects and objects of speech and all forms of cultural exchange, be they text, image, or sound. When Marx, in *The German Ideology,* writes of language as puffs or perturbations of air, he calls attention to the materiality of language—that it only appears in a material form—but strangely he does not raise the question of the change from speech to print. Print is precisely not puffs of air. This is a surprising omission on his part, since print technology was so important to his own work of disseminating the critique of political economy and because the forms of print were undergoing major changes in his day. The introduction and spread of the cheap newspaper brought current political information to the working class, extending considerably the scope of class consciousness, and the introduction of the typewriter later in the century changed work opportunities for women and altered significantly the means of literary production both for writers and readers. The example of Marx's neglect of the problem of technological mediation in the case of print is hardly exceptional. Critical theorists have generally read through and past the message of the medium.

The shift in the material form of the sign from print to computer writing may be approached initially as a change from analogue to digital. This formulation is often posited by technically expert commentators whose understanding of the attendant philosophical questions is often limited. It is crucial for humanists to recognize the technical side of the issue and for engineers to come to grips with its cultural aspects.[2] I shall focus on the analogue/digital distinction, attempting to explore both its technical and the theoretical dimensions.

The term *analogue* refers to an aspect of the relation between a copy and an original. A taped recording of a sound, for example, transforms waves/cycles of air emitted by a person, for instance, into a configuration of metal oxide particles on a Mylar band. This is accomplished by an electromagnetic transducer that responds to the waves/cycles and moves the particles from a random into a patterned configuration. The relation between the configuration of particles on the tape recording to the original waves/cycles of air is one of analogy; that is, the specific density and distribution of particles resembles the characteristics of the waves/cycles in their amplitude and frequency, their loudness and pitch. The same relation of resemblance is found in the older technology of vinyl records. The grooves on the record, in their width and length, form an analogous configuration to the acoustic waves/cycles so that the stylus or needle tracing the grooves reproduces the shape of the sound. Even though the sound recording, on tape or vinyl, is a different material form from the acoustic event of the sound, there remains an isomorphic relation, or one of similitude, between them. Because of this analogy, some individuals are even able to "read" the grooves on vinyl disks and say which piece of music is inscribed in it. In the case of photographic, film, and television images, the analogous relation pertains between light and the recording medium.

Not so with digital reproduction. In this case the sound as waves/cycles is sampled some forty thousand times a second. (This figure allows two results for what is considered the highest frequency available to the human ear, twenty thousand cycles.) The computer changes the input into a series of zeros and ones according to a formula that maps the sound event, both in loudness and pitch. The formula relating the characteristics of the sound to specific combinations of zeros and ones is arbitrary. In the case of digital recording there exists no resemblance, no analogy between the configuration of digits and the sound. The digits in no way "look like" the sound. The relation between the copy and the original in the case of digital reproduction is much more one of difference than in the case of analogue recording. In both cases, let us not forget, the reproduction includes a material transformation of the original, but in the case of digital copying the material configuration of the copy bears no resemblance at all to the original. As an aside it may be noted that many argue that the reproduction of the sound from a digital recording is superior to that of analogue recording in its coincidence with the original. Digital differs from analogue, therefore, in the extent of their correspondence to the original. The advantage of digital copying over analogue derives from some aspect of this difference.

There are two separate but related questions that follow from the analogue/digital distinction. The first concerns the qualities of difference between the analogue and the digital. The second concerns the specific attributes of the digital as a material form, its electronic character, its numeric character, its ability to be reproduced exactly, transmitted at the speed of light, and stored very efficiently. The implications of the answers to these questions are potentially great for social, cultural, and political issues. They raise the specter of nothing short of a revolution in the figure of the author and the reader.

Analogue and digital copying are both material transformations of an original signal or input. A written or printed word is not the same as a spoken word. The latter is fixed in time and space, evanescent and local. Writing, by contrast, as a material trace, is stable in time and movable in place. Handwriting introduces one relation of the writer and the reader to the text; typewriting and print, different ones. Spoken words rely upon the ear for copying and reproduction; writing depends rather upon the eye. Each change in the form of writing is momentous in its effects upon authors and readers; from cuneiform and papyri to codices and books, the history of writing enormously varies the cultural and social forms of its production and reception. Yet the distinction between speech and writing is much greater than the variations in the written form. That much must be conceded. Is then digital writing to be understood as yet another variation within the history of writing, or is it a more momentous change on the order of the shift from speech to writing? I leave this question to the reader to decide, turning instead to the characteristics of the print/digital distinction.

Print relies upon the alphabet, and alphabets are not analogue types of reproduction. Though early alphabets like ideograms are indeed analogue in that they depict in traces what they refer to, the Greek alphabet is composed of units that, in their combination, bear no relation to the meaning of the words they generate. The word *tree* does not look like a tree. Alphabets in this sense are digital in the sense in which I am using the term. All material variations of writing in alphabets like Greek benefit enormously from their liberation from the constraints of analogue reproduction. Contrasted with the thousands of characters that compose ideographic alphabets, the Greek alphabet contains fewer than thirty distinct units. Yet alphabets do bear isomorphic or nearly isomorphic relations with sounds. This is their abstraction, their increased level of generalization, compared with ideographic writing (Porush 1998, 50). An *a* in a certain language is limited to a repertoire of sounds. Yet, as a material trace, the *a* does not look like any of these sounds and in this sense is not in a relation of analogy to it.[3] Nonideographic alphabets introduce a level of articulation beyond that of ideograms, although even ideographic alphabets must include phonetic elements to account for proper names, for example (Ducrot and Todorov 1979, 194). The phonetic elements stress a relation between a written symbol and the thing represented. The Greek alphabet introduces a relation between a written symbol and its utterance, between two forms of language, writing and speech. The relation between the word and thing becomes conventional, arbitrary, whereas the relation within language between trace and voice is stronger, more direct.[4]

Printed forms of writing enable easy reproduction. They change culture by retaining the temporal dimension already evident in older forms of writing, its endurance and stability, but extend considerably its spatial dimension, disseminating texts widely. Print democratizes writing by its mere distribution of texts in space. But print retains the material constraint of earlier forms of writing: the requirement that a trace is produced on an enduring substance like paper, a substance that is scarce. There is no escape from this characteristic, one that drastically limits the inscription of print in time and space. Regardless of the type of technology through which the trace is achieved—from Gutenberg's mechanical contraptions to the most advanced, automated apparatuses— print means inscriptions on durable materials. With print, language is set loose from speech and handwriting but is also bound tightly with the material in which it resides.

Digitization does not surrender the advantages of writing and print in extending language in time and space or of the alphabet in deepening the articulation of language. Digitization introduces yet another level of articulation of language, however, by introducing sequences of ones and zeros as representations of letters. This simple addition would be cumbersome in the forms of writing and print, somewhat equivalent to the disadvantages of roman numerals in comparison with arabic. But by introducing this change to ones and zeros, the material form of language can shift to the microworld of electrons. In Katherine Hayles's words, "When a computer reads and writes machine language, it operates directly on binary code, the ones and zeros that correspond to positive and negative magnetic polarities" (1999, 274). The basic difference introduced by the digital code is that it is translatable into a simple presence or absence and therefore into a minimal physical trace such as a pulse or an electron. Telegraphy achieves some of this reduction but remains tied to the Newtonian, macroworld of sounds. Once the alphabet is translated into digits, it transcends the constraints of printing and enters another, far different, physical regime: electric language. Digitally coded language remains tied to the umbilical cord of the social world where, in the last instance, it will return and enter human writing or speech, being read or heard and perceived by conscious beings. But before this occurs, electric language moves within an imperceptible dimension and is governed by its material determinations. Digitized language may be placed in the electronic form of the computer, and these may be connected through telephone lines or radio waves, enabling the simultaneous presence of words at any point in the globe.

The Book as Machine: Two Views

Digital writing presents a colossal problem of focus: What aspect of the technology should receive priority? Which part of digital writing impinges on the author and reader and in what way does it do so? Is the important aspect of digital writing the computer as machine, the software program, the graphical interface, the network, the programming code, or the binary storage system, to mention a few possibilities? In order to explore the question of focus I shall analyze the work of Friedrich

Kittler and Vilém Flusser, two theorists of the media who paid particularly close attention to the materiality of technology.

Kittler has written several major works on the question of culture and information technologies: *Discourse Networks: 1800/1900* (1985), *Gramophone, Film, Typewriter* (1986), and *Dracula's Legacy: Technical Writings* (1993) present and explore technocultural difference with an originality matched by few others.[5] Kittler contrasts technocultures on the basis of their ability to store, transmit, and compute the real. He does so from a most productive standpoint: retrospectively from the development of networked computing. He looks at book technoculture, for example, in relation to its ability to store the real. Printed books are limited to words in this respect. Unlike phonograph records and tapes they omit sounds, and unlike film they omit moving images. Since sounds and images are features of experience, the reader incorporates them into the reception of the book regardless of their absence. Kittler writes, "Around 1800 the book became both film and record simultaneously—not, however, as a media technological reality, but only in the imaginary of the readers' souls" (Kittler and Johnston 1997, 39). The reader produced the missing information in acts of imagination. In a brilliant passage, Kittler captures the media effect of the material constraint of book technology: "As long as the book had to take care of all serial data flows . . . words trembled with sensuality and memory. All the passion of reading consisted of hallucinating a meaning between letters and lines" (40). In the next century, around 1900, the phonograph and film began to record audio and video, transforming forever the place of books in culture. Kittler writes, "The dream of a real, visible, or audible world arising from the words is over" (44). The book lost its monopoly over the storing and dissemination of cultural material.

With Kittler's framework one can comprehend effectively the difference between cultural media, say, virtual reality systems and novels. Individuals disciplined by, interpellated by, and accustomed to novels in the form of books often find it very difficult to grasp the innovation of virtual reality systems. Such bookish types regard the novel as already a virtual reality system. But this is only so, after Kittler, because these readers of books "hallucinate" the audio and video data missing from the printed word on the page. In the technoculture of the book, these individuals have developed a certain form of imaginary that works to supply the absent information. As subjects constituted in the technology of the power of books, however, they are not aware of this function as related to the material form of the book, assuming its naturalness and inevitability. Yet precisely this productive imaginary is what is changed in later media such as virtual reality systems. Book readers may find no use for virtual reality systems, film, and the rest, even complaining that the book is superior to these media when in fact they merely register their preference for one technology over others. They often fail to see how individuals constituted by other media—film, television, or virtual reality—might prefer these over books because, constituted in a different technoculture, they have developed different capacities of reception, perhaps visual imaginaries, producing cultural meaning out of visual and aural information or data flows. With the mind-boggling multiplication of media technologies in the twentieth century (not to mention what we are likely to witness in the twenty-first), it becomes imperative, in institutions of higher learning especially, to understand the multiple capacities of subjects constituted by various media, instead of blindly and repeatedly insisting that only one media—the book—and only one set of cultural skills—the imagination or rationality—deserves recognition as intelligence.

With regard to the question of the interpretation of digital writing, Kittler makes some choices concerning the pertinent aspects of technology that I think are less than optimal. In certain places, he interprets the change in writing tools from typewriter to computer as one of loss of perception. He characterizes the change as "a rather sad statement" since "written texts . . . do not exist anymore in perceivable time and space but in a computer memory's transistor cells. . . . [Computer writing] seems to hide the very act of writing: we do not write anymore" (Kittler 1997, 40).[6] These perhaps pessimistic conclusions are achieved by configuring digital writing as a machine process. Such writing is invisible to its author, unlike typing, because signs are stored as sequences of zeros and ones in a file format on a disk. Even though the words appear on the computer screen, for Kittler they are really invisible, inaccessible to inspection by the writer because of their tiny location on the machine. Kittler here ignores the connectivity of digital texts in favor of their physical characteristics in an isolated computing machine. He overlooks the distributed network of textual presence in favor of its containment on a hard disk inside a single machine. In short, Kittler limits his interpretation of digital writing to his own relation to his texts stored in *his* computer. He approaches the question as an analogue author and is dismayed to find his presence missing from his writing. One might just as easily take the stance of a digital author and find an anonymous murmur in the links of hypertexts on the Web.

Kittler accounts for the subject constituted by the book in the form of the imaginary. He reinterprets early-nineteenth-century literary culture from a discovery of the imaginary and the consequent depth of the individual as a historical by-product of a certain discourse network. What philosophers and literary theorists of the period celebrated as transcendental interiority, Kittler links to the material constraints of printed volumes. Vilém Flusser (1992) looks instead to the array of traces on the page of analogue texts, the linear progression of letters composing words; of words composing sentences; sentences, paragraphs; and so forth. Also concerned with the material trace of the printed page, Flusser depicts the constituted reader of books as a linear mind, well suited to logical argument and historical explanation. He writes:

> The first examination of writing reveals that the line, the linear sequence of the characters, is its most impressive aspect. Writing appears here as the expression of a one-dimensional thinking, and thus also of a one-dimensional way of feeling, willing, evaluating, and acting.... Writing, this linear stringing together of signs, actually made possible for the first time a historical consciousness. Only if one writes in lines can one think logically, calculate, criticize, pursue science, philosophize—and act accordingly. (11–12)

Contrary to Kittler's understanding of the book as constituting a subject with interiority and an extended imaginary function, Flusser configures the analogue author as having a linear mentality, as one who amplifies certain forms of rationality.

Since the study of print technoculture is in its infancy, it is not necessary to choose between Kittler and Flusser, between understanding the book as constituting subjects through its absence of sound and image or through its linear sequence of signs. At this point it suffices to note the difficult question of focus. The decision about the precise machinic character of media is crucial to the understanding of their cultural consequences. Yet essentially it is impossible to choose. Rather the researcher benefits from exploring a line of investigation—taking a limitation of a media, or its phenomenal appearance—and experimenting with cultural analysis by making links with institutions and figures, with practices and subject positions of a given time and place. My choice is first to broaden the field of study by looking at the figure of the author in relation to copyright, at the complex institutional matrices in which the author emerges in its analogue form.

Analogue Authors

The history of copyright is complex, differing from country to country and from region to region. In all cases, however, the legal system of copyright is connected with the question of the author. At first, copyright concerned books; later other cultural objects, such as film and brand names, would also be included in the question. In its origins, however, copyright developed around the figure of the author, the individual who had created something distinctive, something that warranted special legal protection. In the case of Anglo-American law, however, it may be argued that in effect what was actually protected was not the creative cultural object—idea or work of fiction—but the book, the material casing in which the novel creation was embodied and reproduced (Lury 1993, 25).[7] As long as books were the major or even only instance governed by copyright, the legal distinction between the idea and the book was nullified in cultural practice by the analogue notion of the author, the spirit contained within the book, governing its meaning.

One other feature of copyright needs to be mentioned at this point, and this concerns the technical nature of the book. Mechanical print technology enabled multiple copies. The simple fact that many copies could be produced changed the relation of the author to the reader. The audience lost specificity, becoming more anonymous and general. The author, in turn, internalized a new, vaguer addressee. The distance between the author and the reader led to new practices of writing in which the author was stimulated to develop textual means to control the reading process. More attention had to be paid, in the composition of the text, to methods of leading the reader, one less familiar to the author, in directions the author chose. An analogue of the author was thus implanted in the text in the form of a controlling voice. The authority of the author had to be embedded in the content and structure of the text, as well as in the material layout of the signs. The book took its modern shape as an array of signs in sentences, indentations, paragraphs, pages, footnotes, and illustrations in the context of its mass reproduction, its increased distance of author and reader.

But the emergence of the figure of the author and the normalization of the printed book as an emanation of the author and as a reliable duplicate was not at all sudden. As Nietzsche and Foucault remind us, origins always occur in a field of forces, with the new struggling and adapting to the old, changing and taking shape only in a historical process of birth. Now that the analogue author may be giving way to a digital one, it is important to recall the historical circumstances of the birth of the analogue author. By doing so we can avoid setting up the analogue author as an abstract figure against which the digital author becomes either demonized or celebrated. We can also avoid the confusion of technological determinism.

Of great assistance in the study of the origins of the analogue author is recent work on the beginnings of the printed book (Goldberg 1990). One work in particular I find most helpful, Adrian Johns's magisterial *The Nature of the Book: Print and Knowledge in the Making* (1998). Johns's accomplishment, one that now seems so right and so obvious but that none before him had noticed, is to show that books were first made in the social-cultural-economic world of the guild. The new technology of print was born in the midst of a precapitalist, feudal, artisanal structure. Guilds were organized to produce a consistent quality of a type of commodity without strong attention to the inventive capacities of the individual. Commodities produced by guilds were above all the result of *collective* labor. When we look at the origins and shaping of the analogue author we must understand that its present figuration in the market structure of a fully modern or even postmodern society was the outcome of a long process of transformation, one that began in a context in which authorship as we think of it was impossible.

Our print culture contains two principles, neither of which applied in the first century or so of book production: that the copy one sees in one's hands is an exact duplicate of all others, especially those of the same edition, and that the "author" of the book may be trusted to have written the words one reads. These are the essentials of print culture and they did not exist during the origins of the book. "The first book," Johns writes, "reputed to have been printed without any errors appeared only in 1760. Before then variety was the rule, even within single editions"

(31). Only two hundred and some years after Gutenberg did a reliable book exist. What is more, the practice of artisans in book-producing guilds—practices that Johns spells out in some detail—encouraged what might be called creative compositing. As he says, "A compositor did not just slavishly copy a writer's manuscript. On the contrary, he enjoyed substantial freedom in his settings" (87–88). The writer of the text in those years had little prestige as an "author." Instead the book was credited to the guild that produced it, as was the case with all objects made in the artisanal mode of production. The guild that printed books was the Stationers, within which a long battle for control of the book was played out, not with the author but between the printers and the booksellers. Guild masters were the highest authority in this very hierarchical society, and printing was done in the home of the master, mixing family life and work in the unique blend of early modern European life. The "author" was at best a guest in this setting, someone without much command (102). In the wider society, among the powers that prevailed and among people in general, the Stationers were recognized as the "authors," not the writer of the text (138).

Another general feature of these first two centuries of print that nullified the modern analogue author was piracy. Guilds could not in the end completely control the production of books. Piracy was inherent in the structure of the Stationer's guild, so much so that pirates "at times were among its most prominent and upstanding members" (167). The term *piracy* was applied to books by their users and was an effort by them to designate one aspect of the uncertain status of the object before them. How could one place trust in objects in 1600? In a society that was generally one of face-to-face interactions, that was extremely hierarchical and based on personal relations of allegiance and command, objects only attained the moral status of trust through the individuals and groups who made them. What counted, then, for the reader was the moral fiber of the stationer: "The character of the Christian Stationer was properly assessed in terms of domestic virtue, personal credit, religious constancy, and moderate temperance. . . . links were constantly being constructed between vocation, family life, piety, and soteriology" (143). These qualities of the stationer were what people read on the title page of the book, not the character of the author, and these ensured reliability. In this world of face-to-face relations, oral words alone had epistemic value. If one did not know the Stationer, what one heard from friends framed the value of the printed words on the page. As Johns writes, "Occupying such confined and encompassed premises, surrounded by gossip and conspiracy, a successful book-selling business consequently required the active preservation of delicate systems of trust and honor among people in constant proximity to each other" (113). In this context, piracy was but one element in the mix that constructed a relation of trust between the reader and the words on a page.

Most important in understanding the conditions in which analogue authors emerged is the fact that authors themselves were not cultural figures of great trust. Authors were precisely those one did not know, those whose character was a blank to the reader. The first impulse of people in this world was to distrust authors. What Johns shows so effectively is that the moral act of reading in the early modern period could not constitute epistemic value in the author's words. This trust had to be learned by readers in the course of centuries. When today we question the truth value of words or images on the Internet, we are simply in the same position as readers of books were in the seventeenth century. And perhaps it was more difficult for our forebears to learn to trust authors of printed works than it is for us to learn to trust digital authors on the Net because they made the leap from trust in spoken words uttered in proximate practices to the disconnected splash of ink on paper.

Enormous social and cultural changes had to occur before the analogue author familiar to us would emerge as an important figure. Literacy had to become general, diminishing personal authority relations; markets for books had to expand and replace guilds with capitalist commodities; legal systems of copyright had to be perfected and political regimes had to make such laws effective; and, above all, the cultural sign of the author had to displace the guild master. For this latter to happen, individuals had to be defined as interior consciousness, which could then be externalized first in manuscripts, then in print. The value of originality in consciousness had to grow, and readers had to develop skills to interpret it and render it significant. All of this began to fall into place, Johns contends, in the early nineteenth century. But as we shall see by the end of the nineteenth century, analogue authors began losing their prominence to the captains of the culture industry, who manipulated copyright in their lust for lucre. The irony of this history is that academic disciplines in the humanities became institutionalized just as analogue authors began to lose control of cultural commodities. It has been the burden and the glory of the humanities to preserve the analogue author just as this figure became socially irrelevant.

Analogue Authors in the Regime of Broadcast Media

The special relation of author to copyright changed as new media developed. With the rise of the electronic reproduction of text, voice, and image, limitations on copying characteristic of print gave way to broadcast. The electronic broadcast enabled far greater reproduction, reaching truly mass audiences, from the thousands to the millions. Such a change in the material means of reproduction, as Celia Lury (1993, 51) points out, enlarged the economic scale of cultural objects. With a truly mass audience, cultural works became economically significant. Culture, in Adorno and Horkheimer's words, became an industry. In this new context of material reproduction, the position of the author and the status of copyright shifted: with larger sums of money at stake, those in control of the means of production took a greater degree of control over the production or creation of the cultural object. Displacing the author, the film producer, the radio channel, or the television network intruded upon the process of cultural creation to ensure market success in ways that book publishers of the eighteenth century could not. The media, as Adorno (1978) complained, created the success of the cultural object. The mere repetition of songs on radio stations, he noted, shaped their reception (270–99). With the media playing such a great role in cultural creation, the figure of the author began to decline. In Lury's words, "The commercial exploitation of the new technologies of replication has required a new emphasis on the processes of reception rather than the authorial moment as the basis for defining the terms of intellectual property" (1993, 56).

With the broadcasting model of cultural reproduction, brand names, logos, images, and trademarks displace the author from the center of the cultural object and the focus of copyright (Coombe 1998, 70). The question of intellectual property shifts to these features of the cultural object,[8] but the privileges of copyright are kept. Cultural objects are the second leading export of the economy of the United States, behind weapons. Their importance also resides in the general transformation of all industrial into postindustrial economies, in which information plays a greater and greater role in every level of economic life. Copyright law, with its analogue author, has become, in the broadcast age of cultural reproduction, an entirely different legal structure. Instead of protecting authors and cultural innovation, it is nothing less than the general law of property. Wealth increasingly is defined as information and copyright is its police force. Crimes against property are less and less the appropriation of or damage to a physical object than the illicit copying of text, image, and sound.

Digital Authors

How, then, are authors affected by digitization? As a hypothesis, we may explore the proposition that the shift in the scene of writing from paper and pen or typewriter to the globally networked computer is a move that elicits a rearticulation of the author from the center of the text to its margins, from the source of meaning to an offering, a point in a sequence of a continuously transformed matrix of signification. I say "elicits a rearticulation" rather than "directly *moves* a rearticulation" in order to avoid any hint of technological determinism. If there is one rule that may obtain to the introduction of new technologies, it is not determinism but unpredictability. For example, Marshall McLuhan foretold the disappearance of books with the spread of broadcast media. But one trend that is emerging with computer technology is the oxymoronic digital book. Manufacturers are now falling over themselves to market a computer in the form of a book, a computer that combines the advantages of the book's ease of handling and portability with the computer's strength of storing and manipulating vast quantities of data. One company sells a 2.9-pound, 8 1/2-by-11-inch object that contains the exact format of book pages and is even leather bound! Another company markets a booklike computer that weighs only 1.25 pounds (Silberman 1998, 98, 100–102, 104). This doubling back of new technologies upon old, creating unforeseen combinations, renders futile linear predictions. Whatever happens to the author function will occur through a congeries of discourses and practices that are so complex that they will be an event. Nevertheless a horizon of visibility is at least plausible: the move is or may be one from the author function of modernity to a multiple, unstable author of postmodernity.

Stability of the Sign in Time and Space

The space/time configuration of the analogue author is different from that of the digital author. Set firmly on the printed page, the words of analogue authors speak to readers without a response. The traces of ink on the page are unaltered by the reader response, be it in a cognitive event, a marginal inscription, a printed review, an essay, or a book. In each case, the printed page is unaltered by the reader so that others may read the same page or another copy of the page and see the same traces, the same arrangement of signs. This page also exists uniquely in space and time. This page is here and now. One must physically move it to displace it or one must displace oneself to approach it. The page is an object in the world, obstinately enduring from moment to moment, subsisting in a place through the laws of inertia. Even if there exist multiple copies of the page, each one is subject to the identical conditions of material embodiment. True enough that time wears away at the paper. It shows its age to the reader and to the chemical analyst. That is the way of objects in space. They disappear, however slowly. But for long periods, they are enough the same to yield themselves to different readers with the exact display of traces.

In the digital world, texts are mobile and changeable. I can move a digital text around the world in an instant. Space offers no resistance to bytes on the Internet. A few nanoseconds is all it requires to circle the globe. From the point of view of a reader, a digital text is everywhere at once, so long as the appropriate technical conditions apply. Time constraints of bits are those of electrons. They apply as surely as those that apply to the molecules that compose pages, but they are different laws with different effects on the practice of reading. Insofar as digital texts are everywhere at once, they extend the power and authority of the analogue author. If digital texts did no more than disperse themselves more efficiently and ubiquitously than paper, the analogue author would perhaps be expanded.

But the temporal instantaneity of digital texts undermines their spatial stability. Embodied in computer files, digital texts subsist in space only at the whim of the reader. The author of digital texts loses the assurance of their spatial continuity. Pages of digital text have the stability of liquid. They may be altered in their material arrangement of traces as they are read. They may be combined with other texts, reformatted in size and font, have sounds and images added to them or subtracted from them. And all of this may be done with almost no effort. No doubt about it: bits may be moved, erased, or changed as easily as they are read. Digital texts thus have more permanence than paper in the sense that they may be distributed or copied without alteration. At the same time they have no permanence whatever. Digital texts are subject to a material regime fundamentally different from analogue texts. I contend that the author function of the analogue period of textual reproduction cannot endure the change to the technology of the power of bits.

Analogue authorship took form in the placid world of the printed page. Here signifiers succeeded one another without alteration. The reader could return time and again to the page and reexamine the words it contained. A readerly imaginary evolved that paid homage to this wonderful author who was always there in his or her words, ready to repeat him- or herself, always open to be admired or criticized. The world of analogue authors was leisurely, comforting, reassuring to the cognitive function, and expanding through continuous exercise of the visual function. Authors of printed pages controlled the meaning of the page in Foucault's sense and were invested with aura in Benjamin's sense in good part through the material configuration of pages of paper. A printing industry, a market for books, an educational system all developed around the page and the continuity of its arrangement of ink. Modern culture as we have known it in the West is inconceivable without the space/time constraints of pages and books. As we move into digital authorship, we can expect serious alterations in the author figure and in the readerly imagination evinced by mobile bits and liquid pages traveling at the speed of light. These natural laws of digital authorship are yet only in their beginning stage of development. We can expect that someday they will constitute the formative conditions for a new regime of authorship with its own definition of author's rights; its own practices of distribution, editing, and production; and its own legal, political, and economic configuration. Practices of digital authorship have already begun to bring changes to the character of the text, most notably in hypertext.

Hypertext and Digital Authors

The case of hypertext may be seen to confound copyright law as it affects authors. Legal experts agree that authors deserve copyright in U.S. jurisprudence because they have expressed original cultural ideas in their work; they have implanted analogues of their mental creativity in the text. But digital authorship raises many questions about the relation of an author's creativity to a work. For example, does the translation of an encyclopedia into a hypertext format for publication as a CD-ROM or a Web page constitute new intellectual labor, asks copyright lawyer Pamela Samuelson? She continues: "Someone who designs a hypertext system may be able to speed up delivery of graphic images from the computer's memory to a display screen by using highly efficient graphics compression and decompression algorithms. Would these algorithms be part of the copyrightable 'expression' of the hypertext product?" (1992, 699). Or further, if one makes links in a hypertext, is this an act of authorship that is capable of being subject to copyright? Indeed, perhaps authorship is constituted by the reading of a digitally formatted text, recorded as a series of links or as a rearrangement of the text. And finally, if a hypertext circulates on the Web, undergoing numerous additions and even deletions, who may claim to be the author of the text?

Hypertext may be taken as the paradigm of the digital author. Hypertext is a digital text that may be read not in the fixed direction suggested in a printed book but as a series of links that jump across the presented text in any direction. It may exist on a CD-ROM, a hard disk on an individual computer, or on a site on the Internet, on any medium compatible with digital technology. These links may be provided by the author, by the reader, by previous readers, or by any combination of these. Many scholars have noted the novelty of hypertext in comparison with printed books and its implications for theory and literature (Bolter 1990; Landow 1992; Lanham 1989; Murray 1997; Ryan 1999). Hypertexts may stand alone, being read in a program on a single computer (Joyce 1987; Moulthrop 1991) or be connected to a database, such as George Landow's Dickens project, which combines novels, criticism, history, and philosophy in text and graphic form (Landow 1997).

Katherine Hayles (1997), searching for the limits of the analogue/ digital divide, explores the implications of hypertext even when it appears in the form of print. Hayles insists that hypertext is a form of symbolic expression that appears in all media. For instance, a work like *Dictionary of the Khazars* (Pavic 1988) appears in print but is in many respects hypertextual. Yet Hayles is more convincing when she connects the materiality of the media to cultural formation in her analysis of Shelley Jackson's *Patchwork Girl,* a hypertext that is published in digital form on the Internet. After a stunning analysis of the fragmentary body of the woman in this narrative, its connection with Mary Shelley's *Frankenstein,* with gender theory and the construction of the subject, Hayles argues for the specificity of hypertext to its material manifesta-

tion in networked, digital form: "The construction of multiple subjectivities in this text and the reconfiguration of consciousness to body
are both deeply bound up with what I have been calling flickering signification, constituted through the fluidly mutating connections between
writer, interface, and reader" (1997, 28). Hayles argues eloquently for a
literary analysis that heeds the medium, for changes in the habits of textual interpretation to account for the shift from print to digital hypertext.

At the other extreme from Hayles's argument that hypertext may appear in print form, *American Quarterly* devoted a special issue to the
question of hypertext. The novelty introduced by this official journal
of the American Studies Association was to publish four articles on-line,
solicit responses to the on-line essays, and publish some of the responses
to the on-line articles in print. As the editor of the special issue notes,
the experiment allowed the exploration of the differences between on-
line and print publication (Rosenzweig 1999). The on-line essays, unlike their print versions, included moving pictures, sounds, images, entire databases of documents, and virtual world, or three-dimensional,
images. If publication on-line in hypertext format introduces startling
possibilities, it also entails great technical burdens, such as incompati-
bilities between browsers accessing the pieces, problems that simply do
not exist in the print format.

But in principle the entire World Wide Web may be taken as one hypertext since any site may be linked to any other site. The profound implications of this for the subject of writing are just what Donna Haraway (1997) notices in the case of science and Mosaic, the first Web
browser: "Mosaic was about the power to make hypertext and hyper-
graphic connections of the sort that produce the global subject of techno-
science as a potent form of historically contingent, specific human nature at the end of the millennium" (126). Although many literary critics
are skeptical about the novelty of hypertext in relation to books, the
issue appears in quite a different guise when digital texts are understood
in relation to the totality of the Web. In fact, the principle of hypertext
is easily deduced from the problem of data storage, as Vannevar Bush
(1945) did with his Memex (MEMory EXtender) project in 1945.

Since the issue of digital texts is crucial to the argument of this book,
it is worth dwelling for a moment on positions that deny the importance of the change from analogue to digital texts. Among writers on
this topic there is one who has posed the issues in a most systematic

and interesting form. Espen Aarseth (1997) argues for the unique nature of digital texts, which he calls "ergodic." In this respect he differs from other literary analysts who refuse any difference at all to hypertexts. Yet Aarseth claims that ergodic texts depend for their qualities not on the material structure of the text but on its relation to the reader (59). Aarseth is opposed not only to skeptical literary critics but also to terminology that relies upon what he calls "computer industrial rhetoric"—terms such as *hypertext, interactive, virtual,* and *nonlinear.* His denial of the importance of the material casing of the text is most peculiar. He writes, "The politics of the author-reader relationship, ultimately, is not a choice between paper and electronic text, or linear and nonlinear text, or interactive or noninteractive text, or open and closed text, but instead is whether the user has the ability to transform the text into something that the instigator of the text could not foresee or plan for" (164). But does not the material form of the text dictate whether the user can change it or not? And in the end he reverses himself on the issue of materiality, defining an ergodic text as "one that in a material sense includes the rules for its own use" (179). He even complains that literary theory, including that of poststructuralists, "seldom" accounts for the "materiality of literature" (164–65).

His illustration of independence of the "user-text relationship" from "the physical stratum of the medium" is the change from long-playing records to compact discs, in which, he argues, the shift in the cultural object from analogue to digital "did not change any substantial aspects of the cultural production or consumption of music" (59). As we have seen in chapter 3, the advent of digital music not only changed the production and consumption of music but in fact is stimulating a revolution in this domain of the culture industry. The early shift to digital music did have an impact on the user: it reduced the ability of the listener to influence the quality of the reproduced sound. The introduction of compact discs destroyed the listener's ability to tinker with playback technology. All one could do is buy a better-sounding CD player. With long-playing records, the audiophile had much greater flexibility in extracting sound from the grooves of the storage medium. If anything, the introduction of CDs diminished the ergodic quality of the text, to use Aarseth's term, reducing the user-text interaction to a passive mode of playback.

However, when digital music is extracted from the compact disc and transferred into a file format such as MP3 on the hard disk of the computer, and further when the file is placed on the Internet for exchange and copying between users, the music becomes ergodic to an extent that is unimaginable. Music reproduction, as we have seen, returns to the folk level of participation: the cultural object becomes open to the user for reproduction, distribution, and even transformation. As in digital texts, digital music files transform the user into a creator, a manufacturer, and a distributor. A better example of the profound impact of a change in the material form of the cultural object could hardly be found.

The issue of the digital author must not be reduced to that of hypertext. Hypertext may most profitably be approached as a special case of writing on the Internet. E-mail, chat rooms, MUDs (multi-user domains), MOOs (multi-user domains, object oriented)—all forms of synchronous and nonsynchronous communications in digital form across networked computers raise the fundamental issue of the medium and its reconfiguration of the author. If we restrict the discussion of digital authors to hypertexts, the literary model of authorship plays too much of a role in our thinking. Digital authors are mediated by a vast apparatus of interconnected information machines. Digital authors are not simply separated from their words, as they are in the print media, but reconfigured by their relation to the machinic apparatus. Because digital writing may be rewritten with ease, the stability of words on paper is lost, severing the link between author and text that was established with so much difficulty during the first centuries of print, as we have seen. The cultural practice of taking authors of books as trustworthy authorities, as persons of possibly great creativity, is difficult to reproduce in the case of digital texts on the Internet. This, of course, by no means prevents the establishment of a new cultural practice in which authorship as we know it is somehow sustained. But the case of digital texts does indicate a rupture in existing practices and the need for a new invention of authorship.

When analogue authors were installed in the cultural landscape the modern subject was being articulated in discourse and practiced in daily life. The figure of the analogue author fit well with the emerging sense of the body as private, the self as separate from the world of objects, and the investment in rationality as human essence and consciousness as the source of meaning. It fit well with the practice of distanced relations of the free enterprise market, the theory of representative democracy, and secular education in literacy and mathematics. It fit well, in addition, with the narcissistic arrogance of European superiority and imperialist adventure and with patriarchy in its new articulation in the urban nuclear family. Each of these hallmarks of modernity had its own temporality; by no means was all of this some unified essence, some spirit of the age, or even some revolutionary project of a well-defined group of political agents.

Digital writing emerges at a very different point of history, which might be characterized as follows: The broadcast media, as many have argued, have done much to diminish or even dissolve the rational, autonomous ego. Global capitalism is reconstructing planetary relations along very different lines from older colonialism. The viability and even legitimacy of leading modern institutions is no longer secure, even though alternatives are by no means obvious. Digital authorship arrives, then, in a specific context and the shape it is given in the decades to come will owe much to that context as well as to its material characteristics. It is my contention that the more beneficent configuration of digital authorship can come only from practices that explore its particular potentials, perhaps with an eye to the best that analogue authorship has offered but by no means with a sense that at best we can only repeat its achievements. This is a great moment to experiment with digital forms of writing and communication, even though these experiments will be resisted by the gatekeepers of authorship—the watchdogs of copyright, printing establishments, tenure committees, and so many others.

Visual Texts

As another example of the complex relation of technology to culture in the shift from analogue to digital,[9] let us consider the case of the effects of virtual reality technologies on the classic visual order of Renaissance perspectivism. The discussion of visual culture often focuses on a change from the literary to the visual, from text to image as the dominant form of mediation (William Mitchell 1994). What is often overlooked in this regard is that text itself is visual; the printed page, just like film, is accessed through the eyes. Yet the cultural force of perspectivism obtains in both cases. As long as the culture positions the viewer or reader as an interior subject confronting a discrete object, as Norman Bryson (1988) contends, "vision is still theorized from the standpoint of a subject placed at the center of the world" (87). The Cartesian subject may endure through vast changes in media. Indeed most virtual reality technologies present the viewer with a field of vision that resembles to a surprising degree the drawings of Leon Battista Alberti, a world of space in which Euclidean geometry is enhanced by the illusion of three-dimensionality. The representation of Renaissance perspectivism continues even in the classic novels of cyberspace. As Sandy Stone (1995) notes, "the geometry of cyberspace as Gibson described it [in *Neuromancer*] was Cartesian" (34).

The paradox of virtual perspectivism must not obscure the transformations that are under way. Digital space, as I have argued, introduces underdetermination as the material novelty of the Net, upsetting the cultural coherence of the subject/object split and reconfiguring this relation into a human/machine assemblage. Alberti's Renaissance city does not translate into the medium of the Internet (William Mitchell 1997, 1994). In the simulated three-dimensionality of virtual reality on the Internet such as in Active Worlds, in a game like SimCity, or in the architecture of MOOs, digital space is not experienced as linear or Euclidean. The on-line participant jumps from one location to another in associative moves that are much like those in hypertexts. When the body moves in territorial space or when the viewer images this movement in film and, mutatis mutandis, in printed pages, the eye and flesh construct the horizon as object, one that may be negotiated. Of course there are important exceptions, such as the garden in Daniel Liebeskind's new Jewish Museum in Berlin, where a slanting floor and standing concrete slabs produce disorientation and nausea, where the subject collapses within the field of the object. In digital realms one moves only with the machinic apparatus; one's eyes and flesh incorporate and are incorporated by the space constructed by the networked computer. The "realism" of this domain is virtual and digital (Heim 1998). Just as one may in the domain of discourse ask with Foucault, "What does it matter who speaks?" in cyberspace one may ask, "What does it matter who is on-line?"

Conclusion

Many of the features of digital authorship, as they affect the conditions of work in the humanities, are in some sense anticipated in the modern period. From the novels of Lawrence Sterne to the theoretical practice of Roland Barthes, anticipations of hypertext, for instance, may be gleaned. If the digital imaginary is here foreshadowed, the practice of digital

authorship had to await the material inscription of networked computing. Only when this rearrangement of ink into bits, this profound desta-
bilization of the trace, occurred could the regime of the author function be transformed in countless practices of symbolic culture. Only
then could the Gutenberg Galaxy become overlaid with a universe of
cyberspace.

CHAPTER SIX
Nations, Identities, and Global Technologies

It may have been by the ghostly light of a computer screen that some of the men and women found dead in the Rancho Santa Fe house-turned-temple first got word of the oft-changing cult now called Heaven's Gate.

—Terence Monmaney

Fear and Trembling in the Halls of Power

As a political unit, the nation is facing an ever expanding set of challenges. Modern systems of transportation and communication facilitate global exchanges of commodities, populations, and information, often evading the borders and jurisdictions of the nation-state. Faced with an increasingly interconnected globe, the nation may no longer be able to sustain its territorial hegemony. Some commentators conclude that the nation-state has ceased to be a viable political entity, placing democracy itself in jeopardy (Guéhenno 1995). Most observers, however, note with some trepidation the globalizing trends that put the nation into question. In this chapter I shall briefly examine these trends, look at the various anxieties provoked by globalizing information flows, and attempt to outline a way of conceptualizing the current situation with an emphasis on its emancipatory possibilities. Although I will focus on the anxieties aroused by globalizing trends, I recognize that there are also great expectations in the scene, from the drooling of free marketers at the fading away of tariffs and quotas on commodities, to the broad grin of liberal democrats as dictators disappear from perches of power, to the breathless hopes of technophiles at the prospect of unfettered planetary communications. As bothersome as these optimistic stances are to some, I shall ignore them in order to keep some coherence in my analysis.

Transnational phenomena may be grouped under three headings—commodities, populations, and information. Each has distinct effects upon the nation-state.

International corporations have become multinational and now transnational, with a shift from having subdivisions in more than one nation to integrating production on a worldwide scale, finally verging toward becoming "virtual corporations" whose location in space is increasingly difficult to determine (Mowshowitz 1992).[1] In the first phase of the industrial revolution, as better transport systems emerged, trade expanded between nations, and a global, if unequal, division of labor emerged, with some nations trading industrial goods and others raw materials. In the next phase, firms established branches in foreign countries, dispersing their reach across national boundaries, or peripheral nations set up substitute industries for those of the center. At the same time companies exported labor processes to other countries, so that commodities were produced multinationally. Finally the center of the corporation itself was dispersed by taking advantage of advanced communications systems. Economists have calculated that the process of globalization is the most dynamic sector of many advanced societies (Castells 1993, 37). Increasingly, agglomerations of economic power are global in scope and interest, breaching the historic alliance between the nation-state and national economic institutions. These centers of power are by no means evenly distributed across the globe but are concentrated in key sites: research shows that, in the United States, fully one-half of Internet hosts are found in just five states (Moss 1998, 117).

Along with the globalization of the corporation and of labor, commodities have become transnational, circulating across the planet and bringing the material style and consumer culture of nations into direct juxtaposition. In earlier centuries commodity flows were mainly, though never exclusively, agricultural products and minerals, reflecting climatic and geological differences more than cultural and social ones. Now exchanges include industrial and postindustrial objects, from automobiles to software programs, from soft drinks to films. Along with material objects, cultural meanings and attitudes circulate the planet. If scientific assumptions travel with computers, so do consumerist lifestyles accompany the importation of jeans and music. The intensity of these mixings has resulted in some areas in products that are global in composition, such as world music. But in all areas, as Arjun Appadurai (1990) has argued, the circulation of objects includes a continuous resignification when the imported commodity is appropriated by and integrated into the local society. Goods flow around the earth, and are mapped again locally. The assumptions of foreign cultures are absorbed and new complex, global articulations result. What was once a sign associated with a particular nation becomes a multicultural phenomenon, as will attest the taco made in Minnesota by Kraft Foods.

At the same time people are in motion, emigrating temporarily or permanently across national borders for political, economic, or other reasons. More and more, territorial populations are mixtures of cultures, ethnicities, and races, each group with varying commitments to the national government in their adoptive territory. As the anthropologist Roger Rouse (1991) puts it, "We live in a confusing world, a world of crisscrossed economies, intersecting systems of meaning, and fragmented identities. Suddenly, the comforting modern imagery of nation-states and national languages, of coherent communities and consistent subjectivities, of dominant centers and distant margins no longer seems adequate" (8). Large numbers of peoples are in movement because of the ravages of civil war, as in Burundi, Bosnia, and Kosovo; because of invitations to work or extreme local poverty, as in Turkey and Mexico; because of changing political regimes, as in Vietnam and the former Soviet Union; because of political oppression, as in Central America; or because of hopes for better economic opportunities, as in parts of Asia. This extraordinary mixing of peoples, as evidenced so clearly in southern California, breaks what once may have appeared to be the natural links between the nation-state on the one hand and language and traditions on the other hand (Cheah and Robbins 1998). The taken-for-granted aspects of national institutions and identities are now in doubt. If the nation-state is threatened by loss of control over its economic resources, it is equally challenged to become a guardian of multiple culture—not a melting pot on the model of assimilation but a negotiator between heterogeneous groups.

In addition to the challenges of mobile economic assets and human populations, the nation-state faces another novelty: globalization takes place at the level of culture itself (Tomlinson 1999). The world is increasingly linked by an ever thickening network of communications systems, extending its reach in a capillary-like structure to every nook and cranny of the planet—first the telegraph and the telephone system with its underwater cables, next television with its orbiting satellite technology, and now the Internet, combining all previous communications systems, amplifying them in new ways and integrating them with digitized computer apparatuses (Deibert 1997). The Internet also provides the innovation of combining the decentralization of the telephone network with television's capability of reaching large audiences. And it improves on each of these: the Internet's decentralization is more developed than that of the telephone system since it avoids the controls of a circuit-switched technology. It improves on television's broadcast model because it is a many-to-many, interactive system in which a message sent to a large number of participants may be responded to by an individual or by many individuals. In addition, the digital form of information on the Internet provides the advantage of virtually costless copying, storing, editing, and distribution.

The digital form of Internet communications is crucial to the complications it poses to the nation-state. One may hypothesize that the nation-state's ability to interpellate individuals into national identity is only possible in an analogue media system (Morely and Robins 1995). How is this so? In principle, digital information enables infinite, costless, perfect reproduction. National laws governing culture presume a material form that limits reproduction to the presence of an original. In order for national laws to control culture (intellectual property), there must be an original object that exists in a material form that cannot easily be reproduced. Yet once digitized, the original cultural object loses its privilege, its ability to control copies of itself, escaping the laws that would manage it.

In addition, digital information may be transported without regard to the posts the nation established to monitor and control its movement. Digital information may include instructions about its destination that permit it to flow within a decentralized network. Aside from speech, analogue information flows could be controlled by nationally instituted stations. Post and telegraph offices, telephone circuitry, broadcast licenses, and film and record distributors easily conform to the power systems that derive their authority ultimately from the nation. Not so with digital culture. On the Internet, information is contained in multiple packets, each with delivery instructions. A packet communicates with automated switching points that are not fixed. The address on a letter passes through determinate postal stations, a flow that can be regulated or interrupted at any point. An analogue telephone conversation requires an open circuit that can be monitored. A digital message—text, voice, or even moving image—travels autonomously to its destination without regard to instituted points of control. In these ways digital culture becomes detached from the powers of the nation, moving globally at the speed of light (assuming enough bandwidth) in an unregulated sphere of communication. The change in the material form of culture from analogue to digital in principle enables information to bypass existing, national relations of force.[2] One commentator goes so far as to characterize the nation's relation with new technology as warfare: "While regulation and design of technological artefacts and of their use are neither impossible nor useless, we are increasingly unable to extend this traditional technology-taming approach to some of our major innovations. Society therefore has no choice but to defend itself against unknown dangers flowing from our technological achievements. We are at war with our own products and with our overwhelming technological skills" (Lenk 1997, 133).

Although the Internet began as an instrument of U.S. Cold War strategy, it is now beyond the control of any nation-state, and its sharply increasing usage consistently ignores national borders and their jurisdictions. The Internet is becoming a paranational culture that combines global connectivity with local specificity, a "glocal" phenomenon that seems to resist national political agendas and to befuddle national political leaderships. The level of ignorance on the part of many political leaders about the Internet, as late as mid-1996, was evident in a campaign speech by Bob Dole. He said at one point in the campaign, "The Internet is a good tool to use to get on the Net."[3]

Postnational Anxiety

These three massive transformations—economic, demographic, and cultural—of the past several decades induce various types of anxiety in national populations and governments. The patriotic white male Timothy

McVeigh, who, fearing a multiracial society, bombed the federal building in Oklahoma City in April 1995, and the U.S. government, with its fear of terrorists, local and foreign, while apparently in opposition, are in fact responding to the same conditions of postnationalism. Without identifying the bomber and the U.S. government, they are nonetheless in a strangely similar position regarding globalization. The bomber is confused by the same circumstance as is the government. Neither knows how to respond to the process of globalization. The U.S. government's very effort to secure its borders from "terrorism" (one might see terrorism as an aspect of globalization) is similar to the fantasy on the part of the bomber in Oklahoma of an America secure from the "contamination" of foreign bodies. If the U.S. government were able effectively to safeguard its national sovereignty to the extent that it was able in the nineteenth century, the fear of the bomber would diminish. But neither side can reverse the trend toward globalism, and both will no doubt continue to struggle with each other, blindly and tragically.

I shall explore the question of the anxiety raised by globalization, specifically in relation to the Internet. I shall do so at three levels: the individual in daily life, the national government, and the intellectual. I shall interpret these anxieties in relation to the destructuring of national institutions and cultures and with a view to understanding how, in their negative reaction, they foreshadow a new politics of globalization. The anxieties aroused by the Internet are a revealing index of its novelty, of how different it is as a mediator of communication, and therefore of the changes it might bring to human relations in general. Certainly globalization is a complex topic, and certainly the effects at the economic, demographic, and cultural levels are distinct, even opposed to some extent. In what follows I am primarily concerned with the cultural aspect of globalization and its effects upon the nation-state.

As an aside it is well to recall that new technologies often arouse deep fears. In the United States in the 1920s and 1930s, radio, for example, was perceived as a threat, especially by some parents. They feared that their children would be exposed to dangerous ideas. And they were right, since radio, like television a few decades later, brought into the privacy of the home ideas and cultural forms that could not easily be monitored by parents. But there were other forms of anxiety, as well. In Berlin a newspaper in 1925 reported that women feared listening to the radio because the strained expression it required when the reception was poor resulted in "radio wrinkles," or even worse "a radio face."[4] Comparable fears accompanied the introduction of the telephone in the nineteenth century[5] and film in the twentieth. In each case an important component of the anxiety is a sense of threatened authority: the new device puts into uncertainty those who are in authority. Social figures in positions of command often do not understand the new technology, whether these are parents of humble social station or leaders of nations and industry. A sense of confusion easily leads to a fear of the machine. Younger people—who by definition are not holders of authority—often tend to respond more openly to the new technologies, accepting them more easily than their elders as part of the social landscape. In these respects the introduction of the Internet and its reception continues in a long line of historical experience.

Let us first look closely at the anxieties aroused by the Internet. My purpose here is not to celebrate the Internet, nor is it to dismiss the cautions and worries that it elicits. Instead I suggest that there is a historic process under way that does involve changes and losses but that also affords new opportunities and new political articulations. I see the strong anxieties aroused by the Internet as a defensive and less than optimal response by those who hold on to forms of social and cultural life that indeed may be lost in the maelstrom of change. My hope is that a clarification of the issues at stake in the globalization of culture through the Internet may open new political directions that might facilitate the emergence of postnational forms of political authority. At the same time such a clarification might assist in developing a discourse that serves to alleviate at least a bit the anxieties of those who look with disfavor on the demise of the nation.

First one must recognize that the nation is no natural or universal entity.[6] It is a grouping of human beings that emerged in the West in the process of modernization, and its emergence meant the destruction of earlier forms of association, such as the tribe and the feudal empire. One of the most destructive effects of national forms of political power today is, ironically, the denial of the historicity of the nation. The interpellation of the individual into the nation, the formation of the bond between the individual and the nation, and the creation of national identity include the simultaneous denial of their occurrence. The individual recognizes him- or herself as a member of the national group in a manner that forecloses awareness of the discursive and social process through which this occurs. An example would be schoolchildren in the United States reciting the Pledge of Allegiance. The unconscious quality, the activity of putting into forgetting, of the formation of national identity is strongest among those who live in the nation where they were born. But it may be just as powerful an effect among those who are immigrants and go through the stages of "naturalization," the term itself suggesting the problem. What is actually a process of Americanization, for example, is placed under the sign of the natural, of becoming "naturalized," of being made into a "natural" creature, where before one was presumably "unnatural" or foreign. If one recognizes the nation as a historic construction, one may suffer less from the prospect of its disappearance. One may also more readily recognize that what is happening today is that another process is emerging, with a new form of human association coming into being, one that includes a louder note of the global than was sounded during the age of the nation, but one that does not necessarily exclude local levels of identification and participation.

Portraits of Anxiety: Daily Life

Imagine, if you will, the following scene: a person sits alone in a partially lit room, secluded from the company of family, friends, or any other humans, withdrawn equally from public space and from nature, from sunlight and fresh air. How shall we evaluate this person's situation? Shall we regard it with disgust, or even alarm, bemoaning the progressive isolation of the individual in contemporary society? Shall we blame new media and new technologies like television and the computer for this egregious shunning of community? But what if I were to add to the description of the scene that the person is not crouched over a computer or lifeless before a TV set but is reading a book, no matter what book. Then our evaluation might change; we might reconsider our response and even applaud this same, wretchedly isolated individual for elevating his or her mind, for contributing to the progress of mankind, for enriching the imagination, and so forth. I only want to indicate that, in our response to this fictional scene, there is found today a tendency to regret a supposed loss of community, of the copresence of bodies in space, and to blame the computer for it when in fact this alleged loss of community is a process that began much earlier in the history of modernity and was once associated with the liberation of the mind from the force of hierarchical relations, from the stifling closeness of copresent bodies. Yet this judgment of the computer as asocial is far too characteristic of the moralism with which the introduction of information technologies is greeted.

Anxiety over the loss of the nation, another form of this moralism, is connected with the spread of globalization, which in turn is connected with the computerized communications of the Internet. To understand these anxieties, let us first look closely at the fears elicited by others working at computers. I remember, back in the early 1980s, the first time I watched a dear friend sitting before a computer screen in rapt attention. I had not yet used a computer, but I was very familiar with people watching screens, be they in the media of film or television. Yet I had never seen anyone so intent, so locked into what he was viewing. And what he saw was hardly comparable to the wondrous images on the silver screen, or even the banalities of the boob tube. He was completely concentrated on a few green letters on a black background. It was the intensity of this concentration that I both envied and found somewhat frightening. The bond between human and machine, I now think, underwent a profound modification with the introduction of the computer. A symbiotic practice emerged in which the human and the machine constitute a new assemblage in social space. I believe now that my confusion and fear at watching my friend at the computer derived from a perception, however subconscious, of that new bond emerging in history.

If the human-computer interface may induce anxiety, how much greater might be that feeling when the computer part of the assemblage is itself connected to a network including tens of millions of people around the world. What monstrous new being appears in the gaze of a person watching another at a computer that is connected to unknown, unseen, untold others? At present, at the turn of the millennium, a majority of people in the United States use computers, mostly at work but also in the home. The number of people who communicate by computer, however, is still small, and the number of those who communicate not by e-mail but in real-time chat modes is still far less. This emergent practice of connectivity, planetary in scope, is the source of a great deal of unsettled feelings and is associated with the general question of globalization.

The Internet raises anxieties among parents since it upsets their authority with their children. Always alert to report on new fears among the populace, the print and television media regularly and ambivalently announce and amplify the dangers and the hopes. These older media may be acting out of jealousy and fear of the Internet as a new medium, out of their regular urge to exaggerate so as to attract attention, ratings, and dollars, or out of some unintended effect of their structure as media. Whichever is the case, the following example is instructive. In July 1994, while in Berlin, I viewed a CNN report that pictured a boy of twelve or so at his computer. The male voice-over, serious in tone, warned that parents might regard such a scene as innocent or even educational, but they would be naive. This boy, the voice intoned, is connected to the Internet, where he may find obscene materials and instructions on building bombs. The report continued about boys in a small New England town who had downloaded such instructions, built explosive devices, and played pranks in the community, destroying mailboxes and in one case the boy's own fingers. The message to parents was clear: "The Internet is a danger to youth. Beware!" In 1999, *Time* printed a special essay of advice to parents about children's use of the Internet, including statistics on teen surfing habits and an elaborate rating system for various types of sites on the Net. What is noteworthy about the piece is that its author concluded that many, if not most, parents are incapable of monitoring their children's use of the Internet and that many children are able to circumvent whatever devices of control the parents can muster (Okrent 1999).

If relations of authority between parents and children are shaken by the Internet, so are relations between spouses and partners. The *Los Angeles Times* printed an article entitled "Daily Life's Digital Divide," in which the reporter, true to journalism's standards of objectivity in which one is fair to both sides of the argument, described a new class division between those who avidly communicate by computer and those who are terrified of such communication. One wife, whose husband habitually communicated by computer, was resentful and fearful about his practice. This woman complained, "It's a real sore point with me. I get a peck on the cheek and he's in the bedroom and the computer's on, he's checking his e-mail. He tells me I should learn it but, you know, I really don't want to. I don't want to be addicted like that" (Harmon 1996). The husband's connection with his networked computer—in the bedroom, no less—appears to her as an "addiction," which in some cases may be true, but here "addiction" might be her projective term to defend against her fear of the bond between her husband and the machine, as if a new attractive person was drawing his attention away from her or as if he were morphing into a new being, a cyborg.[7]

In a third example, the print media again broadcasts the danger of networked computing. In this case an obvious fact is presented as a lurking threat. The *Los Angeles Times*, presumably again with calm objectivity, ran a piece entitled "Technology Lets Tentacles of Terrorism Extend Reach." The simple truth that the Internet allows anyone to connect more easily with anyone else becomes the source of a new danger. The subtitle was "Cellular phones and Internet help militants connect. Even charities are suspected as fronts" (Dahlburg 1996). The subtitle was accompanied by a small drawing of a masked Arab terrorist, rifle in hand, with the caption "a global scourge." There is no way to understand this sort of reporting other than as itself a form of terrorism upon the readership. This article has but one rhetorical effect: to produce fear in the audience about a phenomenon that the majority of the readers know a little about but have never experienced. At a broader level of intermedia struggles, the newsprint in this piece is at war with the Internet. The discursive effect of the article is to draw the reader to newspapers as a defense against a new enemy: the Internet.

Portraits of Anxiety, II: Nation-States

Frightened parents, lovers, ministers, and ordinary folk are matched by national governments in the anxiety of their response to the Internet. The Chinese leadership announced in June 1996 that all users of the Internet must register with the local police! And in early September 1996 it added that many sites on the World Wide Web would be interdicted for its citizens because, this government of progressive ideology claimed, the Internet sites were "spiritual pollution."[8] By 1999 the government was incarcerating individuals for distributing prodemocracy materials on the Internet (Farley 1999). Such authoritarian reactions from the People's Republic might be greeted with knowing smiles in capitalist countries. Yet "free" societies and societies with open economies hardly have a better record. The Singapore Broadcasting Network justified its move to ban Internet sites by claiming that they were "subversive." Also in September 1996 the German government banned "access for all" (xs4all) sites in the Netherlands for their alleged "illegal" political viewpoints.[9] The leaders of the leading democratic regime, the Congress of the United

States, enacted a law (the Communications Decency Act with its Exxon Amendment) in 1996 to prevent all citizens from accessing sites on the Internet deemed to be obscene. The senators and representatives who voted in favor of this law, as well as the president, who signed it, had little experience with the Internet. This unfamiliarity, however, did not prevent them from voting for a statute that well might abrogate the fundamental basis of freedom in the nation, the First Amendment to the Constitution. New technologies, in their rapid proliferation and dissemination, outstrip the slow pace of legislative deliberation. Fortunately this law has been overturned, first by a federal court in Philadelphia and later by the Supreme Court. Meanwhile in China, the Net itself proved unmanageable by the government. After the U.S. bombing of the Chinese embassy in Belgrade on May 7, 1999, Chinese chat rooms were flooded with criticism of the U.S. government, a protest the Chinese regime was helpless to stop (Pomfret 1999).

The best example of the response of nation-states to the introduction of the Internet is that of the so-called Clipper Chip.[10] Here the level of paranoia by a national government is especially high. Since 1993 the Clinton administration, which purportedly supports the dissemination of the Internet as, in Vice President Al Gore's term, an "information superhighway," has attempted to enact into law a requirement that all messages on the Internet be encoded by the Clipper Chip device.[11] This would ensure, according to the administration, that messages could be decoded by their intended receiver but also by (and only by) the U.S. government. And all messages could be so decodable, not merely those decreed dangerous to national security by a court of law. Since one cannot know in advance which transmissions are dangerous and which are not, all messages become possible threats to the nation. Other systems of encryption, those designed or used by individuals or groups that are not decodable by the U.S. government, have in fact become illegal, and their export—considered as a form of munitions—has been treated as a traitorous act. So far the administration has been defeated in its efforts to enact this law, but, in keeping with its fear, it stubbornly persists in its efforts.

One can question the motivation of politicians of nation-states who wish to attempt to monitor (and to have the exclusive capability to do so) the millions of messages that daily course through electronic networks. Intelligent, thoughtful politicians who value freedom respond to the Net not as a new opportunity to extend free speech to a new medium, as well they might given the political ideology of this nation, but rather as a threat to national security. In this way, the Clinton administration develops a need to control all communications over the Net, which is, after all, an impossible feat of surveillance. What target of animosity renders the administration eager to risk the privacy of all citizens on the chance—the very unlikely chance—that they can intercept the message of some unknown enemy of the nation? The easy answer to these questions is, of course, "terrorism," although only seven years ago the same engine of ideological discourse would pronounce the term "communism" and the same mystifying discursive effects would occur. In both cases, diverse phenomena are grouped under a label and demonized. The Soviet Union, Salvador Allende's Chile, and Vietnam war protesters were all equally "communists." Similarly a lone disgruntled and confused individual like the Unabomber, devout Muslims in certain groups, and leaders of some small nations are mixed in the pot of "terrorism." Since "communism" turned out not to be the threat it was thought to be, perhaps the same might be said of "terrorism." Or perhaps "terrorism" is just like "communism," and both have nothing to do with either bombings or alien forms of government but instead with the other side of the nation, with the black hole of fear outside the safe territory of the homeland, with the other as Other. No doubt both claims have merit. In the present case the Other takes the form of the Internet. Its specific characteristics do indeed allow one to conclude that it is Other, different from almost all beings and machines, objects in general, on the face of the Earth. In its difference, the Internet may be unassimilatable to the nation, unterritorializable, in the sense of Deleuze and Guattari, undomesticatable, un-"naturalizable," in short, the first real alien we have encountered.

Portraits of Anxiety, III: Discourse

If the discourse of politicians about the Internet is mired in inexperience and fear, perhaps a better vantage point is provided by intellectuals. Unfortunately there are problems in this domain, as well. Leading intellectuals of the spectral cultures of television and film, Jean Baudrillard and Paul Virilio, respectively, display an ignorance and fear of the Internet which, if not equal to that of the politicians, is not significantly an improvement. If the leading intellectuals of the mass media have great difficulty with the Internet, it becomes even more difficult to grasp the relation of new media to the nation.

Take the following example from a recent interview with Baudrillard. Note Baudrillard's forthright admission of ignorance and fear. The interviewer, Claude Thibaut, asks: "From your point of view, what potential do the new technologies offer?" and Baudrillard responds:

> I don't know much about this subject. I haven't gone beyond the fax and the automatic answering machine. I have a very hard time getting down to work on the screen because all I see there is a text in the form of an image which I have a hard time entering. With my typewriter, the text is at a distance; it is visible and I can work with it. With the screen, it's different; one has to be inside; it is possible to play with it but only if one is on the other side, and immerses oneself in it. That scares me a little, and Cyberspace is not of great use to me personally.[12]

The hyperreality that Baudrillard understands as the consequence of broadcast media apparently does not warrant the fear induced by the Internet. But Baudrillard registers the difference of the typewriter, which he configures as an object that can be mastered by a subject-author, from a computer screen, presumably with a word-processing program in active memory, which refuses a subject-object relation and demands that the subject become like the object, that the author "enter into" the screen. The screen is a permeable, seductive interface that joins computer and person into a synthetic cyborg. This is what Baudrillard fears and refuses.

But what if the computer has a chat program in active memory, not a word processor, or a bulletin board on-line? The interface then is presumably even more compelling, more enticing and insistent of the merging of person and computer. In the case of computer communications, two or more cyborgs are interacting, and that must be even more dreadful than a relatively simple merging with a machine. In both cases the subject, which Baudrillard would continue to be, is transformed; the individual who maintains autonomy from and mastery over machines disappears into the postmodern assemblage of person-computer-communications network. And with this disappearance, I argue, so vanishes the citizen of the nation, the subject formed in the bosom of the nation-state in the age first of print, then of broadcasting.

Similar difficulties detract from Paul Virilio's recent writings on advanced technologies, from his brief interview, "Alarm," to his major work, *La vitesse de libération.* In the latter work he speculates fearfully that on-line chat groups will destroy love relations and the institution of the family. Social organizations that have accompanied the formation of the nation-state, like the family, are endangered, Virilio thinks, by new communications technologies. But the danger is not conceptualized as that of a historic arrangement—the nuclear family—but as one that impinges upon love itself. The threat does not come from one social practice toward another but rather toward the human as such. The discursive register thus shifts in his text from critique to ideology.

For Virilio (1995) the Internet represents a new phase in the space/time continuum of life, a "third interval" governed by the speed of light that supersedes and annuls distances of space and time. Duration and separation disappear in the instantaneity of an interval that is no interval, a gap without extension. He writes, "Speed in the new electro-optical and acoustic milieu becomes the ultimate void (the void of speed), a void that does not rely upon an interval between places, things and thus the extension itself of the world but on the interface of an instantaneous transmission of distant appearances, on a geographic and geometric constraint in which all volume, all relief disappears" (48). On the basis of this new fundament of the human condition, societies and cultures will be recalibrated. In such a new world, information generates a virtual reality that, Virilio estimates, "supplants the geography of nations" (106). Enabling and promoting relations without physical presence, the Internet destroys existing forms of love and families. "The end of the supremacy of physical proximity in the megalopolis of the postindustrial era," he writes, "will not simply encourage the spread of the single-parent family. It provokes a further more radical rupture between man and woman, threatening directly the future of sexual reproduction.... the Parmenidean rupture between masculine and feminine principles broadens to allow remote acts of love" (130). We have thus attained, Virilio fears, a zero point of life: on-line sex replaces lovemaking, and the human species, for want of reproduction, disappears. Virilio's hyperbolic anxiety, like Baudrillard's dogged resistance, blocks an understanding of the effects of cyberspace on modern institutions.

Among general intellectuals who comment on globalization, not media critics like Virilio and Baudrillard, ignorance of global communications is often more pronounced. An essay by Jürgen Habermas attempts to defend the principle of democratic solidarity by uncoupling it from the nation-state at a time of the latter's decline in the face of globalizing trends.[13] Accepting these trends, he evinces little nostalgia for the nation-state and its forms of identity. In perceptive comments on Habermas's paper, Timothy Mitchell (1998) and Wendy Brown (1998) effectively refute his purpose of defending democracy. They easily show that democratic solidarity—citizenship—was possible only with nationalist, imperialist, racist, and sexist identifications. Be that as it may, what is of interest in the context of this essay is Habermas's misunderstanding of Internet communities. In search of new sources of solidarity to replace the waning nation-state, he turns to the Internet. "The publics produced by the Internet," he warns, surely with the advantage of never having experienced one, "remain closed off from one another like global villages" (411). Alluding to McLuhan's global village, Habermas equates Internet communities with medieval European hamlets, where peasants, as Marx quipped, enjoyed the solidarity of a sack of potatoes. But Habermas clearly has got things wrong. Whereas peasant villages were isolated in time and space, Internet communities, embedded in a web-like electronic structure, are no more distant from one another than a keyboard stroke or a mouse click. The communications logic of the Internet is interconnectedness, not autochthony. By contrast, Habermas sees "the logic of networks" as "a completely decentered world society that splinters into a disordered mass of self-reproducing and self-steering functional systems" (414). While Habermas is surely correct to worry about the shape of new systems of political solidarity in a globalizing context, his uninformed, offhand remarks do not do justice to his topic and reflect badly on a scholar like himself, whom Brown rightly characterizes as having "unmatched erudition and analytic comprehensiveness" (425). Too bad this dedication to seek the truth does not extend to the basic principles of contemporary communications. But again Habermas is hardly exceptional in this regard.

French Fears of American Neoimperialism

If anxieties about the Internet are an index of the novelty of computerized communications, the example of some French reactions illustrates how national identity is in question. French worries about the demise of their culture and language were evident in the GATT negotiations of the mid-1990s. As a defense against threats to local industries and the hegemony of their native language, French government officials insisted on quotas on American cultural products such as films and television shows. Worldwide interest in American popular culture, from clothing and food to music and the mass media, aroused particular fears in France. Perhaps the strength of French high culture and the weakness of its popular culture contributed to the intensity of the reaction. Students of France have noted for some time both a concern to preserve French things and a wariness about American influence.[14] Fredric Jameson, for instance, praises French resistance to the hegemony of American popular culture, recommending it as nothing less than "a fundamental agenda for all culture workers in the next decade" (1998, 60). In any case one finds in France a sharp sense of the boundary of the local and a strong desire to preserve what is inside it. At the same time, France has long associated its culture not with localism but with the universal, an irony that should not be lost in the current discussion.

With these reactions in mind, French suspicion of the Internet ought to come as no surprise. France has but half the Internet hookups and hosts as Germany, which itself can boast no more than one-eighth that of California. Rates of growth in participation in the Internet are higher in Mexico than in France. With 80 percent of sites on the World Wide Web in English compared with 2 percent in French, there might be cause for concern. The Internet might well be viewed not as a force of globalization but as an extension of American imperialism in the electronic mode of information. Some French negativity toward the Internet is posed as a preference for the conviviality of face-to-face relations over the coldness of the computer interface (Harmon 1997). Technophobia, however, is too simple an excuse for the simple reason that the French were the first to experiment with computer-mediated communications. The Minitel, developed in the late 1970s by a French government determined to modernize its communications infrastructure, was broadly used in France for remote intimacy, electronic conversation, and virtual sociability long before Americans took to the Internet. The current pose of some French opponents of the Internet that French culture lacks enthusiasm for technology is surely disingenuous.

The perceived threat to national identity by some French people indicates instead a failure to come to grips with contemporary conditions of life. The defense of the local need not by any means imply a rejection of the global. French defensiveness, along with that of many others (including Americans), toward planetary communications suggests to me a combination of compulsive clutching to the local and demonizing misrecognition of the global as alien or other. This regrettable failure of the imagination gives up on the possibility of developing a level of global interconnectedness that is outside the aegis of both the nation-state and the transnational corporation. It perpetuates a false view of globalizing communications technologies as a threat to local differences. Here is Baudrillard's jeremiad: "Triumphant globalization sweeps away all differences and values, ushering in a perfectly in-different (un)culture. . . . all that remains is the all-powerful global technostructure standing over against the singularities" (1998, 14).

English is now the dominant tongue of the Internet, no doubt reflecting U.S. world power, but this is not necessarily the case forever. After all, there is nothing especially English about digital code. It is no more difficult to set up a Web page in other languages as it is in English. And if English does become a widely used language of international communication, one can dismiss it only if one rejects bilingualism in general or if one petulantly insists that one's language should take the place of English. Behind the high-minded concern for national identity and national culture lurks simple parochialism and fear of the new. The Internet offers an opportunity for a planetary articulation. It does not legislate an end of the local.

Nation and Nationalist

Let us now examine the nation as a historical formation in relation to the question of identity formation and attempt to set up an analysis that compares the role of print to that of the broadcast media and finally the Internet. Let us do so in a spirit that openly seeks new possibilities of political organization that are both transnational and subnational, acknowledging that such possibilities are encumbered by serious risks.

The form of government known as the nation is a modern phenomenon, coming into existence in Europe over several centuries.[15] One aspect of the process was the destruction of regional and local powers by monarchies and the formation of legislative institutions as a compromise between powerful, contending groups. Far from a universal form of political organization, the nation-state is but a few hundred years old.[16] The second process was the formation of bureaucratic apparatuses attached to the monarchies. These sets of offices and their personnel, in complex relations with the monarch, became, as Foucault (1991) has shown, the basis of a form of power known as governmentality. With its legislative and executive functions in place, the nation-state defined itself as a territory, with precise boundaries, in relation to other nation-states, doing so primarily through a sequence of wars. The political problems of the internal structure and external relations of the nation-state presented one degree of difficulty. An entirely different and perhaps more difficult question concerned the cultural formation of the population as committed members of this community.

A change had to be effected in each individual from local, kinship identification based on a relational culture of correspondences to a form of less geographically immediate but no less intense attachment to the nation. How could the individual be wrenched from the thick network of village connections to emerge as a modern citizen, one who took this status as so important, so natural that he or she was ready to die and have loved ones die for so distant a point of power? I have raised this question as if it were perceived as such by historical agents ready to adopt policies to achieve its solution. This was not at all the case. The formation of the modern, national subject was an immensely complex process in which heterogeneous agencies and unintentional practices intersected in complex manners. The process was in this sense "chaotic." Yet a few of its conditions may be mentioned, especially with an eye to discerning the part played by the media and the implications of this historic role for new media and possibly new political formations. I am by no means attempting to account completely for the rise of national identification but only to raise the question of the role of the media in the process of its formation.

The question turns on the figure of the citizen, for this is precisely the name for the subject of the nation. Citizens were forged in the heat of the American and French revolutions of the late eighteenth century, unbinding ties of monarchical subjects. More was at stake, however, than simply substituting one political relation for another. For the individual's relation to the monarch was always mediated by a thick network of local authorities (noble, village, kin), each of which entailed hierarchical statuses and deeply personal allegiances. As Tocqueville (1955) argued in his classic *The Old Regime and the French Revolution,* these affiliations dissolved or at least diminished so that a relatively homogeneous nation could emerge and become the focus of individual identification. The new state and its political fitures were nominally mere representatives of the nation. Along with these large-scale social transformations went the cultural change by which the individual was abstracted from the specificities of older links and statuses to emerge as an autonomous creature capable of connecting with the nation. The nation presupposed free individuals, atomic (male) units who could act in the public sphere and belong only to the people.

Such an autonomous being had been articulated as the nature of man in the Enlightenment, achieving its best expression in Descartes. A being separate from the world of material objects, defined by rationality, outside any social integument—this Cartesian subject was the prerequisite of the citizen. The complexities, difficulties, and ironies of this historic change are captured well by Étienne Balibar (1991) in his term "citizen subject." For this subject was a transformation of the older "subject" of the monarchy, a relative and subordinated being, into an active, independent, and universal agent. The argument for such a radical redefinition of the term was accompanied, however, by the historic need to exclude women, children, slaves, and nonwhites more generally. The citizen subject then was of necessity somewhat indeterminate, a category between the universal and the empirical, at once real and effective enough to make a revolution but also contingent and empty enough a sign to remain a possibility for the future.[17] The citizen subject came into being not as an emanation of a Cartesian idea but in the dilatory, imperfect forge of massive political transformation.

The nation is now being superseded, challenged, and displaced by processes of globalization, as Saskia Sassen (1998) convincingly argues, both in its territoriality and its sovereignty (81). Multinational and transnational corporations cause nation-states to adjust to their imperatives. New global organizations like the World Trade Organization and the World Intellectual Property Organization, however much they are influenced by the United States and other powerful nations, bypass national juridical institutions in the regulation of trade. Similarly, international rights organizations, Médecins du monde, and other nongovernmental organizations (NGOs) impose political relations outside national control. Cities, as Sassen (1997) argues, are becoming new centers of power, along with these transnational structures. In each case the territory of the nation is bypassed. She observes, "Economic globalization and the new information technologies have not only reconfigured centrality and its spatial correlates, they have also created new spaces for centrality" (5). Finally and above all, the citizen is being surpassed by the person, and earthlings are beginning to be recognized as such. In this context, when claims for human rights are successfully constructed, we need to examine the role of the media as globalizing practices that construct new subjects.

Imprinting the Nation

The media technology associated with the interpellation of individuals into national citizens, is of course, print. Print technology afforded distant governments the tools for reaching dispersed populations with the same messages. Political processes, national and international, could be received, reviewed, and discussed by citizens, by individuals presumed to be actively concerned with public affairs. As an instrument of information distribution, print was essential to the national unit, in the same way that gossip was essential to the village. But print served the formation of the nation in another, unintended manner. The press strove for independence from the government, reporting political events but also commenting critically upon them. A unique feature of the nation-state is that it was never able to communicate with the sovereign, the demos, except through the mediation of the press. There has never been a direct, face-to-face relation between national leadership and the voters but only one produced in practices of readership in the material channel of print. The specific form of this mediation is crucial to the formation of the public sphere.

Habermas's widely influential analysis (1989) of the public sphere as a political domain apart from institutional politics, an informally constituted region on the model of the ancient Greek agora, pays tribute to print media but misconstrues its effect. Habermas perceived newspapers as a tool of face-to-face dialogue, one that enhanced the critical potential of that dialogue. In coffeehouses, salons, and such places, persons, independent of their socially determined status, read the print of newspapers, broadsheets, and tracts, debating political issues of the day. For Habermas the crucial aspect of the public sphere was the community dialogue, irrespective of money or power, but in conversations ruled by critical reason. In his analysis, it must be noted, the materiality of print, mediating between government and citizenry, evaporates before the scene of dialogue and debate. Reading and writing are, for him, subordinate to speech. Consequently in Habermas's thesis the misleading portrait emerges of the public sphere as a logocentric community, rather than one dependent upon the space/time deferrals of print.

Habermas's disregard for the materiality of the media is further evident in his discussion of its role in the formation of national identity. The mere fact that national consciousness may only be sustained through information machines leads him to conclude that it is inauthentic. Habermas says: "Nationalism is a form of collective consciousness which both presupposes a reflective appropriation of cultural traditions that... spreads only via channels of modern mass communication... [This lends] nationalism the artificial traits of something that is to a certain extent a construct, thus rendering it by definition susceptible to manipulative misuse by political elites."[18] Habermas sees mediations as false constructions. To defer the face-to-face meeting of minds is to corrupt reason, to open the door for manipulation by politicians. On the contrary: the question is posed just where Habermas cannot look for it— within the constructedness of the mediation. National identity must not be referred back to an ontological foundation of reason, against which it is found lacking, but analyzed as a construction of the subject in regimes of rationality formed through the media. Only in this way can one raise the question of national identity as a historical problem in relation to which new forms of collective subjects may be seen emerging in relation to new media.

Compensating for Habermas's presentist public sphere, Benedict Anderson (1983) underscores the mediating function of print by his insistence on the nation as an imagined construction. For him unity of the nation could not be constituted in a time/space continuum of full presence but only through the mediation of print technology: "All communities larger than primordial villages of face-to-face contact (and perhaps in even these) are imagined. Communities are to be distinguished, not by their falsity/genuineness, but by the style in which they are imagined" (6). Without the parenthetical remark, Anderson dangerously approaches Habermas's ideal of the agora. But it is clear that the problem for Anderson is how the imagined identification of the individual with the group is structured, not in contrast to one without an imagined element but as variations within the imagined. The unfortunate aspect of the term "imagined" is that it immediately suggests a relation of opposition with a "real." I prefer the concept of mediation to that of the imagined because I find it easier to insist upon the universality of mediation and to focus on the question of its technocultures as opposed to a supposed unmediated presence than to wrestle with the question of the real. Also, the term "imagined" implies a model of consciousness, whereas that of mediation allows a turn to a level of complex articulations or technologies of power within each medium. In either case the issue is one of the construction of the nationalist individual through the media.[19]

Insisting on print (the newspaper and the novel) as essential to the cultural formation of the nation, Anderson remains sketchy on the precise connections between the two. He mentions important aspects of print as a medium: the stability of the sign, the hollowing out of time as a result of this stability, and other technical features that made the nation a possible sign to be represented. But he does not adequately elaborate upon the specific features of the materiality of print and indicate how these are related to the formation of the national subject or the citizen. In contrast, Michael Warner's *The Letters of the Republic* (1992), on print in eighteenth-century American society, comes much closer to these issues.[20] Adeptly avoiding the problem of technological determinism, Warner argues for a reciprocal play of influences between the medium of print and the public sphere. He shows, for example, that print was not a universal technology, open to all, and shows how practices of reading were defined as a white, male practice so that printed materials folded within the preexisting racial and gender lines, affecting each group differently (14). The formation of the public sphere through print then favored the participation of some groups and not others. Also in the religious communities of New England, print was inserted in oral practices, like the sermon, being engulfed by it rather than being the occasion for the formation of a public sphere. Again, preexisting social relations were too strong to allow the new technical practice to develop a new kind of political practice.

Yet print publications in the form of tracts, broadsheets, newspapers, and books did enable and promote a new political space and new identities within it. The crucial feature of the new media was the impersonality of voice that it constituted (38). An individual might now air his views to others as if they were not limited by particular concerns. Writing a letter to the editor of a newspaper or composing a piece for publication opened a space of communication in which the individual was a citizen, a general member of the community, presenting an argument that anyone might consider. In Warner's words, "The difference between the private, interested person and the citizen of the public sphere appears both as a condition of political validity and as the expression of the character of print" (43). If in the ancient agora one spoke face-to-face with the community on the issue of the public good, in the new United States, print made possible a public sphere in which millions imagined themselves to be orators of the republic. The public sphere of modern democracy substituted for the embodied presence of the collective the mediated community of ink and paper. The public sphere would exist nowhere but in the practices of reading print, and those habituated to do so would be the citizen subjects of modernity. This argument does not negate other factors from contributing to this process, so that even the illiterate, a large part of the population in the eighteenth century, might participate in national identification.

If today we find the public voice of the print-based citizen unconvincing, "idealistic," even phony, and suspect authors of printed materials of nothing more than personal interests, we are beholden to the broadcast media. Our suspicion is an index of our constitution as political subjects by electronic mass media—radio, film, and television. Persons participating in these first electronic media are interpellated not as universal, rational citizens, but, as Andy Warhol so presciently showed, as celebrities, those who are also absent subjects yet mediated by sound and image, not text.[21] I suspect that electronic mass media have drawn print media within their system of subject constitution, drowning the latter's effects in favor of those of the former. The issue we face is the possibility of a second electronic media age, that of the Internet, and of a move beyond both the citizen of print and the celebrity of TV.

Electronic Embodiment and the Globe

The discussion of the relation of print to the nation is circumscribed by the limits of the material form of this mediation. When electronic forms of mediation such as the Internet are introduced, one can go back to the question of print and discern issues that remained hitherto untheorized. As Marx writes in the *Critique of Political Economy* (and I cite it without adopting the progressivism of his formulation), "The anatomy of man is a key to the anatomy of the ape" (1970, 211). Digitized, globally interconnected information flows raise the issue of the relation of the individual to the community in a compelling manner, for print confirmed the power of the function of representation in a way that intersected with the self-understanding of the Cartesian subject. The excessive aspects of print, its qualities of rhetoric, fantasy, and imagination, could be contained within the modern subject position of autonomy, rationality, stability, and centeredness. Even though in potential the mediation of print *might* have effected a sense of difference between the individual and the nation, a sense of the unfoundedness of the nation and the inessential link of the individual to it, the historic play of print served rather to suture together individual and nation, to foreclose the ambiguity and fragility of this link and to produce a politically effective bond of citizenship. As we have seen in the discussion of Warner's work, such a constructed determination also excluded many from this social figure—the illiterate, children, nonwhites, women, non-Westerners.

There has been a lively discussion of late concerning the globalization of identities. Numerous works have appeared concerned with changes in the structure of identity—racial, national, and global identity, postcolonial identity, postmodern identity.[22] In particular, deconstructive analyses of the hybrid postcolonial subject, the antiessentialist subject of feminist theory and the multiple subject of postmodern theory have been linked with studies of globalization from a cultural studies perspective. Stuart Hall (1996), for example, outlines the tendencies toward deessentializing identity associated with globalization and the prospect of postmodern, multiple subjects ironically becoming a new planetary, homogeneous type. These are subjects dispersed by global commodities, drinking Coke and wearing Levis all over the world. But Hall also finds qualifications to this argument in countertendencies such as a reemergence of ethnic identifications. He concludes that the danger of global uniformity is unlikely. Instead he anticipates "a new articulation between 'the global' and 'the local'" (623). He goes further and raises the important question about identity as such: "The problematization of identity, the opening of identity to an understanding of identification itself as a process is what we need to understand. How do people come to identify at all?" (1995). How then does the understanding of globalizing processes assist in confronting the question of identity? In response I propose to look at the role of the Internet and global information flows in the process of identity construction.

The Internet enables the exchange of images, sounds, and text across national borders, as if those borders did not exist as political units. (Differences of language and culture nevertheless persist.) It forges links between individuals and groups of different, even antagonistic, nationalities. It produces the effect of global connectivity or planetary relations. It erases the distances of space and time in an unprecedented manner. It enables every receiver of a message to produce a message, every individual to disseminate messages to a mass. But it achieves these transparently instrumental effects at a tremendous cost of cultural dislocation and innovation. If print extracted the citizen-author from the face-to-face community, it forged a bond between the citizen-reader and the material object of the text. The Internet also enables disembodied community, but it places individuals in relations of interdependence with information machines; it introduces into the landscape of human society a profound bond with machines; it draws attention to the mediation of this bond in a way that deconstructs the modern subject position, undermines the relation of representation to the real, introduces a machinescape of underdetermined objects, and of cultural artifacts with such a degree of plasticity that issues of authorship, canons, authority itself are put into suspension and reconfigured. Far from an extension of man in McLuhan's sense, the Internet forebodes a reconstruction of the basic elements of human culture. No wonder there are doubts, fears, and anxieties.

How then will the Internet construct subjects and how will these subjects become political agents? What will be the effect of being on-line in cyberspace upon the existing forms of interpellation, specifically upon national identity? Will the conditions of global interconnectedness, interactivity, and the instantaneity of electronic communication generate new forms of the subject that entail planetary selves? Writers from Teilhard de Chardin to Pierre Lévy foresee a collective intelligence, a noosphere of human spirituality encircling the Earth as a consequence of electronic communications. I urge a less visionary interpretive move, one that attempts to gauge the potential of new forms of postnational identity, of dispersed and multiple subjectivities that have a component of cosmopolitanism. At the same time one must recognize that the Internet creates new invisibilities, filters out those who are not wired to its machinic tentacles, disempowers those who cannot afford the start-up fees, those who belong to communities that reject modernizing technologies or are too poor to distribute them, those who prefer literate culture of the nineteenth century or couch-potato practices of the mid-twentieth. The Internet is no more universal than print was in eighteenth-century America. Perhaps it is less so.

Yet the Internet is growing in popularity, changing in its configurations, decreasing in its costs. It is also incorporating earlier media (from print to television) and being incorporated by them as in WebTV and pointcast or push technologies. It is likely that we are at the beginning of its spread and its influence, and we might well note its potential for globalizing politics, not without some fear, but also with a good portion of hope. If the Internet represents a new form of universalism,[23] one must understand this not as a closure of human history, a final realization or telos or dialectic moving from parochialism to cosmopolitanism. Instead Internet globalization suggests an articulation of the universal and particular at a level at once more general and more local than the nation-state. In that configuration rest the prospects for a humanity different from those of earlier times.

The difference the Internet may make is neither absolute nor certain. One must avoid a too sanguine stance that opposes nation and global in a binary relation. From its inception the nation-state was enmeshed with international, if not global, relations. Its sovereignty was never perfect, always relative to laws and obligations forged through transnational mechanisms. The Internet to some degree is an extension and deepening of the imbrication of the nation in international exchanges. What is more, the dangers to the nation to adjust to outside forces derives far more from transnational corporations and international finance than from the communications flowing in the Internet. If cyberspace offers the possibility of a new universalism, this emerges in a transnational ocean that is rife with the sharklike predators of the great corporations whose frenzied, voracious feeding upon workers of all colors and conditions is curbed only by the nation-state. Finally the nation-state is not a fixed institution. It has changed in the past and may change again in response to globalizing trends. Perhaps it will soften its claims to territorial sovereignty, following the model of borderlands with their blurring of boundaries and ambiguous political status or that of an emerging European community with its weakening state boundaries. Perhaps nations will transmute into both larger aggregations and fragment into smaller ones, as in the case of the Netherlands, where networked computing leads to smaller-scale bureaucracies and local autonomy (Frissen 1997).

These cautionary speculations must not discount an appreciation of the potential for new planetary connections, exchanges, links, and relations enabled by the Internet. Perhaps a new form of nomadic culture will emerge in the circuits of the Internet, as Rosi Braidotti (1997) suggests. We remain at the cusp of an age of global interactions whose density and scope has never before existed and never before been materially and technically possible. One cannot say how Internet technocultures will become inscribed in history, what specific institutional matrixes will be invented to shroud them, and how existing institutions will appropriate them or transform themselves in the process of doing so. Yet one can expect, from the bowels of the new constellation of elements, the birth of a monster, of a human-machine assemblage whose contours may be feared as those of an alien but who surely will be yet another incarnation of ourselves.

CHAPTER SEVEN

Theorizing the Virtual: Baudrillard and Derrida

Your telephone is you. In a moment it multiplies and projects your personality to many different places and many different people, near or far. Part of your very self is in every telephone message—your thoughts, your voice, your smile, your words of welcome, the manner that is you. You use the telephone as you use the power of speech itself, to play your full part in a world of people. With it in your grasp, you are master of space and time. You are equal to emergency, ready of opportunity, receptive to ideas, equipped for action. The extraordinary fact is that the more you use your telephone, the more it extends your power and personality.
—American Telephone and Telegraph Company print ad, July 1933

The Limits of the Virtual

Virtual reality systems continue the Western trend of duplicating the real by means of technology. They provide the participant with a second-order reality in which to play with or practice upon the first order. Flight simulators in their military and game varieties, architects' "model" houses and medicine's computer bodies—to mention only the most prominent virtual reality applications—provide substitutes for the real that are close enough to the real that its conditions may be tested without the normal risks. In these cases technology provides prostheses for the real in order to better control it, continuing the Enlightenment project of modernity. Yet this doubling, as many have noted, puts the original into question: the virtual upsets the stability of the real in ways that were perhaps unintended but certainly unwanted by proponents of the modern.[1]

A careful examination of the technology makes this clear. Virtual reality (VR) extends the line of technologies of the sensorium, as Jonathan Crary has shown. Like the stereoscope, the panorama, and other nineteenth-century visual apparatuses, virtual reality addresses the peculiar traits of human perception, for example, the way binocular vision constructs a field of depth (Crary 1992). It does not assume that sensation provides a basis for objective truth about the world, as in the model of the camera obscura. It does not assume the neutrality of the technologies of the human senses, as in Lockean epistemology. Instead virtual reality technology provides sensations for the eyes in line with the manner in which they process this information. But virtual reality goes one step beyond the stereoscope: it bypasses the system of light reflecting off objects to bring directly to the eye patterns of light generated by the computer, an alteration in the process of perception in which the machine has been integrated within the body at a new level of symbiosis (Holmes 1993). Beginning, then, with the late modernist acceptance of senses as constructing the real for the human body, virtual reality engenders a new combination of a human-machine that places in question the fixity and naturalness of the human perceptual apparatus.

Reactions to virtual reality technologies are, as one might expect, extreme. Jaron Lanier, one of the founders of the apparatus as head of Virtual Programming Language, Inc., celebrates it:

> Virtual Reality exists so that people can make up their reality as fast as they might otherwise talk about it. The whole thing with Virtual Reality is that you're breeding reality with other people. You're making shared cooperative dreams all the time. You're changing the whole reality as fast as we go through sentences now. Eventually, you make your imagination external and it blends with other people's. Then you make the world together as a form of communication. And that will happen. (1990, 46)

With almost the same level of expectation Michael Heim affirms: "Cyberspace is more than a breakthrough in electronic media or in computer interface design. With its virtual environments and simulated worlds, cyberspace is a metaphysical laboratory, a tool for examining our very sense of reality" (1993, 83).

Observers more attached to modern perspectives are skeptical of these claims. One Marxist critic notes that virtual reality was extended beyond the narrow confines of the military and science fiction only through the discursive effect of advertising. Chris Chesher (1995) writes, "VR's appeal has largely been due to its marketing. It proposed a paradigm shift: that computers can be 'reality generators,' not just symbol processors. This shift allowed VR to become associated with a far broader range of cultural tropes than computers had been before." And in the end this simply reproduces and extends the baleful imperatives of capital in the age of global commodification (Stallabrass 1995). Others find in VR not simply a marketing success but dangerous and threatening possibilities. Ken Hillis, in what may be the subtlest critique of virtual reality systems to date, presses the proponents of VR to specify the benefits for society of the new technology: "What is lacking in arguments advanced by those promoting this profoundly individuated virtual 'freedom' and 'pleasure' to play with identities, subjectivity, and geographies is a sustained consideration of the meaning and context of self-control of our actions, along with any sustained interrogation of the consequences for social relations beyond the scale of individual access" (1999, xxxi). Opponents of VR, from presidential contender Pat Robertson to the pope, discern effects such as ontological insecurity, moral confusion, sexual impotence, political apathy, irrationality, dehumanization, and narcissism.[2]

The term *virtual reality* quickly spread beyond "computer-generated immersive environments" (the helmet-glove-computer assemblage) to include, first, certain communications facilities on the Internet—bulletin boards, MUDs, MOOs, Internet Relay Chat—and then to the Internet more broadly—including e-mail, databases, newsgroups, and so forth—also known as "cyberspace." In these cases, as distinct from helmet-and-glove VR, the salient trait of the virtual is community—electronic cafés, cybersalons, "places," in short, where conversation takes place either in "real" time or by message facilities. Those who are critical of the helmet-and-glove variety of virtual reality because of its seeming narcissism, even solipsism, need to note that virtual reality in cyberspace tends to be preeminently social, at least in the sense that many people participate. Yet one must be careful using terms like *social* in regard to virtual reality unless it is kept in mind that the interactions at issue are purely electronic. VR in either case is not disembodied, since the messages or signals are composed by human beings, but the VR meeting place does exclude bodily presence. As sound and images are added to the textual communities on the Internet, skeptics may be forced to reconsider the nature of these exchanges. Those who dismiss them today as "disembodied" need to ask themselves if full video and audio will make a difference and, if so, why?

More generally still, the term *virtual reality* began to expand its associations to all electronically mediated exchanges of symbols, images, and sound, so that a second world is constituted over against the "real" world of sensory proximity. The mode of information, as I have termed this virtual world, is one way of conceptualizing the cultural significance of the new phenomenon. In some discussions of virtual reality, especially among some literary critics, the term refers not simply to electronically mediated communication but to all reality. The term *virtual reality*, in many of these discussions, so destabilizes the real that the real itself is understood as "virtual," as provisional, constructed, and mediated by processes of signification or interpretation. Hence for these literary interpreters, virtual reality is not a new technology with general cultural significance that would put reality into question. Here reality is "always already" virtual, while the helmet-and-glove technology is a mere machine. In the hands of certain literary theorists the virtual becomes transcendental and founds the real in its own image. Thus novels are just as much virtual realities as computer-generated immersive environments. And since novels are more "real" than experience, fiction more true than facts, a new disciplinary foundation for literature is constructed. In discussions of virtual reality it is imperative to guard against the "transcendentalist gesture," as I would like to call these discursive maneuvers, by keeping in mind the material basis of the term, the machinic assemblages of cyberspace and helmet-and-glove apparatuses.

As a preliminary step toward an examination of virtual reality in cyberspace I will analyze the theory of the virtual in Jean Baudrillard and Jacques Derrida. Although others could have been selected for this purpose, I believe these two thinkers have made important contributions to understanding the problem of the virtual, and the difficulties in their positions are illustrative of the issues that need to be explored further.

Baudrillard's "Crime" against Reality

Baudrillard's work has proven enormously suggestive in the interpretation of the media and of cultural phenomena such as Disneyland generally, which seem in some ways to be like electronic media (Nunes 1995). His notion of simulational culture, later termed *the hyperreal,* captures as no social theorist before him the linguistic gestures and the unique configurations of electronic media as they course through the wired capillaries of the postmodern body social. Beginning with *Simulacra and Simulation* of 1981 and continuing at least through *The Illusion of the End* in 1992, Baudrillard interrogates the cultural forms of media communications from a consistent if ambivalent standpoint. For Baudrillard of the 1980s our culture is simulational. Driven by the media, especially television, popular culture preempts the exchange of symbols between individuals, introducing another layer of experience that undermines the subject's ability to define and to grasp the truth. Electronic mediation cripples the modern system of representation, folding it into a new mode of signification in which signs are divorced from their referents in the object world, becoming reorganized into a "hyperreal" of screen surfaces.

It might appear that the terms *simulation* and *virtual reality* are equivalent, each suggesting a sign system in which cultural objects are divorced from their referents, in which words and images appear in their electronic reproduction without firm connection to a prior "real" world, thus functioning not as representations but as objects themselves, as entities whose meaning resides within. For Baudrillard in 1981, "The age of simulation begins with a liquidation of all referentials—worse: by their artificial resurrection in systems of signs" (Poster 1988, 167). This revolution in the structure of language unsettles thought systems of an earlier epoch. Simulation, Baudrillard contends, threatens the distinction between truth and falsehood: "Truth, reference and objective causes have ceased to exist" (Poster 1988, 168). In dramatic, totalizing prose, Baudrillard discounts the multiplicity of language games at play in the seeming infinite complexity of the social in favor of a one-dimensional theory of the hyperreal. In any case, simulation denotes a major cultural change.

Baudrillard's writing begins to be sprinkled with the terms *virtual* and *virtual reality* as early as 1991. But he uses these terms interchangeably with *simulation* and without designating anything different from the earlier usage. Concerning the Gulf War of 1991, for example, he writes: "In our fear of the real, of anything that is too real, we have created a gigantic simulator. We prefer the virtual to the catastrophe of the real, of which television is the universal mirror" (Baudrillard 1991b, 25).[3] The virtual is equivalent to the hyperreal or to simulation. In all cases the electronically mediated communication stands in a double relation to "reality." Mediated communication both reflects reality by delivering signals from a sender to a receiver that are somehow about it and substitutes for reality in the sense that it never simply represents reality but puts forth its own reality. Simulations and the virtual, for Baudrillard, are different from reality but always stand in a certain relation to it.

With *Le crime parfait* (1995a), however, things have changed. To paraphrase Marx speaking of communism as the solution to the riddle of history, Baudrillard has become virtual and knows himself to be such: he argues that his critical theory of simulation has become nothing less than the principle of reality.[4] The world has become virtual; Baudrillard's theory is no longer true, but real. What use then for Baudrillard's writings in the age of virtual reality machines?

> The idea of simulacrum was a conceptual weapon against reality, but it has been stolen. Not that it has been pillaged, vulgarized, or has become commonplace (which is true but has no consequence), but because simulacra have been absorbed by reality which has swallowed them and which, from now on, is clad with all the rhetoric of simulation. And to cap it all, simulacra have become reality! Today, simulacra guarantee the continuation of the real. The simulacrum now hides, not the truth, but the fact that there is none, that is to say, the continuation of Nothingness. (Baudrillard 1995c, 146)[5]

Since simulation is now the dominant form of culture, Baudrillard's concept of simulation, he thinks, no longer functions as a concept. Somewhat immodestly he suggests that "theory [his own] that realizes itself is no longer a theory" (1995, 19). Unsympathetic critics may find lurking in this revisiting of the Hegelian dialectic synthesizing itself in and for itself a whiff of Marx's comment about Napoleon III: repetition as farce.

Baudrillard is too competent a social theorist not to see the problem he is raising in its general significance. If the concept of simulation is now reduced to mimetic description, critical theory (and Enlightenment discourse more generally) is nullified:

> We have lost the advance that ideas had on the world, that distance that makes an idea stay an idea. What to do then? What is there to do when suddenly everything fits the ironic, critical, alternative, and catastrophic model that you suggested (everything fits the model you gave beyond any hopes you had because, in a sense, you never believed it could go that far, otherwise you would never have been able to create it)? (Baudrillard 1995, 146)

Baudrillard argues that a "crime" is responsible for the current predicament, the perfect crime alluded to in the title of the book. This crime is the theft of reality by virtual reality. Much of *Le crime parfait* is a demonstration of the new circumstances through analyses of cultural figures (the usual suspects) such as Madonna and Andy Warhol and a playing with the concept of perfect crime in the context of the virtual. What can a "perfect crime" be if the image "is the real" and the real is virtual reality? What sort of jurisprudence fits with this brave new world? You can imagine the fun Baudrillard has with his criminally violated world.

Baudrillard understands the passage from the hyperreal to virtual reality as an intensification in kind rather than a new direction. Virtual reality equals simulation as cultural dominant, to use Jameson's term. Here is Baudrillard's compelling description of the culture of virtual reality: "It is as if things swallowed their mirrors, and became transparent to themselves, entirely present to themselves, in the light of day, in real time, in a pitiless transcription. Instead of being absent from themselves in illusion, they are forced to inscribe themselves on millions of monitors at the horizon of which not only the real but the image has disappeared" (1995, 17). The culture of the screen has now become the norm of culture itself, according to Baudrillard. The consequence is that reality is lost, and along with it go critical thought and the concepts that defined an emergent screen culture, such as simulation and the hyperreal.[6]

What then is the difference between Baudrillard's theory of simulation and virtual reality? For one critic, C. J. Keep, the difference between Baudrillard's concept of the hyperreal and virtual reality is this: "Where the 'hyperreal' is constituted by the play of surfaces, by a paralytic fascination with exteriority, the 'virtual' offers images with depth, images which one can enter, explore, and, perhaps most importantly, with which one can interact" (Keep 1993). The difference enunciated by Keep is one between a passive or specular hyperreal (television technology) and an active or interactive and immersive virtual reality (headset-glove-computer technology). There is much to this argument because Baudrillard does not define virtual reality in relation to any particular technology but to a certain stage of technology in general. In fact the one place where he actually describes helmet-and-glove VR using the English phrase "body simulation," he does not mention the term *virtual reality* (1995, 174). Instead we have a Heideggerian lament: "With Virtual Reality, and all of its consequences, we are delivered over to the extreme of technology, to technology as an extreme phenomenon" (56). Or again in an allusion to McLuhan, Baudrillard warns that the logic of technology as extension of man is carried to the point where it goes beyond itself and becomes "virtuality without limit." All of this sounds surprisingly like an old-fashioned humanist's jeremiad against the evils of technology. Indeed the great weakness of Baudrillard's effort to theorize VR is his inability to recognize practices that involve assemblages of humans and machines and account for their differential realizations. Instead Baudrillard is the unconscious ideologist-theorist of the television screen, imposing that vision upon cybernetic technologies.[7] It may be that the conservative overtones in the political implications he draws from the new order of virtual reality in part 2 of *Le crime parfait* derive from his failure to come to grips with the new level of human-machine imbrication represented especially by the "virtual communities" of the Internet and VR technology.

Critical reflection upon new technologies requires some exploration of the domain of the computer and some experience with the communication patterns it affords. One needs to do more than expatiate upon VR as a metaphor; one must look closely at its forms. One needs to differentiate between the TV screen and the computer screen. Such research often yields suggestive models that begin to come to grips with the true novelties we are confronted with. For instance, Kate Hayles argues compellingly that virtual reality technologies require and put forth new epistemologies: "The new technologies of virtual reality illustrate the kind of phenomena that foreground pattern and randomness and make presence and absence seem irrelevant" (1993). The shift in the location of the body in cybernetic technologies, Hayles suggests, reorganizes the field of analysis and the categories one may deploy to render it intelligible. Another example of a discourse on VR that speaks to its peculiar features is Marie-Laure Ryan's analysis of the relation of fiction and new technologies. If VR is distinguished by the immersion of the individual into computer-generated space, does not the novel also bring the reader into another world, a virtual world? Ryan sorts through this issue in relation to technologies of both immersion and interactivity, not simply being within a world but also acting upon it to change it. Though she is quite cautious about certain features of the new technologies, such as the limits imposed by the computer code upon the VR experience, in the end she recognizes important differences between literature and VR, as well as between different applications of VR itself. She concludes, "The most immersive forms of textual interactivity are therefore those in which the user's contributions, rather than performing a creation through a diegetic (i.e. descriptive) use of language, count as a dialogic and live interaction with other members of the fictional world" (Ryan 1994). VR enables, indeed requires, the individual to participate in constructing the world as she or he experiences it, rendering it distinct from reading a fixed text. As with Hayles, Ryan's analysis of VR begins to locate the specificity of the experience in terms that are not beholden to face-to-face or print modes of cultural practice.

Baudrillard's response to VR, by contrast, is to invent a new kind of discourse, dubbed "radical thought," in order to maintain his distance from it, to preserve his place in front and ahead of VR, in short, to repeat the gesture of the avant-garde. The problem he sees with "critical thought" is that it takes a stance in opposition to the real, setting up a dialectic of negation. But the real itself is structured in that way so that the gesture of opposition is already nullified. As an alternative Baudrillard offers radical thought as "the putting into play of this world, the material and immanent illusion of this so-called 'real' world—it is a noncritical, non-dialectical thought" (Baudrillard 1995). Thinking for him would be a nonoppositional alterity to the real, one that, through its difference from the real, exposes it, mocks it, destabilizes it.

Baudrillard takes language as his model for radical thought. "Language," he writes, sounding very much the poststructuralist or even Derridean, "is an illusion in its very movement, ... it carries this continuation of emptiness or nothingness at the very core of what it says, and ... it is in all its materiality a deconstruction of what it signifies" (1995). The insubstantiality of language allows it to escape the "evil transparency" of the real, its logic of identity, fullness, and performativity (Baudrillard 1993). Such a position would restore the world as illusion rather than as real. As illusion, the world takes many forms, among them the virtual reality of today, the "apocalypse of simulation."

Against his critics, Baudrillard denies that radical thought is nihilist. Refusing to defend himself, he still insists that "we have to fight against charges of unreality, lack of responsibility, nihilism, and despair. Radical thought is never depressing" (1995, 148). His apparently outrageous pronouncements, such as "What are you doing after the orgy?" or "The Gulf War did not take place" (Baudrillard 1983, 1991a)[8] are not examples of cynical reason but a sort of desperate playfulness in the face of extreme phenomena. Radical thought is not a failure to decipher or decode the world but to stand as witness in poetic and ironic enunciations of language. But is not language itself taking on new forms in the era of virtual reality and cyberspace? Can one rest with a self-styled deconstructive stance when the material infrastructure of the sign is being so drastically reconfigured? Baudrillard's virtual reality has not taken into account, with enough rigor and seriousness, the condition of the body, the material, the trace. Though he calls for a "fatal strategy" of the object, this object is without substance, depth, and resistance, so that the reconfigured cultural world of the mode of information remains, to him, a distant, threatening horizon of America, the desert.

In the end his world of totalized simulation remains limited by the model of simulation. Simulations rely upon their difference from representations. If simulations refute the logic of representation—its dualism of active subject, passive object—they maintain the linguistic stability of representations. Simulations are coherent sets of meanings, even if they are detached from referents and precede their objects. From first-level simulations, like maps, to third-level simulations, like the televised Gulf War, this cultural form retains its fixed matrix of meanings. TV shows and theme parks organize a cultural world that the individual consumes. What distinguishes VR from simulation is its transformational structure: subjects and objects interactively and immersively construct cultural spaces and events. They do so not in the present/absent logic of the first media age but in the informational logic of pattern/noise of the second media age. The cultural space of VR is not preceded by the model, as in simulations, but is continuously invented and reinvented through the material parameters of the media apparatus. As cybervillage and helmet-and-glove construct, VR discombobulates earlier cultural and social forms in order to recombine them in a new constellation, one not without its own constraints but with constraints that are peculiar to it and immune from complaints by modernist viewpoints.

Derrida's Ghosts

In *Specters of Marx* Derrida engages the issue of virtual reality, connecting it with the general question of politics, the media, and their interpretation. He first shows how the virtual is the supplement to the real: "*What is* a ghost? What is the *effectivity* or the *presence* of a specter, that is, of what seems to remain as ineffective, virtual, insubstantial as a simulacrum?" (1994, 10). Deconstructive analysis will show that the virtual is essential to the real, that "ghosts" haunt the full presence of the real in the forms of the debt to the past and the promise of justice in the future. Derrida announces a theory of "hauntology" to indicate the imbrication of the virtual in the real and declares the foundation of a "new international" to promote the aims of this promise, to sustain the alterity of justice against those who proclaim the "good news" of an uncontested liberalism, to foster the secular messianism of the virtual against the claim of the full presence of democracy.

If virtual reality is always already inscribed in the event, rendering history forever a "time out of joint," resisting the transparency of the real, it is also, for Derrida, a particular exigency of our age. Today virtual reality takes the form of the media and technology more generally. Derrida praises Marx's *Communist Manifesto* for its acumen on this score: "No text in the tradition seems as lucid concerning the way in which the political is becoming worldwide, concerning the irreducibility of the technical and the media in the current of the most thinking thought" (13). *Specters of Marx* consistently affirms the centrality of new media to a comprehension of the present age. The analysis of public space today, he writes, must take "into account so many *spectral* effects, the new speed of *apparition*... of the simulacrum, the synthetic or prosthetic image, and the virtual event, cyberspace and surveillance, the control, appropriation, and speculations that today deploy unheard-of powers" (54). Or again, "The logic of the ghost... points toward a thinking of the event" and is "demonstrated today better than ever by the fantastic, ghostly, 'synthetic,' 'prosthetic,' virtual happenings in the scientific domain and therefore the domain of the techno-media and therefore the public or political domain" (63). And again, Western democracy "is exercised with more and more difficulty in a public space profoundly upset by techno-tele-media apparatuses and by new rhythms of information and communication, by the devices and the speed of forces represented by the latter, but also and consequently by the new modes of appropriation they put to work, by the new structure of the event and of its spectrality that they *produce*" (79). The speed of the media and their pervasiveness "produce," Derrida contends, a condition of virtual reality that undermines modern institutions and evokes the need of a "new international" to assert the claims of justice.

The term *virtual reality* oscillates in Derrida's text between a general, transcendental aspect of the event and a particular configuration of the present associated with a specific set of technological apparatuses. On the one side, Derrida insists that his "hauntology" is "not an empirical hypothesis," relevant only to an age of computers, for example (161). As the term *iteration* suggests, a given technology may be redeployed elsewhere, by an other, and therefore "projects it *a priori* onto" all scenes of technique, media, and so forth. On the other side, Derrida, with equal vehemence, insists that he is not advocating an undifferentiated virtuality, "a general phantasmagorization" in which all technological cows are gray, (163) in which immersive virtual realities are the same as fictional worlds of novels. Rather he calls for new concepts that are more refined than those we presently have, concepts that would specify the different structures of virtual reality, the different forms of haunting in each technological apparatus. He writes, "The differential deployment of *tekhnē*, of techno-science or tele-technology... obliges us more than ever to think the virtualization of space and time, the possibility of virtual events whose movement and speed prohibit us more than ever (more and otherwise than ever, for this is not absolutely and thoroughly new) from opposing presence to its representation, 'real time' to 'deferred time,' effectivity to its simulacrum, the living to the non-living, in short, the living to the living-dead of its ghosts. It obliges us to think, from there, another space for democracy" (169). Unlike Baudrillard, Derrida senses the need to account for differential materialities of the media, for the ways in which the ghosts of television structure subjects differently from the virtualities of computer screens, for the ways in which Internet communities are different from helmet-and-glove computer-generated worlds. As in his earlier works, Derrida is attentive to the trace and to its material manifestations.

But Derrida does not provide the concepts needed for the analysis of the new technologies, and his discussion of "the virtualization of space and time" tends to preserve the philosopher's taste for the general over the cultural analyst's penchant for the particular. For instance, just after insisting upon deconstruction's actuality, that it is no mere "critique of a critique" but a positive intervention, establishing new institutions (an international) and new categories (for the analysis of the spectrality of the media), Derrida warns that this is all nothing new, that there will always be the need for new concepts, for "constant restructuration" (162).

The questions that remain then are these: Can hauntology take the next step and begin to specify the criteria by which these new concepts would be evaluated? And even further: Can it specify which are the pertinent domains of materiality that can be differentiated and analyzed in their effectivity? Instead of this initiative Derrida provides strings of hyphenated terms, "tele-technology" or "techno-scientifico-economico-media" (70), that vaguely point in a direction without guiding the virtual traveler in any particular direction.

There is at least one place, however, where Derrida has begun an analysis of the "teletechnological": his essay "Archive Fever: A Freudian Impression" (1995). Here Derrida does more than name the phenomena or point to it. He specifies its characteristics and determining features. If an archive is a necessary "supplement" of discourse, as Derrida argues, its specific form, its technical level, determines its effectivity as archive, its ability to preserve information both in time and in extent. Electronic databases, he surmises, would have changed the Freudian movement by their abilities in this regard alone. Second, the electronic archive also determines *what* can be preserved: "The technical structure of the *archiving* archive also determines the structure of the *archivable* contents" (Derrida 1996, 17). Whatever can be digitized can be stored. For example, audio- or even videotapes of meetings of the Psychoanalytic Society and of sessions with clients might be archived. In particular Derrida muses that electronic mail, with its automatic archiving function, changes stored memory in particular for a group such as psychoanalysts because of their extensive correspondence. But more than any of these features, the impact of teletechnology is most exigent in its transformation of what Derrida calls the public and the private. In his words, "electronic mail today, and even more than the fax, is on the way to transforming the entire public and private space of humanity, and first of all the limit between the private, the secret (private or public), and the public or phenomenal" (17). Derrida does not elaborate on this suggestive claim. Still, many have observed this phenomenon and have commented extensively upon it. Electronic surveillance and computer databases reduce, if not erase, the domain of the private. Computers are not alone in working to erode the privacy of the modern era. Television also, as Joshua Meyrowitz (1985) argues, by its framing structure and its location in the family living room, transforms public, formal occasions and spaces into intimate, private ones. The modern subject's sense of its exclusive awareness of its own thoughts and inclinations, however much a historical construction, as Francis Barker shows, is restructured by electronic communication systems so as to render nugatory its private, interior space (Barker 1995).

In these ways Derrida enumerates specific features of one teletechnology, e-mail, as it profoundly affects the question of the archive. Yet he does so in relation to a discussion of Freud and the early psychoanalytic movement, when there was no e-mail. Derrida takes a current topic of great urgency and controversy and reviews its character not in the present but in a hypothetical time, even an anachronistic time. For him, in a discursive act that he labels "retrospective science fiction," e-mail would have changed psychoanalysis. But why transform e-mail first into science fiction in order to set it up as a topic of analysis when it is in full use today? Perhaps Derrida requires this rhetorical move in order to energize his hauntology, in order to animate the ghost in Freud's archive with an anachronistic "teletechnology"? Or perhaps "teletechnology" may enter deconstruction only indirectly, through the temporal distance inserted by Derrida's discourse, the temporal distance of a "retrospective science fiction"? This making absent of e-mail and of the teletechnological, displacing it from its moment of inception and dissemination, occurs while the librarians at the University of California, Irvine, are accumulating the manuscript corpus of deconstruction for future scanning into an electronic archive.[9]

In *Specters of Marx* Derrida discusses an example of a teletechnology: the "visor effect" or "helmet effect" of the ghost in Shakespeare's *Hamlet*. Derrida is concerned to portray the materiality of the ghost through its partial or evanescent visibility. Ghosts refute the transparency of the "real" body, resist the perception of objectivity of the everyday. In Derrida's words, the ghost presents "the furtive and ungraspable visibility of the invisible . . . the tangible intangibility of a proper body without flesh" (7). If an ordinary ghost evinced such chaos in the visible, then the helmeted ghost of Hamlet's father, with his visor preventing certain identification, plays worse havoc with the real and does so in another material region: the ghost with helmet. This "helmet effect" offers "incomparable power" to its bearer, "the power to see without being seen," the power of hiding "his identity" (8). But is the Danish king's helmet a "real" helmet? Do ghosts wear metal on their heads or only simulations of metal? In Shakespeare's play, no doubt this distinction makes no difference, at least when it is performed in the seventeenth century. But at the close of the twentieth, when we possess "teletechnologies," would a film of Hamlet be required to make a visible distinction, since it is technically possible, between the ghost's helmet and a nonghost's helmet?

The materiality of the helmet emerges when we consider another user from the canon: Wagner's Alberich from *The Ring of the Nibelungen*, in which gold is fashioned into a magical helmet (the *tarnhelm*) that makes its wearer invisible. In this case the material for the helmet, gold, is itself a specular material, containing fantastic powers not visible on its surface but inscribed in the social imaginary of Western (and other) society. The gold is reshaped by a master craftsman (Mime, who is Alberich's brother), evoking the society of guilds and the power of human labor to infuse matter with special, even unimaginable, qualities. Finally, Alberich uses the *tarnhelm* to control his laborers, his invisibility providing an extra amount of power. This capitalist imaginary, with panoptic surveillance capacities, refunctions yet again the material of the helmet effect, introducing into Wagner's music-drama the contest between patriarchs of the feudal and capitalist variety. Ghostliness and materiality again combine in unanticipated ways.

The problems left by deconstruction's hauntology are particularly acute when the issue of political analysis is raised. Derrida provides a reasonable tablet of the ten major ills of present-day capitalist democracy: from unemployment and homelessness to market irrationalities, arms dealing, ethnic wars, and international law. Yet this analysis requires no hauntology or even deconstruction. Basic Marxism, or even left liberalism, would suffice for enumerating the political and economic plagues of the waning years of the millennium. Derrida admits as much, presenting this analysis with explicit debts to Marx. He writes, "Without necessarily subscribing to the whole Marxist discourse... one may still find inspiration in the Marxist 'spirit' to criticize the presumed autonomy of the juridical and to denounce endlessly the *de facto* take-over of international authorities by powerful Nation-States, by concentrations of techno-scientific capital, symbolic capital, and financial capital, of State capital and private capital" (85). But if Marxist categories suffice for such a discourse, is not hauntology little more than a "critique of a critique," a reminder of the ghost, an insistence on alterity, and a vigilance against ontologizing presence? In Sue Golding's words (1994), "When

Derrida speaks of a virtual limit, he replaces the politics of virtual being-there with 'the logic of the ghost.'" If he does not "replace" the one by the other, he certainly opens his analysis to that danger.

The question remains of deconstruction's purchase of justice when Marxist analysis depicts injustice so well.[10] Why does justice require Derrida? What it is about deconstruction that gives it a claim to witness justice? If the ghostly promise of justice to come is to haunt the present world, why must it appear in a specifically Derridean guise? Or should its identity even be known? Ought not Derrida, when announcing the New International and avowing its dedication to justice, hide himself in a visor or present himself in a virtual form? What necessary connection exists between the critique of the logocentric tradition, for which deconstruction is as fine an instrument as exists, and justice? Is Derrida's commitment to justice consonant with deconstruction or a departure from it?

In his review of *Specters of Marx,* Jameson raises this question in a particularly acute manner: "Whether the new figurality, the figured concept of the ghost or specter, is not of a somewhat different type than those that began to proliferate in Derrida's earlier work, beginning most famously with 'writing' itself and moving through . . . terms like dissemination, hymen" (Jameson 1995, 79). Does the introduction of the ghost in the *mise-en-scène* of deconstruction cause an alteration in its theoretical composition? Jameson reasons that it does because Derrida's messianism harkens to the "postmodern virtuality" of new communications technology, in other words to a reconfiguration of materiality (108). And I agree. To the extent that the mode of information restructures language and symbols generally into a configuration that is aptly termed *virtual reality,* the particular form of the messianic, of our hope for justice, must go through this technological circuit and must account for the difference between writing and e-mail, dissemination and the Internet, the parergon and the World Wide Web. Unless such an account is provided, deconstruction may return to its minimalist position as critique of critique, as disavowal of ontology, forever incapable of an affirmative sentence.

Specters of Marx instantiates an equivalence between the defense of the virtual, deconstruction, and justice. Evoking Nietzsche's prophetic yea-saying, Derrida writes, "A deconstructive thinking, the one that matters to me here, has always pointed out the irreducibility of affirmation and therefore of the promise, as well as the undeconstructibility of a certain idea of justice" (90). Very much like Foucault in "What Is Enlightenment?" affirming "a permanent critique of our historical era" (1984, 42), Derrida posits "a new Enlightenment for the century to come," animated by "an ideal of democracy and emancipation" (90). The poststructuralists link themselves tightly with a Nietzschean spirit of critique, Nietzsche as an affirmative philosopher of the will to power, the transvaluation of values, the creative soul who celebrates giving birth to a "dancing star." Yet this side of Nietzsche's thought has been noticeably absent from the poststructuralist appropriation, beginning with Gilles Deleuze's *Philosophy of Nietzsche* (1962) and continuing with Foucault's "Nietzsche, Genealogy, History" (1971) and finally Derrida's *Spurs: Nietzsche's Styles* (1978).

The danger of Derrida's association of democracy, Enlightenment, emancipation, and justice with deconstruction, all in a New International, is pointed out by Ernesto Laclau in his review of *Specters of Marx.* The danger is an automatic association of deconstruction with justice. Deconstruction becomes an ethical practice equivalent to emancipatory politics. Laclau writes, "The illegitimate transition is to think that from the impossibility of a presence closed in itself, from an 'ontological' condition in which the openness to the event, to the heterogeneous, to the radically other is constitutive, some kind of ethical injunction to be responsible and to keep oneself open to the heterogeneity of the other necessarily follows" (1995, 92–93). In this case, the ontological moment that Derrida would avoid returns through the back door of hauntology. The ghost loses his or her partial invisibility and becomes a witness of justice and bearer of the messianic promise. This strategy may stave off those critics of deconstruction, and poststructuralism more generally, who find in it an opening to "neoconservatism" or even neofascism, but it risks a theoretical step backward into the very ontological security these positions at their best have always sought to avoid. A commitment to justice and democracy is not in question. What is at issue is the way these are linked to theoretical strategies. If there is to be a New International, who will be part of it? What will be its aims? And what will be its strategies and methods? None of these questions is confronted in *Specters of Marx,* and until they are, it is difficult to see in what sense a New International exists.

Derrida's work, from *Writing and Difference* to *The Postcard* is informed by a sense of being in a new context, a transitional period in which what is emerging cannot be clearly discerned but dimly appears in the form of a monster. Writing in the late 1960s, Derrida positions himself clearly at a point of historical uncertainty:

> For my part, although these two interpretations [of interpretation] must acknowledge and accentuate their difference and define their irreducibility, I do not believe that today there is any question of *choosing*—in the first place because here we are in a region (let us say, provisionally, a region of historicity) where the category of choice seems particularly trivial; and in the second, because we must first try to conceive of a common ground, and the *différance* of this irreducible difference. Here there is a kind of question, let us still call it historical, whose *conception, formation, gestation,* and *labor* we are only catching a glimpse of today. I employ these words, I admit, with a glance toward the operations of childbearing—but also with a glance toward those who, in a society from which I do not exclude myself, turn their eyes away when faced by the as yet unnameable which is proclaiming itself and which can do so, as is necessary whenever a birth is in the offing, only under the species of the nonspecies, in the formless, mute, infant, and terrifying form of monstrosity. (1978, 293)

The historical question for Derrida is the naming of the "unnameable," the "nonspecies" that is emerging. And it cannot be done and ought not be done. In 1967 Derrida thinks within the process of the birth of a world, and deconstruction bears the marks of its term of gestation as the philosophy of the undecidable. In this context the old metanarratives and totalizations are no longer credible, but neither are new general political stances perceptible. In such a condition the deconstruction of Western culture labors in the horizon of the undecidable. With the avowal of emancipation and the declaration of a New International, Derrida, it would seem, collapses the critical ambivalence of the 1970s and 1980s into a positivity that is well-meaning, to be sure, but without much force of conviction.

The question of politics in the age of virtual reality must depart from a new materialism, a new theory of the imbrication of technology and culture, one that comes to terms with the transformation of mechanical machines into smart machines, into "artificial intelligence," self-regulating systems, and digitizers of images, sounds, and text; it must commence from an appreciation of the dissemination of these software-hardware systems throughout social space and the installation of interfaces that unite humans and machines in new configurations of agency.[11] This gigantic task of conceptual-empirical development no doubt relies in part on deconstruction, especially in its hauntology phase. But it does not guarantee a politics of emancipation, however much one would wish it were so. While Marxist and liberal critiques continue to have important but limited effectivity, a general new politics of radical democracy must await the substantial analysis of an emerging global mode of information. The reconfiguration of time and space, body and mind, human and machine, imagination and reason, gender and ethnicity, and the virtual and the real must congeal into a postmodern relation of force before critical theory's owl of Minerva takes flight.

CHAPTER EIGHT

Virtual Ethnicity

Global Ethnicity

Ethnicity and *race* are much contested terms today. Once, when Enlightenment discourse retained its hegemony, these terms were easily dismissed as idols of outmoded eras and primitive societies, as irrational myths, at best as regrettable ideals of minds incapable of ascending to their own humanity. Today spontaneous identification with one's local group, a sort of natural parochialism, is precluded by the saturation of daily life with globalized media: one is continually confronted with people who are not of one's tribe, kin, ethnicity, race, or community in any sense. Yet the desire for ethnic identification, at least in some quarters, is strong. Perhaps this is a postmodern ethnicity, mediated by an increasingly technologized social world.

The celebration of what some call neoethnicity extends to critical discourse. With a purpose of supporting oppressed groups in their struggles against domination, many critical thinkers wary of essentializing ethnicity as a stable, presocial center of identity nonetheless discover there a resort for resistance to domination. For example, Lisa Lowe, in *Immigrant Acts* (1996), recognizes that "oppositional solidarity movements have been organized around racial identities because of social and economic oppressions that have targeted those identities" (15). Yet this defensive identification does not prevent her from attributing to such communities "resistance cultures" on the basis of those identifications (23). She argues that inequalities of class, race, and gender contravene absorption into the abstract position of national citizenship. "Asian American particularity," she contends, "returns a differently located dialectical critique of the universality proposed by both the economic and the political spheres" (28). And at the cultural level, she continues, "the contradictory history of Asian Americans produces cultural forms that are materially and aesthetically at odds with the resolution of the citizen to the nation" (30). For Lowe, race and nation are in antagonism.

But race and nation are not in singular opposition.[1] A global economy and global communication complicate and disrupt this site of struggle. When Lowe adds the global into the stew of cultures of resistance the dish changes flavor: ethnic and racial identification become questionable supports of emancipation. She writes, "The current global restructuring—that moves well beyond the nation-state and entails the differentiation of labor forces internationally—constitutes a shift in the mode of production that now necessitates alternative forms of cultural practice that integrate yet move beyond those of cultural nationalism" (171). When the reference point is global, ethnicity becomes an impediment to alliances of solidarity, not an inspiration to resistance.

Local identifications are increasingly linked with planetary configurations of economy and media. Ethnic differentiation now mixes with transnational formations. Ethnocentrism becomes ethno*excentrism*. A culture of resistance must engage with the other in global configurations. Instead of a localism oriented to an original, pure ethnicity, globalism impels us to conceive a new localism profoundly affected by the grace of the link with other. In *Primitive Passions* (1996), Rey Chow offers a concept of translation as a model for such cultural restructuring. Chow takes the linking of nations, races, and ethnicities in global configurations as an opportunity, not a threat. The occasion is now offered to us to understand how our language, heritage, and traditions partake, in their specificity, of the general capacity for such phenomena. When we translate we learn new things about ourselves, not simply about the other we encounter. To translate is not to copy an original, represent it, appropriate it as our own, or to fail to do so. It is the chance, Rey reminds us, borrowing from Benjamin, to enhance our experience of our own culture. Understood in this manner, ethnicity becomes neither an originary resort of identification nor a primitive incapacity to attain universality. It becomes a moment of self-construction through the other, just the sort of practice fitting with a thickening global landscape.

The term *virtual ethnicity*, like Chow's translated ethnicity, suggests one of the great questions confronting us at the beginning of the twenty-first century: Is there a new form of planetary culture alongside existing ones that appears in the "space" of electronic communications? Does "globalization" imply a "noosphere" in Teilhard de Chardin's sense (1959), a new layer of hominization, as he calls it, that inhabits the earth in underground wires, floats in the air over the planet as high-frequency radio waves and under the water in cables, all variations of communications technologies? Can there be a form of culture that is not bound to the surface of the globe, attaching human beings to its particular configurations with the weight of gravity, inscribing their bodies with its rituals and customs, interpellating their selves with the force of traditions and political hierarchies? Is virtual ethnicity an alternative to the binaries of particularism and universalism, parochialism and cosmopolitanism, inserting itself between nations and communities, earthly ethnicities and races? Is virtual ethnicity a transgression of essentialism in all its forms, including that of Western rationalism? Does virtual ethnicity betoken a new age, a "postmodernity" that spawns multiple, dispersed, heterogeneous subjects as well as global communities? These are some of the fascinating questions inspired in me by the emergence of forms of ethnicity in the global communications network known as the Internet.

An approach to these questions requires a double interrogation: first, of the term *virtual* and its formulation in relation to its apparent opposite, the real; and second, the term *culture* and its related terms, *ethnicity, nationality*, and *race*.

In Wellington, New Zealand, in April 1994, a Maori reporter for a Maori radio station asked me, in an interview about new technologies, what the implications were if a Western company produced a CD-ROM on Maori culture and sold it throughout the world? Could Maori culture survive if its sounds, images, and texts were controlled by a non-Maori entrepreneur? Could her social world survive if people from other cultures obtained the CD-ROM and learned the stories, customs, and secrets of her culture without participating in them in real life? It appeared to her that her world was being threatened by CD-ROM technology; that the integrity of her way of life was at stake in an era of high technology; that the autonomy and coherence of Maori identity could easily be shattered and dispersed by information systems that disseminated cheaply the sacred rites of her group, the secrets and precious beliefs and practices that defined and held together her ethnicity. She implied that ethnic identity and global information were incompatible. If Marshall McLuhan celebrated the spread of electronic media as the dawn of a "global village," a retribalization of humankind, this Maori feared that same future as the devastation of her tribe.

An altogether different attitude toward information technology was expressed at a different time, in a different place, by a person of a different background. In this instance the question of ethnicity evaporates before a universalist vision of rationality. Here are the words of one white American male of the mid–nineteenth century:

> It has been the result of the great discoveries of the past century, to effect a revolution in political and social life, by establishing a more intimate connexion between nations, with race and race. It has been found that the old system of exclusion and insulation are stagnation and death. National health can only be maintained by the free and unobstructed interchange of each with all. How potent a power, then, is the telegraph destined to become in the civilization of the world! This binds together by a vital cord all the nations of the earth. It is impossible that old prejudices and hostilities should longer exist, while such an instrument has been created for an exchange of thought between all the nations of the earth. (Briggs and Maverick 1858, 21–22)

This sanguine vision of a pacified and unified Earth, shorn of ethnic particularism as a consequence of the proliferation of communication technologies, exemplifies the dominant metanarrative of liberal thought, the hallmark of the telos of progress.

In the one case the globalization of Maori culture through CD-ROM technology incites a threat of dissolution; in the other the telegraph promises to unite into harmony the peoples of the Earth. Is this an opposition between tribal parochialism and Western Enlightenment, between particularism and universalism, between difference and sameness, between localism and globalism? Are these the only alternatives before us as electronic communications technologies multiply and spread across the globe? What then is the fate of ethnicity in an age of virtual presence?

Culture is now technologically processed. Machines that process symbols, sounds, and images install mediations between human beings that permit remote intimacy, exchanges at a distance, spatial simultaneity. The computer, communications satellites, telephones, and now television are being linked into a new cultural processing assemblage. This assemblage in turn is connected by a network architecture that extends, however unevenly at present, over the globe. And this network is decentralized so positions of speech and reception cannot easily be restricted or even hierarchized. The assemblage is digital so that messages travel, when bandwidth is adequate, at the speed of light. And it is packet-switched so that each message has no prescribed path but follows any available route to its destination. What is known as cyberspace is sustained by this entire apparatus. Though it is not a finished product with definite specifications and fixed features, one may characterize cyberspace, because of the characteristics that have emerged thus far in its configuration, as the virtual territory. If an argument can be sustained that a virtual realm has been set into place, can there be a "virtual ethnicity"? Does such a virtual ethnicity imply a new articulation of the relation of individual to community, or is it a "false" ethnicity, as some would have us believe? Are the Maori reporter and the Western progressivist really in opposition, or do they both present ethnic identity as essentialist? Do virtual technocultures challenge this essentialism, and if so, how?

Language and the Virtual

The first question confronting the analysis of virtual ethnicity is that of language. To what extent and in what ways do virtual technologies alter the gap or *différance* already inserted between identity and ethnicity by language? Friedrich Nietzsche (1986) theorized language as itself a second or virtual world standing against and outside "the real." Nietzsche writes, "The significance of language for the evolution of culture lies in this, that mankind set up in language a separate world beside the other world, a place it took to be so firmly set that, standing upon it, it could lift the rest of the world off its hinges and make itself master of it" (16).[2] Here language is not only separate from "the world" but also "master of it." At every moment symbolic coding intercedes between individual consciousness and experience, rendering human culture a double world of mediated immediacy.

There are three separable assertions in Nietzsche's statement: (1) that language mediates humanity's relation to the world, (2) that in doing so it alters that world, and (3) that this alteration takes priority over any immediacy of the world. Today, decades after the linguistic turn, the first position may be accepted without argument. The third is essentially an empirical question, one that is not at the heart of the issue in this essay.

The second, however, leads into my central concern. In what way does language alter experience? More particularly, how does the form in which language is exchanged between individuals and groups affect the cultural construction of the world and subject positions within it? In addition, this question must be expanded beyond language proper to include all mediated symbolic structures, comprising, in addition to language, images (both still and moving), animations, and sounds.

Walter Benjamin argued that the technical[3] reproduction of art alters the nature of art by changing the relation of the audience to the author, the conditions of reception, and the authority of the author. A similar claim may be sustained for culture taken in the anthropological sense of symbolization in general and in the Foucauldian sense of the construction of the subject. The technical reproduction of culture then transforms the constitution of identities,[4] even ethnic or national identities. If these claims are accepted, the next step in the argument is to divide the term *technical* into its various aspects: mechanical/electrical and broadcast/networked.

The mechanical/electrical distinction (for example, print versus television) affects considerably the ease of diffusion of fixed materials. In both cases production is greatly centralized and cut off from reception. The mass distribution of objects requires, for technical reasons independent of their social location, a preformed content whose reception may be contested and resymbolized, as Michel de Certeau demonstrates,[5] but whose material form is not altered in the reception. Even if I critique an advertisement on television or in the newspaper, everyone still receives the same content, regardless of the brilliance of my response to it. The ability to disseminate widely cultural objects appears to curtail the ease of their transformation. Both print and electronic mass media install a monologic discursive regimen in the heart of everyday life. Cultural and social critics, however, have tended to register complaints against such centralization, not with the advent of newsprint but rather with the spread of electronic media.[6]

The second distinction concerns broadcast versus networked wrappings of language. In this case cultural objects may be distributed centrally or not. In the case of the telephone and the Internet, a highly decentralized practice of distribution replaces the hierarchy and monology of the broadcast model. While the telephone generally confines decentralization to a one-to-one pattern of sending and receiving, the Internet allows broadcasting or multiple distribution in addition to decentralization. Various techniques available on the Internet, from asynchronous listserves and newsgroups to synchronous electronic cafés, with or without graphics and sound, permit a many-to-many dialogic practice to be instituted in a global environment of exchange. How might such an alteration of the way language is packaged and exchanged affect the constitution of ethnic identities?

One caveat is necessary before pursuing this question. These differences in the material inscription of language are not to be taken as technological determinisms. Technical forms are never "independent variables" but always already inscribed in social and cultural processes.[7] However, technical forms do open possibilities and do contain constraints. One cannot fly from London to Vienna on a cigar, however symbolically charged in the unconscious might be the relation between airplanes and cigars. Nonetheless one might do just that in a virtual reality technology, except that "Vienna" would be computer generated and one's feet would remain firmly planted in London. It might be useful to distinguish and to bear in mind four levels of technological inscription:

1. The constraints of the medium, its material limits
2. The pretechnological conditions for the introduction of the medium; perceived needs that inspire innovation
3. The general *cultural* determinations of the medium, for example, the difference between the introduction of print in Europe and in China
4. The determinations of the medium through practices, that is, how people symbolize their experience with the medium

If these are kept in mind, the problem of technological determinism may be held at bay.

As a working hypothesis I will assume that technologies of symbolization are positioned in complex relations to other social practices, are mutually transforming through historically specific articulations, but also have limits to their material forms that seriously affect the way they are so inscribed. Before developing this hypothesis in relation to the issue of virtual ethnicity, it is necessary to consider an opposing position: that the virtual is not real.

No Virtuality

There are many ways to deny the virtual, to elide it or repress it, to claim that it represents nothing new, that it does not challenge the existing order of things in any way. Here is Slavoj Žižek's version of such a stance, one that may stand in not so much for psychoanalysis in general but for the propensity, widespread in many registers of discourse and daily life, to normalize and to disavow the strange and the novel:

GEERT LOVINK: In your speech during the Ars Electronica conference, you emphasized the fact that after a phase of introduction, the seduction of the new media will be over and so will "virtual sex." So the desire to be wired will be over soon?

SLAVOJ ŽIŽEK: The so-called "virtual communities" are not such a great revolution as it might appear. What impresses me is the extent to which these virtual phenomena retroactively enable us to discover to what extent our self has always been virtual. Even the most physical self experience has a symbolic, virtual element in it. For example playing sex games. What fascinates me is that the possibility of satisfaction already counts as an actual satisfaction. A lot of my friends used to play sex games on Minitel in France. They told me that the point is not really to meet a person, not even to masturbate, but that just typing your phantasies is the fascination itself. In the symbolic order the potentiality already gives actual satisfaction. In psychoanalytic theory the notion of symbolic castration is often misunderstood. The threat of castration as to its effects, acts as a castration. Or in power relations, where the potential authority forms the actual threat. Take Margaret Thatcher. Her point was that if you don't rely on state support but on your individual resources, luck is around the corner. The majority didn't believe this, they knew very well that most of them would remain poor. But it was enough to be in a position where they might succeed.

The idea that you were able to do something, but didn't, gives you more satisfaction than actually doing it. In Italy, it is said to be very popular during the sexual act that a woman tells a man some dirty phantasies. It is not enough that you are actually doing it, you need some phantasmatic, virtual support. "You are good, but yesterday I fucked another one and he was better..." What interests me are the so-called sado-masochistic, ritualised, sexual practices. You never go to the end, you just repeat a certain foreplay. Virtual in the sense that you announce it, but never do it. Some write a contract. Even when you are doing it, you never lose control, all the time you behave as the director of your own game. What fascinates me is this *Spaltung*, this gap in order to remain a certain distance. This distance, far from spoiling enjoyment, makes it even more intense. Here I see great possibilities for the VR stuff.

In the computer I see virtuality, in the sense of symbolic fiction, collapsing. This notion has a long tradition. In Bentham's panopticon we find virtuality at its purest. You never know if somebody is there in the centre. If you knew someone was there, it would have been less horri-

fying. Now it's just an "utterly dark spot," as Bentham calls it. If someone is following you and you're not sure, it is more horrible than if
you know that there is somebody. A radical uncertainty.[8]

In the first sentence of his reply to Geert Lovink's question, Žižek dismisses Internet communications: it is no "revolution." In the second sentence, he universalizes it: everything is always already virtual so while it
is everywhere, it is also nowhere. He does this by equating the virtual
with the symbolic, an interesting proposition but one that dangerously
occludes the material forms in which the symbolic is wrapped. Beginning in the third sentence, Žižek incorporates "virtual communities"
within the principle of psychoanalysis: that virtual sex is real sex was
already known to psychoanalysis in its understanding of the imaginary
component in all psychic phenomena—that the threat of castration is,
in a very important sense, castration. In this way the virtual becomes one
more example of the truth of psychoanalysis, not at all a new register
that might be the occasion for a rethinking or even restructuring of the
Freudian position. Žižek's discursive move in this passage illustrates the
classic gesture of ideology: when faced with an apparent novelty, a seeming "revolution," to use his term, place it under the cover of one's already existing position. Two feats are thereby accomplished: the threat
of the new is dissolved and one's position is expanded and strengthened.

His last position, that the computer, far from sustaining a "revolution"
in virtual communities, actually dissolves the virtual, goes one better.
Now we find that actually existing psychoanalysis has not simply discovered the virtual in advance of modern technology, but that modern
technology destroys the virtual, in contrast to psychoanalysis, which defends and sustains it. In order to achieve this theoretical reversal, Žižek
switches the scene to Bentham's panopticon, hardly the latest development in Western technology but one that nonetheless represents to Žižek
"virtuality at its purest." The "utterly dark spot," the "black hole in cyberspace"[9] of the prison tower, with its position of surveillant authority, whose guard may be present or absent but in either case effectively
real for the prisoner caged in his cell, this "virtuality" is somehow the
"real" virtual, if this oxymoron will pass the reader's scrutiny, compared
with the alleged false virtual community on the Internet. Žižek has here
moved outside of the psychoanalytic paradigm into that of deconstruction: a conflation of presence and absence replaces the effective power

of the imaginary as absence. Such a conflation does not seem to give Žižek pause for reflection as the interview moves on to other matters. Yet it does illustrate an incoherence or, if one prefers, a consistent shifting of registers within the same argument, a shifting that reminds one of the movement of unconscious in Lacan's version of it rather than of the ego function of the discursive method.

Perhaps the most interesting position expressed by Žižek in response to Lovink's query appears just before the turn to Bentham where he announces that he sees great possibilities for "this VR stuff" because it "intensifies" the "gap" or "distance" between announcing an act and doing it. At last Žižek finds an aspect of the virtual communities of the Internet that he defines as new (at least in its intensity, even though Italian women have already mastered the art for the pleasure of their men) and as positive, as something that contains "possibilities." But at precisely this point in his answer to the question Žižek slips from speaking of the virtual in any meaningful sense. He is simply presenting the imaginary, the "symbolic fictional," as he previously said. "This VR stuff" must be taken as the real in order for it properly to be virtual. When one is online in an erotic exchange with a partner, one must play the game of the conversation as a form of "virtual" conversation. Instead Žižek reduces Internet sex games to being a "director" of one's own play, of simply exaggerating the real with special effects for the purpose of manipulating the audience that is oneself into greater orgiastic pleasure. The problem is that one does not control or "direct" conversations on bulletin boards any more than one does in RL (real life), face-to-face dialogue, or on the phone. What is virtual about Internet community is not the intensification of the role of director, but the simultaneity without physical presence, even the physical presence of the voice.

I have taken this digression from the discussion of virtual ethnicity to the path of Žižek's answer to the question of the virtual not to expose the limitations of his thought—his text comes from an off-the-cuff interview, after all, not a carefully prepared statement—but to illustrate the practice of the denial of the virtual. We must acknowledge the possibility that the globalization of a new communications network may not amount to much except the instrumental purpose of speed of interchange. Since the installation of virtual technologies is at an early stage, no firm judgment about its effectivity is possible. However, I will assume the opposite of Žižek, that is, that virtuality represents an occasion for the articulation of new figures of ethnicity, nationhood, community, and global interaction. Only on the basis of this assumption is it possible to perceive the novelty of virtual ethnicity and evaluate its import. And I will attempt to avoid the naturalization or normalization of the virtual, the discursive practice through which it emerges in writing as always already given. For the "natural" is only what we are used to, but it is so in the form of denying that we are used by it, transformed and constituted into something historically articulated, something emerging in time, something new; in short, an event.

"Real" Ethnicity

Is there a real or true ethnicity against which a virtual ethnicity may be measured as a fall or an advance? My aim is not to pose this question but instead to construct a theoretical object of ethnicity as a multiple historical articulation without privileging any of its specific configurations except to highlight the emergence of a new form of ethnicity in the age of electronically mediated communications and to examine its political import in relation to contemporary claims of ethnic authenticity. Virtual ethnicity then is a historically emergent form that, like all cultural figures, bears a relation of force to what has preceded it. The problem, then, is to define the specific categories of communication that render intelligible the pertinent forms of ethnicity in their differential aspects. The understanding of ethnicity found in electronic communities on the Internet must be able to delineate its difference from low-technology, tribal ethnicity.

The historian Pierre Nora, in *Les lieux de mémoire* (1989), provides a useful starting point for this analysis. Nora wishes to theorize a new kind of history, one that is self-reflective and has come to terms with the deeply transformed conditions of writing history at the waning of the twentieth century, conditions that profoundly discourage the sort of history written when it could be assumed that individuals formed their identities in good part through an attachment to a national past. He distinguishes what could be called a "modern" practice of writing history in which the historian innocently constructs in discourse the past of the nation, from a "postmodern" practice of history, in which the narrative link of the individual to the nation is problematic at best.[10] In doing so, however, he first distinguishes the prehistorical from the historical as a distinction between a context in which individual identity is formed into ethnicity through "real environments of memory" (the prehistorical) and one in which it occurs through "sites of memory" (the historical) (7). French peasant culture is his chief example of the former; it is presented as "true" and "immediate." Here the identification of the individual with the group or ethnicity is formed "in gestures and habits, in skills passed down by unspoken traditions, in the body's inherent self-knowledge, in unstudied reflexes and ingrained memories" (Nora, 13). By contrast, historical, national, modern identity is "indirect" and mediated. The salient mediation of national identity, for Nora, is the material trace, particularly the written trace found in the archive. For the modern individual, national identity is principally constituted in historical discourse, Nora contends, perhaps betraying to some extent the myopia of the historian. Today a third stage in the story has emerged "with the help of the media." Electronic communication "has substituted for a memory entwined in the intimacy of a collective heritage [the modern] the ephemeral film of current events" (7–8). Today "a completely new economy of the identity of the self" (15) disrupts and reconfigures ethnicity through electronic encoding and storage of memory in "the omnipotence of imagery and cinema," in "televisual memory" (17). As a result ethnicity is no longer a collective phenomenon but is individualized: it is "as if an inner voice were to tell each Corsican 'You must be Corsican'... [or] to be Jewish is to remember that one is such" (16).[11]

From the standpoint of the practicing historian, Nora searches for a way to theorize changing forms of ethnicity in relation to the configurations of memory as they in turn change from face-to-face to print and finally to electronic communications.[12] He wants to open a project of rewriting history for a postmodern age. No doubt there is much of value in his proposal, as testify the full volumes of *Les lieux de mémoire* (Nora 1984), with their rich analyses of reconfigured historical objects. For an understanding of virtual ethnicity, however, Nora in one sense does not go far enough and in another goes too far. He does not go far enough because his consideration of postmodern ethnicity includes only mass media (film and television), not newer technologies of the computer—their network of communications and virtual reality systems. He goes too far in the sense that his opposition of "true" and "indirect" sites of ethnic identification first privileges the premodern, peasant structure and then, when the comparison is drawn between the modern and the postmodern, privileges the modern, nationalist phase.

We cannot begin with an opposition of immediate/mediated because this discursive move misconstrues the premodern as the authentic, which is exactly what Nora does. Such a binary opposition fails to account for the *mediations* within face-to-face communities, the way they are technologies of power that constitute subjects and their ethnic identities through material, symbolic practices. In the passage cited above Nora errs in attributing to peasant culture "unspoken traditions," whereas these cultures have specific narratives of origin that are spoken, performed, and repeated time and again in barns and churches. We must understand these premodern ethnicities not through a binary opposition of immediate/ mediated but through different configurations of mediation, with particular attention to the material element in the mediation. While it certainly appears to be the case that premodern ethnicities, in their predominately verbal pattern of symbolic formation, were relatively stable, providing the individual with a fixed ethnic identification, this ethnicity still had to be produced and reproduced in discourses and practices, and it remained subject to change, to doubt, and to alteration. It had to be inscribed.

By the same token, Nora's premature ending in film and television preempts the innovation of computer-mediated communication, leading him to sketch the present conjuncture in seriously limited ways. He understands contemporary forms of ethnic identity through the model of consumption: one chooses one's ethnic heritage the way one chooses a pair of shoes or an automobile. He concedes far too easily the voluntary character of the process, thereby losing sight of the socially constituted material patterns at play in such practices. In addition, he comprehends the late twentieth century to some extent as no more than an extension of the modern period, with its practice of archiving written materials. "What began as writing ends as high fidelity and tape recording," he writes, continuing to avoid the computer as a model of storage (1984, 13). We need to ask, then, how do tape recording, e-mail, and electronic communities constitute a structure through which, to take his example, the Jew remembers to be a Jew? Nora notes the recent phenomenon of nonpracticing Jews reviving their ethnic heritage, but he in no way accounts for the material communicational and political structures through which this became a possibility or even an urgency. In the end the outer chapters of Nora's story, the premodern and the postmodern, are dependent upon and determined by the historian's predilection for the modern, for the period of national identity, for the time when it fell to the historian to narrate the past of the nation—at least this is the view of the historian—as a discursive interpellation for national identity. The task for us, then, is to extract from Nora's account the problematic of ethnic identity in relation to material, symbolic configurations and to reshape this category, articulating its attributes, to allow the comprehension of virtual ethnicity in relation to earlier ethnicities, and finally, to open this project with a sense of the political dimension of new formations, the relations of force necessarily at play, and the pathos of individuals searching for a better life.

The Global Village Reaffirmed

In order to comprehend the phenomenon of virtual ethnicity, it is necessary to approach contemporary forms of social life at least to some extent on their own terms, to view them without the modernist lenses through which they are perceived as massified, inert, passive. This is the important achievement of the current of cultural studies of recent decades,[13] of urban anthropology, and of some individual figures such as Michel de Certeau. While risking a new romanticism of the popular and the everyday, these intellectual strains bring us closer to the strange new world of the postmodern quotidian and enable us to glimpse the contours of mass society without the defensive reaction of Olympian disdain that marks so much of critical theory. By the same token, other thinkers, such as Marshall McLuhan, Jean Baudrillard, and Paul Virilio also pioneered the "descent" in mass culture. McLuhan (1964) in particular opens a promising path to virtual ethnicity with his celebration (at times ambivalent, to be sure) of a new tribalism, a global village of electronic communication in which the sense ratio of individuals alters from a dominance of the visual in modernity to a dominance of the tactile in what we may now call postmodernity. McLuhan's position, developed mainly in the early 1960s, was limited by, among other things, its focus on the broadcast media, appearing before the dissemination of computers and their communication networks.

Writing in the late 1980s, Michel Maffésoli suffers no similar handicap. In *Les temps des tribus* he renews McLuhan's initiative in a more developed postmodern environment, opening critical discourse to an understanding of virtual ethnicity. Maffésoli begins by reaffirming McLuhan's claim of a change from "an optical period" to "a tactile era of proximity, from the global to the local" (Maffésoli 1988, 51). Very much like McLuhan, he also discerns a new "orality" in daily life amid a chaos of "micro-groups" he calls tribes. More clearly than McLuhan, Maffésoli perceives the social as a realm of increasing massification but also and at the same time increasing heterogeneity, increasing "sameness" *and* increasing differentiation at the micro level. Maffésoli locates the new tribalism "in diverse sports gatherings,...in consumerist fury in department stores, supermarkets, commercial centers,...on the avenues of large cities" (125). Although he provides no detailed analyses of these "pivots" of postmodern daily life, he discerns within them "a constant going and coming between tribes and masses" (126).

According to Maffésoli, the new tribalism is characterized by proximity, "the unsaid," "the residue," very much along the lines of Nora's community of "true memory." Maffésoli insists that the tribes are beyond modern "individualism," are determined by forms of feeling, "auras" of togetherness that refute the logics of identity and subject/object dualism. The tribes are "nonrational," not "irrational," but also contain "a new form of rationality" that is a combination of proximity, intensity, "both linking people and letting them be" (178). The tribes represent a new Fourierism of postmodern passionate attraction. They are characterized above all by mobility of connection, Charles Fourier's "butterfly passion," the desire constantly to change partners and associations. In this respect they are, for Maffésoli, different from the counterculture of the 1960s, with its dream of stable communities. Although Maffésoli bases his understanding of the tribes on premodern, even archaic principles of closeness, contact, and exchange of feeling, he avoids Nora's ideology of presence: "The fusion of the community...does not imply a full presence to the other...but establishes rather...a *tactile relation*" (94). Even with this caution he slips at times from his own analytic perch. He does, in places, ontologize the tribes, finding in them a new realization of fullness of being: "Participating in a multiplicity of tribes... each person will be able to live his *intrinsic* plurality" (182; emphasis added). Here the postmodern vision of the multiple, decentered self amplifies into the redemption of man, the recuperation of lost unity, the completion of the metanarrative of progress as "plurality" becomes "intrinsic." The tribes are, for Maffésoli, clearly an improvement upon the autonomous, rational subject of modernity. The edge of a differential analysis is given over to a comic trope of a happy ending.

The use of the term *tribe* is perhaps one source of the problem. In the postmodern context, *tribe* cannot designate the anthropologist's society of kinship. Maffésoli's tribes are urban, not rural; dispersed within wider relations, not isolated; subject to the modernizing processes of the division of labor and institutional differentiation, not combined in the unity of spatial and functional solidarity; penetrated by processes of commodification and telecommunications, not restricted to production for use and face-to-face symbolic exchange; and disciplined by the nation-state, not governed by hereditary hierarchies. Nothing could be farther apart than the human ecologies of the late-twentieth-century Western world and the hunter-gatherer societies normally known as tribes. Even Maffésoli's insistence on the emotional ties of the new tribes suggests a break, not a continuity, from the old tribes. The former, after all, gather into groups on a purely voluntary basis, not through the prescriptions of local myths.

These cautions aside, Maffésoli is able to incorporate a sense of computerized communications into his vision of the proximate, local new tribe. He surmises, "The feeling of tribal belonging can be comforted by technological development. . . . potentially, 'cable,' electronic bulletin boards (playful, erotic, instrumental, etc.) create a communication matrix where groups with diverse configurations and objectives emerge, are fortified and disappear; groups which recall the archaic structures of tribes or village clans" (171–72). Global relations on the Internet become local neighborhoods for Maffésoli, very much in the spirit of McLuhan. Maffésoli finds the sociability and amorousness of the Minitel's *messagéries* compatible with shopping at malls, attending football games and rock concerts, and joining raves and hanging out on street corners. His new ethnicity is one without virtuality, a tribalism that conquers the alienations and isolations of life in postmodern capitalism, overcomes the loneliness and passivity of mass culture in a novel, flexible, and multiple individualism, a sociability that, shorn of bourgeois individualism, celebrates what is, after all, predominantly youth culture with no sense of its difficulties, suicides, drug abuse, identity confusion, racism, gang warfare, and so forth. His generous appreciation of "new tribalism" fails to provide a materialism of the mediation, an articulation of the complex structuring of each aspect of everyday life, a sense of how, for example, watching a television show like *The X-Files*, then, during the commercial break, connecting by computer modem to a Usenet group on that subject to enter comments or see what others are saying, and finally going to the mall to buy an *X-Files* T-shirt are each differential engagements that constitute subjects in highly heterogeneous ways. I want to ask not how a new, unified image (new tribalism) is emerging but how specific figures of ethnicity are altered by their electronic constitution in virtual spaces.

Underdetermination Again Briefly

At what point in the history of technologies of symbolization is it appropriate to speak of "the virtual"? Everything depends upon how the virtual is understood. There are currently many concepts of the virtual to clarify this issue,[14] but I will turn to the work of Pierre Lévy, *Qu'est-ce que le virtuel?* (1995a),[15] because of the way it deals with the basic distinction between real and virtual. Two tendencies above all must be avoided: to celebrate the virtual as an evolutionary or dialectical "next stage" beyond the real or to dismiss the virtual as a false instantiation of the real. Instead the virtual must be understood as a historical articulation of the real, fully as actual as any other such articulation but one connected specifically with computer-mediated communication technologies. Lévy productively theorizes this relation by distinguishing between the oppositions real/potential and actual/virtual, which he finds in the Western philosophical tradition. The difference between the two sets of terms is that the former is more algorithmic: that is, the potential easily becomes the real, or better, its possibility to become real is "predefined." In the latter case the relation is more "problematic," requiring more "invention" for the virtual to become actual. This distinction, taken from Deleuze (1994, 208–14), is useful merely to indicate relative degrees of uncertainty and complexity. But Deleuze deploys the distinction to the category of ideas, whereas Lévy relates it to the Internet.

Lévy's innovation is to argue that today a reversal is taking place: instead of the virtual becoming actual, the actual is becoming virtual. We have moved to a condition in which what is actual is now virtual, articulating an undefined set of possibilities rather than a fixed state of things. "Virtualization," he contends, "is not a derealization (the transformation of a reality into an ensemble of possibilities) but a mutation of identity, a displacement of the center of ontological gravity of the object in question: instead of being defined principally by its actuality (a "solution"), the entity henceforth finds its essential consistency in a problematic field" (chap. 1, 2). He gives the example of a hypertext[16] in which the determination of the text, its sequential structure and meaning, and its logic of associations are, in comparison with the book, to a great extent at the discretion of the reader. We thus find objects before us whose determination is to a very considerable extent underdetermined.

Jews in Space

The Internet is not a homogeneous social object. It contains records of information, databases, which construct identities of individuals outside their consciousness, with their (unwitting) participation, yet inscribed in institutional and practical contexts. I have called this phenomenon the "superpanopticon," modifying Foucault's analysis of disciplinary surveillance.[17] In these electronic interpellations, ethnic identities are sutured or attached to individuals, in some cases multiplying but always dispersing their selves. Yet these inscriptions are not fully virtual because they are relatively fixed, formed by the objectified processes of computer-generated files. The Internet also includes electronic mail exchanges in which individuals and groups exchange messages generally with fixed addresses attached, addresses that refer to the identity the individual has already determined in nonelectronic, social space. Here, ethnicity, to the extent that it emerges at all, is associated with the legal name of the individual. The situation becomes more ambiguous in the hypermedia zone of the Internet known as the World Wide Web. In the Web individuals compose "home pages" that present themselves to anyone who is on-line. They may include pictures, sounds, and texts that offer a version of who they are, including their ethnicity, either inherited or self-defined. Still other sectors of the Internet are more prone to virtualizing ethnicity. These are bulletin boards and MOOs (multiuser domains, object oriented), where real-time exchanges of textual messages occur. In the MOOs identities are constructed by participants requiring a name and a gender, but self-descriptions may include ethnic characteristics. Such identities are further formed and reformed in the actual exchanges of messages, in dialogues with others, and are not therefore simple expressions of interior consciousness. Since the bodily markers of ethnicity (physical attributes and vocal accent) are invisible on MOOs, such ethnicity as exists in these electronic communities is fully virtual,[18] although the predominance of white American users often leads to the presumption that one is interacting with a white American person.

It would seem, then, that interactions on the Internet would tend to dissolve ethnicities to the extent that they are based, as Nora argued, on presence in space and on ancient, common rituals. The fixity of ethnicity as an attribute of the self would appear to be the opposite of the identities constructed in the virtual spaces of the Internet. I explored this question by subscribing to a listserve, a messaging system in which all subscribers receive messages sent by any other subscriber, called "CyberJew." Initiated by someone in Israel but including individuals from the United States and other countries, CyberJew explicitly raises the question of ethnicity on the Internet.[19] One participant asks if a "cyber seder"[20] is a real seder. "How and what aspect of the high touch aspects of the Mitzvot [blessing] are at all possible in a cyber mode?" he asks. To what extent is the intimacy of face-to-face presence a requisite for the spiritual effects of the meal?

I was raised in a family of Eastern European Jewish working-class immigrants. My grandfather's generation was secular, so we did not perform Jewish rituals like seders, but when his siblings and other relations visited Jewish ethnicity permeated the air. They spoke Yiddish, ate Jewish meals, and also reflected ways of being that were clearly different from that of "America." My father, however, was a thorough-going Americanizer. He wanted to have no accent, to dress in the latest fashion, and to raise his socioeconomic standing. He remarried (my mother had died) a woman from a more religious Jewish background. In her family I began to attend seders. Yet I saw them almost as an outsider since I came to them late (around age ten), and I experienced them through what I imagined was my father's dislike and my grandfather's politically motivated disdain. Even with these contradictory mediations, the seder was somehow for me a natural, necessary event. I had become a Jew in America.

Years later, after not practicing any Jewish rituals or attending any religious service for decades, I still passively regard myself as Jewish. I believe this ethnic identity "stuck" with me because of my early presence before people of my grandfather's generation who, without believing in any religious doctrine, were steeped in Jewish culture from Europe. The smells of food, intonations of voice, bodily gestures and ways of touching (pinching my cheek and calling me "boychick," a practice I did not much appreciate)—these micropractices of everyday life made me Jewish, and these are, I believe, the factories of ethnicity. To answer my question posed above, then, the intimacy of face-to-face presence during childhood appears to be a sufficient condition for ethnic identification. If that is the case, is a "cyber-Jew" possible?

The "cyber-Jew" quoted above hypothesized that the Internet is not a dissolvent of ethnicity but represents a new stage in the history of the Jews. He writes, "My sense is that we are in an analogous period when the Temple was destroyed and the Rabbis had to reinvent Jewish worship and came up with tefillah and what later became the Synagogue. Are we in a new Yavneh time period?"[21] The question is more pertinent than it might appear to be because one of the stages of Jewish history is the Diaspora, a time precisely when Jewish ethnicity was not associated with spatial proximity. In fact, anti-Semitic writings in Europe often rebuked Jews as the deracinated people, those without a homeland, without roots in the soil, without the conditions that Nora thinks are essential to ethnic identity. Jews are thus the displaced people par excellence. Unlike nomads, whose relation to space is one of movement and change, Jews, until the establishment of Israel, have no space. When Nora writes that Jews must remember to be Jews, as we saw above, he dissociates ethnicity from place in a manner that opens the possibility that remembering might occur through nonspatial mediations, such as the Internet.

This is precisely the argument of many CyberJew participants: the Internet, far from dissolving ethnicity, enables all Jews, wherever they are on the planet, to connect with one another. The Internet here is a neutral instrument of community, connecting preestablished ethnic identities. Numerous home pages established by Jews, such as The Federation of Greater Toronto (http://www.feduja.org) and Chabad (http://www.utexas.edu/students/cjso/Chabad/houses.html), as well as by other ethnic and religious groups, including the Roman Catholic pope, testify to the powerful expectation that cyberspace provides a neutral arena of community solidarity, a place of stabilizing individual commitments to groups, of congealing ethnic identity in a gossamer, electronic medium. As one participant in CyberJew puts it, "Modern communications, including airplanes and computer networks, are doing something else: creating the potential for Jews the world around to be part of an inte-

grated Israel (the people, not the state)." A further example of the facil-
itating character of the Internet is the exploration of distance learning
in MOOs. One participant reported:

> So, let me tell you briefly about the Judaic Studies Center that I am
> building on Diversity University. So far, I have built a classroom, a room
> focusing on the Hebrew calendar, and a room focusing on Jewish stories
> where the person reading the story becomes a character in the story and
> occasionally has to talk to the other characters in the story. A few
> members of DU from Connecticut to Hawaii gathered last Chanukah to
> light candles together, eat latkes, etc.

In MOOs one may learn about Jewish history and also enter into the
Bible as a character. In cyberspace, past and present ethnicities merge
into the bitstream of pixels on the screen. In the words of Barbara Kirshenblatt-Gimblett (1996), an anthropologist examining Jewish virtual
ethnicity, "New communication technologies have made possible the
gathering of vast and far-flung following in new forms of assembly."

Countless difficulties confront the would-be cyber-Jew. How is one
to know that participants in electronic communities are Jews? Or does
participation constitute ethnic membership? How can traditional practices of Judaism subsist in cyberspace? Otherwise trivial practices become impossible predicaments when transferred to cyberspace, where
not only space but also time is problematic. One participant in the listserve asks: "The time for prayer is tied to earth time and it is tied to the
cycle of a day experienced by someone standing on the earth—in other
words the 12 or whatever hours between sunup and sundown. Being in
space would change one's relation to the sun, but it wouldn't need to
change the concept of a 'day.'" Conundrums over the basic features of
Jewish practices assail ethnicity in cyberspace. It would seem that the
transplantation of social forms that arose in preindustrial contexts into
high-tech contexts would be a matter of great difficulty. As one skeptical
CyberJew participant wrote, "Precisely because in cyberspace we do not
meet face to face, the standards of decent communication break down
far more easily." Many had suspicions that cyberspace was not conducive
to any form of ethnicity.

Others were more sanguine but placed their hopes for the Internet
in a global spiritual renewal, rather than in a simple transformation of
Judaism. Here is one participant's formulation of the new possibilities:

We have been treating "cyberspace" as possibly an important new technology thru which the Jewish community around the world may have to reexamine and reshape its communal form.

I want to ask whether it may be EVEN MORE than that: a token, along with many others, of a great surge of God-consciousness into the world, which requires us to shape not only new forms of Jewish community but new Jewish images (i.e. Names) of God, new forms of prayer, new ethical understandings, new shapes of Torah as different from the Oral Torah of the Rabbis as that was from the Written Torah of Tanakh. . . . inventing the Internet and Cyberspace. This is not just a change in human history, but in its fabric—a shift in the life-cycle of God. . . . a "new paradigm" of Judaism.

A "shift in the life-cycle of God" poses the question of virtual ethnicity in its most extreme form: If the Internet represents the possibility of a spiritual "change in human history," are we still speaking of ethnicity in any recognizable form or are we speaking of some new global consciousness, such as Teilhard de Chardin's "noosphere" or Pierre Lévy's "collective intelligence"? If cyberspace is the occasion of a great spiritual renewal of the planet, have we not surpassed in some sense the historic forms of ethnic identity and begun to move toward some as yet unknown relation of individual to group? In the following passage Lévy envisions a new collective intelligence in cyberspace far different from any historical or even conceivable ethnicity:

If we were to take the route of the collective intelligence, we would gradually invent techniques, systems of signs, social forms of organization and of regulation permitting us to think together, to concentrate our intellectual and mental power, to multiply our imaginations and our experiences, to work out practical solutions for the complex problems affronting us in real time and on all levels. We would progressively learn to orientate ourselves in a new cosmos, constantly transforming itself and drifting, to become its authors as much as we can, to invent collectively ourselves as a species. Collective intelligence does not aim at the mastery of selves through human collectives but at an essential loosening of the grip [and] changing the very conception of identity, the mechanisms of domination and of the breaking out of conflicts, the unblocking of confiscated communication, the mutual launching of isolated thoughts. (Lévy 1995b, n.p.)

Lévy's perhaps breathtaking concept of the Internet as "collective intelligence" situates the individual in a virtual object, an unfinished, contingent state where identity is a temporary, fluid link to a process of creation, an *underdetermined* entity whose recognition is never a mis(s) because it never congeals into permanence, a subject position that is "never before" rather than "always already." Linked to continuously shifting global processes of textual, graphic, and aural formations, individuals in cyberspace cannot attach to objects in the fixed shapes of historic ethnicity.

CHAPTER NINE

CyberDemocracy: Internet as a Public Sphere?

I am an advertisement for a version of myself.

—David Byrne

The Stakes of the Question

The discussion of the political impact of the Internet has focused on a number of issues: access, technological determinism, encryption, commodification, intellectual property, the public sphere, decentralization, anarchy, gender, and ethnicity. While these issues may be addressed from a number of standpoints, only some of them are able to assess the full extent of what is at stake in the new communications technology at the cultural level of identity formation. If questions are framed in relation to prevailing political structures, forces, and ideologies, for example, blinders are being imposed that exclude the question of the subject or identity construction from the domain of discussion. Instances of such apparently urgent but actually limiting questions are those of encryption and commodification. In the case of encryption, the U.S. government seeks to secure its borders from "terrorists" who might use the Internet and thereby threaten it. But the dangers to the population are and have always been far greater from this state apparatus itself than from so-called terrorists. More citizens have been improperly abused, had their civil rights violated, and much worse by the government than by terrorists. In fact, terrorism is in good part an effect of government propaganda; it serves to deflect attention from governmental abuse toward a mostly imagined, highly dangerous outside enemy. If the prospects of democracy on the Internet are viewed in terms of encryption, then the security of the existing national government becomes the limit of the matter: what is secure for the nation-state is taken to mean true security for everyone, a highly dubious proposition.[1] The question of potentials for new forms of social space that might empower individuals in new ways is foreclosed in favor of preserving existing relations of force as they are viewed by the most powerful institution in the history of the world, the government of the United States.

The issue of commodification also affords a narrow focus, often restricting the discussion of the politics of the Internet to the question of which corporation or which type of corporation will be able to obtain what amount of income from which configuration of the Internet. Will the telephone companies, the cable companies, or some amalgam of both be able to secure adequate markets and profits from providing the general public with railroad timetables, five hundred channels of television, the movie of one's choice on demand, and so forth? From this vantage point the questions raised are as follows: Shall the Internet be used to deliver entertainment products, like some gigantic, virtual theme park? Or shall it be used to sell commodities, functioning as an electronic retail store or mall? These questions consume corporate managers around the country and their Marxist critics alike, though here again, as with the encryption issue, the Internet is being understood as an extension of or substitution for existing institutions. While there is no doubt that the Internet folds into existing social functions and extends them in new ways, translating the act of shopping, for example, into an electronic form, what are far more cogent as possible long-term political effects of the Internet are the ways in which it institutes new social functions, ones that do not fit easily within those of characteristically modern organizations. The problem is that these new functions can only become intelligible if a framework is adopted that does not limit the discussion from the outset to modern patterns of interpretation. For example, if one understands politics as the restriction or expansion of the existing executive, legislative, and judicial branches of government, one will not be able even to broach the question of new types of participation in government. To ask, then, about the relation of the Internet to democracy is to challenge or to risk challenging our existing theoretical approaches and concepts as they concern these questions.

Others have attempted to define the uniqueness of politics on the Internet by examining how political action is carried out in cyberspace. Here the question is no longer so much the expansion of existing institutions such as representative democracy or the discursive power of existing political theories (Marxism or liberalism). Instead some scholars have looked at actual organizing and mobilizing efforts on the Net. Laura Gurak (1997), for instance, examines the use of e-mail, listserves, and Usenet groups in two cases of political action: the resistance to Lotus's Marketplace (a consumer database for businesses) and the Clinton administration's effort to enact the Clipper Chip, an encryption device, as we have seen, that would enable the U.S. government alone to decode all messages on the Net. In these examples, protest movements originated on the Net, one from popular forces and one from political groups, and were considerably effective in bringing about change: Lotus Marketplace was removed from the market and the Clipper Chip has not passed into law. She argues that traditional political categories do not capture the specific attributes of politics on the Net. Instead politics on the Net is unique. Gurak argues, "Two rhetorical features, community ethos and the novel mode of delivery on computer networks, are critical to rhetorical online communities because these features sustain the community and its motive for action in the absence of physical commonality or traditional face-to-face methods of establishing presence and delivering a message" (5). Gurak's work is a reminder that the politics of the Net is a break of a fundamental nature with things as usual, and this break might warrant the category of the postmodern.

If one places in brackets political theories that address modern governmental institutions in order to open the path to an assessment of the "postmodern" possibilities suggested by the Internet, two difficulties immediately emerge: (1) there is no adequate "postmodern" theory of politics, and (2) the issue of democracy, the dominant political norm and ideal, is itself a "modern" category associated with the project of the Enlightenment. Let me address these issues in turn.

Theorists such as Philippe Lacoue-Labarthe (1990) and Jean-Luc Nancy (1991) have pointed to the limitations of a "left/right" spectrum of ideologies for addressing contemporary political issues. Deriving from seating arrangements of legislators during the French Revolution of 1789, the modern ideological spectrum inscribes a grand narrative of liberation that contains several problematic aspects. First it installs a linear, evolutionary, and progressive history that occludes the differential temporalities of non-Western groups and women and imposes a totalizing, strong interpretation of the past that erases from view gaps, discontinuities, improbabilities, contingencies, in short a panoply of phenomena that might better be approached from a nonlinear perspective. Second, the Enlightenment narrative establishes a process of liberation at the heart of history that requires at its base a presocial, foundational, individual identity. The individual is posited as outside of and prior to history, only later becoming ensnared in externally imposed chains. Politics for this modern perspective is then the arduous extraction of an autonomous agent from the contingent obstacles imposed by the past. In its rush to ontologize freedom, the modern view of the subject hides the process of its historical construction. A postmodern orientation would have to allow for the constitution of identity within the social and within language, displacing the question of freedom from a presupposition of and a conclusion to theory to become instead a pretheoretical or nonfoundational discursive preference. Postmodern theorists have discovered that modern theory's insistence on the freedom of the subject, its compulsive, repetitive inscription into discourse of the sign of the resisting agent, functions to restrict the shape of identity to its modern form, an ideological and legitimizing gesture of its own position rather than a step toward emancipation. If a postmodern perspective is to avoid the limits of modern theory, it is proscribed from ontologizing any form of the subject. The postmodern position is limited to an insistence on the constructedness of identity. In the effort to avoid the pitfalls of modern political theory, then, postmodern theory sharply restricts the scope of its ability to define a new political direction. This theoretical asceticism is a contemporary condition of discourse imposing an unusual discipline and requiring a considerable suspension of disbelief on the part of the audience. To skeptics it can only be said that the alternatives, those of "modern" positions, are even less desirable.

But there are further difficulties in establishing a position from which to recognize and analyze the cultural aspect of the Internet. For postmodern theory still invokes the modern term *democracy*, even when this is modified by the adjective *radical*, as in the work of Ernesto Laclau (1990). One may characterize postmodern or post-Marxist democracy in Laclau's terms as one that opens new positions of speech, empowering previously excluded groups and enabling new aspects of social life to become part of the political process. While the Internet is often accused of elitism (two hundred million users), there does exist a growing and vibrant grassroots participation in it, organized in part by local public libraries (Polly and Cisler 1994). But are not these initiatives, the modern skeptic may persist, simply extensions of existing political institutions rather than being "post," rather than being a break of some kind? In response, I can assert only that the "postmodern" position need not be taken as a metaphysical assertion of a new age; that theorists are trapped within existing frameworks as much as they may be critical of them and wish not to be; that in the absence of a coherent alternative political program, the best one can do is to examine phenomena such as the Internet in relation to new forms of the old democracy, while holding open the possibility that what might emerge might be something other than democracy in any shape that we may conceive it, given our embeddedness in the present. Democracy, the rule by all, is surely preferable to its historic alternatives. And the term may yet contain critical potentials, since existing forms of democracy surely do not fulfill the promise of freedom and equality. The colonization of the term by existing institutions encourages one to look elsewhere for the means to name the new patterns of force relations emerging in certain parts of the Internet.

Decentralized Technology

My plea for indulgence with the limitations of the postmodern position on politics quickly gains credibility when the old question of technological determinism is posed in relation to the Internet. For when the question of technology is posed, we may see immediately how the Internet disrupts the basic assumptions of the older positions. The Internet is above all a decentralized communication system. Like the telephone network, anyone hooked up to the Internet may initiate a call and send a message that he or she has composed, and may do so in the manner of the broadcast system, that is to say, may send a message to many receivers, and do this either in "real time" or as stored data or both. The Internet is also decentralized at a basic level of organization, since, as a network of networks, new networks may be added so long as they conform to certain communications protocols. As a historian I find it fascinating that this unique structure should emerge from a confluence of cultural communities that appear to have so little in common: the Cold War Defense Department, which sought to ensure survival against nuclear attack by promoting decentralization, the countercultural ethos of computer programming engineers, who had a deep distaste for any form of censorship or active restraint of communications; and the world of university research, which habitually exchanges and shares ideas and data. Added to this is a technological substratum of digital electronics that unifies all symbolic forms in a single system of codes, rendering transmission instantaneous and duplication effortless. If the technological structure of the Internet institutes costless reproduction, instantaneous dissemination, and radical decentralization, what might be its effects upon the society, the culture, and the political institutions?

There can be only one answer to this question, and that is that it is the wrong question. Technologically determined effects derive from a broad set of assumptions in which what is technological is a configuration of materials that effect other materials and the relation between the technology and human beings is external, that is, where human beings are understood to manipulate the materials for ends that they impose upon the technology from a preconstituted position of subjectivity. But what the Internet technology imposes is a dematerialization of communication and in many of its aspects a transformation of the subject position of the individual who engages within it. The Internet resists the basic conditions for asking the question of the effects of technology. It installs a new regime of relations between humans and matter and between matter and nonmatter, reconfiguring the relation of technology to culture and thereby undermining the standpoint from within which, in the past, a discourse developed—one which appeared to be natural—about the effects of technology. The only way to define the technological effects of the Internet is to build the Internet, to set in place a series of relations that constitute an electronic geography. While this may be true as well for other communications technologies, none but the Internet so drastically reconfigures the basic conditions of speech and reception.

Put differently, the Internet is more like a social space than a thing, so that its effects are more like those of Germany than those of hammers: the effect of Germany upon the people within it is to make them Germans (at least for the most part); the effect of hammers is not to make people hammers, though Heideggerians[2] and some others might disagree, but to force metal spikes into wood. As long as we understand the Internet as a hammer, we will fail to discern the way it is like Germany. The problem is that modern perspectives tend to reduce the Internet to a hammer. In this grand narrative of modernity, the Internet is an efficient tool of communication, advancing the goals of its users, who are understood as preconstituted instrumental identities.

The Internet, I suppose like Germany, is complex enough so that it may with some profit be viewed in part as a hammer. If I search the database functions of the Internet or if I send e-mail purely as a substitute for paper mail, then its effects may reasonably be seen to be those on the order of the hammer. The database on the Internet may be more easily or cheaply accessed than its alternatives, and the same may be said of e-mail in relation to the post office or the fax machine. But the aspects of the Internet that I would like to underscore are those which instantiate new forms of interaction and which pose the question of new kinds of relations of power between participants. The question that needs to be asked about the relation of the Internet to democracy is this: are there new kinds of relations occurring within it which suggest new forms of power configurations between communicating individuals? In other words, is there a new politics on the Internet? One way to approach this question is to make a detour from the issue of technology and raise again the question of a public sphere, gauging the extent to which Internet democracy may become intelligible in relation to it. To frame the issue of the political nature of the Internet in relation to the concept of the public sphere is particularly appropriate because of the spatial metaphor associated with the term *public sphere*. Instead of an immediate reference to the structure of an institution, which is often a formalist argument over procedures, or to the claims of a given social group, which assumes a certain figure of agency that I would like to keep in suspense, the notion of a public sphere suggests an arena of exchange, like the ancient Greek agora or the colonial New England town hall. If there is a public sphere on the Internet, who populates it and how? In particular, one must ask, What kinds of beings exchange information in this public sphere? Since there occurs no face-to-face interaction, only electronic flickers[3] on a screen, what kind of community can there be in this space? What kind of peculiar, virtual embodiment of politics are inscribed so evanescently in cyberspace? Modernist curmudgeons may object vehemently to attributing to information flows on the Internet the dignified term *community*. Are they correct, and if so, what sort of phenomenon is this cyberdemocracy?

The Internet as a Public Sphere?

The issue of the public sphere is at the heart of any reconceptualization of democracy. Contemporary social relations seem to be devoid of a basic level of interactive practice that, in the past, was the matrix of democratizing politics: loci such as the agora, the New England town hall, the village church, the coffeehouse, the tavern, the public square, a convenient barn, a union hall, a park, a factory lunchroom, and even a street corner. Many of these places remain but no longer serve as organizing centers for political discussion and action. It appears that the media, especially television but also other forms of electronic communication, isolate citizens from one another and substitute themselves for older spaces of politics. An example from the Clinton health-care reform campaign will suffice: the Clinton forces at one point (mid-July 1994) felt that Congress was less favorable to their proposal than was the general population. To convince Congress of the wisdom of health-care reform, the administration purchased television advertising that depicted ordinary citizens speaking in favor of the legislation. The ads were shown *only in Washington, D.C.*, because they were directed not at the general population of viewers but at congressmen and congresswomen alone. The executive branch deployed the media directly on the legislative branch. Such are politics in the era of the mode of information. In a context like this one may ask, Where is the public sphere, where is the place citizens interact to form opinions in relation to which public policy must be attuned? John Hartley (1992) makes the bold and convincing argument that the media *are* the public sphere: "Television, popular newspapers, magazines and photography, the popular media of the modern period, are the public domain, the place where and the means by which the public is created and has its being."[4] The same claim is offered by Paul Virilio (1994): "Avenues and public venues from now on are eclipsed by the screen, by electronic displays, in a preview of the 'vision machines' just around the corner" (64). "Public" tends more and more to slide into "publicity," as "character" is replaced by "image." These changes must be examined without nostalgia and the retrospective glance of modernist politics and theory.

Sensing a collapse of the public sphere and therefore a crisis of democratic politics, Jürgen Habermas published *The Structural Transformation of the Public Sphere* in 1962 (Habermas 1989). In this highly influential work he traced the development of a democratic public sphere in the seventeenth and eighteenth centuries and charted its course to its decline in the twentieth century. In that work and arguably since then as well, Habermas's political intent was to further "the project of Enlightenment" by the reconstruction of a public sphere in which reason might prevail, not the instrumental reason of much modern practice but the critical reason that represents the best of the democratic tradition. Habermas defined the public sphere as a domain of uncoerced conversation oriented toward a pragmatic accord. His position came under attack by poststructuralists like Lyotard (1984), who questioned the emancipatory potentials of its model of consensus through rational debate. At issue was the poststructuralist critique of Habermas's Enlightenment ideal of the autonomous rational subject as a universal foundation for democracy. Before deploying the category of the public sphere to evaluate democracy on the Internet, I shall turn to recent developments in the debate over Habermas's position.

In the 1980s Lyotard's critique was expanded by feminists like Nancy Fraser (1989, 1990), who demonstrates the gender blindness in Habermas's position.[5] Even before the poststructuralists and feminists, Oskar Negt and Alexander Kluge (1993) began the critique of Habermas by articulating the notion of an *oppositional* public sphere, specifically that of the proletariat. What is important about their argument, as demonstrated so clearly by Miriam Hansen in her foreword to their book (ix–xli), is that Negt and Kluge shifted the terrain of the notion of the public sphere from a historical-transcendental idealization of the Enlightenment to a plurality and heterotopia of discourses. This crucial change in the notion of the public sphere assumes its full significance when it is seen in relation to liberal democracy. The great ideological fiction of liberalism is to reduce the public sphere to existing democratic institutions. Habermas's critique of liberalism counterposes a radical alternative to it but one that still universalizes and monopolizes the political. Negt and Kluge, in contrast, decentralize and multiply the public sphere, opening a path of critique and possibly a new politics.[6]

The final step in the development of the concept of the public sphere came with Rita Felski's synthesis (1989) of Negt and Kluge with both feminist gender analysis and the poststructuralist critique of the autonomous subject. For Felski the concept of the public sphere must build on the "experience" of political protest (in the sense of Negt and Kluge), must acknowledge and amplify the multiplicity of the subject (in the sense of poststructuralism), and must account for gender differences (in the sense of feminism). She writes:

> Unlike the bourgeois public sphere, then, the feminist public sphere does not claim a representative universality but rather offers a critique of cultural values from the standpoint of women as a marginalized group within society. In this sense it constitutes a *partial* or counter-public sphere.... Yet insofar as it is a *public* sphere, its arguments are also directed outward, toward a dissemination of feminist ideas and values throughout society as a whole. (167)

Felski seriously revises the Habermasian notion of the public sphere, separating it from its patriarchal, bourgeois, and logocentric attachments perhaps, but nonetheless still invoking the notion of a public sphere and more or less reducing politics to it. This becomes clear in the conclusion of her argument:

> Some form of appeal to collective identity and solidarity is a necessary precondition for the emergence and effectiveness of an oppositional movement; feminist theorists who reject any notion of a unifying identity as a repressive fiction in favor of a stress on absolute difference fail to show how such diversity and fragmentation can be reconciled with goal-oriented political struggles based upon common interests. An appeal to a shared experience of oppression provides the starting point from which women as a group can open upon the problematic of gender, at the same time as this notion of gendered community contains a strongly utopian dimension. (168–69)

In the end Felski sees the public sphere as central to feminist politics. But then we must ask how this public sphere is to be distinguished from any political discussion. From the heights of Habermas's impossible (counterfactual) ideal of rational communication, the public sphere here multiplies, opens, and extends to political discussion by all oppressed individuals.

The problem we face is that of defining the term *public*. Liberal theory generally resorted to the ancient Greek distinction between the family or household and the polis, the former being "private" and the latter "public." When the term crossed boundaries from political to economic theory, with Ricardo and Marx, a complication set in: the term *political economy* combined the Greek sense of public and the Greek sense of private, since *economy* referred for them to the governance of the (private) household. The older usage preserved a space for the public in the agora, to be sure, but referred to discussions about the general good, not market transactions. In the newer usage the economic realm is termed *political economy* but is considered "private." To make matters worse, common parlance nowadays has the term *private* designating speeches and actions that are isolated, unobserved by anyone, and not recorded or monitored by any machine.[7] Privacy now becomes restricted to the space of the home, in a sense returning to the ancient Greek usage even though family structure has altered dramatically in the interim. In Fraser's argument, for example, the "public" sphere is the opposite of the "private" sphere in the sense that it is a locus of "talk," "a space in which citizens deliberate about their common affairs" and is essential to democracy (Fraser 1990, 57). There are serious problems, then, in using the term *public* in relation to a politics of emancipation.

This difficulty is amplified considerably once newer electronically mediated communications are taken into account, in particular the Internet. Now the question of "talk," of meeting face-to-face, and of "public" discourse is confused and complicated by the electronic form of exchange of symbols. If "public" discourse exists as pixels on screens generated at remote locations by individuals one has never and probably will never meet, as it is in the case of the Internet with its "virtual communities," "electronic cafés," bulletin boards, e-mail, computer conferencing, and even videoconferencing, then how is it to be distinguished from "private" letters, print, and so forth? The age of the public sphere as face-to-face talk is clearly over: the question of democracy must henceforth take into account new forms of electronically mediated discourse. What are the conditions of democratic speech in the mode of information? What kind of "subject" speaks or writes or communicates in these conditions? What is its relation to machines? What complexes of subjects, bodies, and machines are required for democratic exchange and emancipatory action? For Habermas, the public sphere is a homogeneous space of embodied subjects in symmetrical relations, pursuing consensus through the critique of arguments and the presentation of validity claims. This model, I contend, is systematically denied in the arenas of electronic politics. We are advised, then, to abandon Habermas's concept of the public sphere in assessing the Internet as a political domain.

Against my contention, Judith Perrolle (1991) turns to a Habermasian perspective to look at conversations on bulletin boards and finds that the conditions of the ideal speech situation do not apply. She contends that these conversations are "distorted" by a level of machine control: here validity "claims of meaningfulness, truth, sincerity and appropriateness... appear to be physical or logical characteristics of the machine rather than an outcome of human negotiation" (351). The basic conditions for speech are configured in the program of the virtual community and remain outside the arena of discussion. She continues, "Most computer interfaces are either not designed to allow the user to question data validity, or else designed so that data may be changed by anyone with a moderate level of technical skill" (354). While this argument cannot be refuted from within the framework of Habermas's theory of communicative action, the question remains whether these criteria are able to capture the specific qualities of the electronic forms of interaction.

Now that the thick culture of information machines provides the interface for much if not most discourse on political issues, the fiction of the democratic community of full human presence serves only to obscure critical reflection and divert the development of a political theory of this decidedly postmodern condition. For too long critical theory has insisted on a public sphere, bemoaning the fact of media "interference," the static of first radio's, then television's, role in politics. But the fact is that political discourse has long been mediated by electronic machines: the issue now is that the machines enable new forms of decentralized dialogue and create new combinations of human-machine assemblages, new individual and collective "voices," "specters," "interactivities," which are the new building blocks of political formations and groupings. As Virilio (1993) writes, "What remains of the notion of things 'public' when public *images* (in real time) are more important than public *space?*" (9). If the technological basis of the media has habitually been viewed as a threat to democracy, how can theory account for the turn toward a construction of technology (the Internet) that appears to promote a decentralization of discourse, if not of democracy itself, and appears to threaten the state (unmonitorable conversations), mock at private property (the infinite reproducibility of information), and flout moral propriety (the dissemination of images of unclothed people often in awkward positions)?

A Postmodern Technology?

Many areas of the Internet extend preexisting identities and institutions. Usenet newsgroups elicit obnoxious pranks from teenage boys; databases enable researchers and corporations to retrieve information at lower costs; electronic mail affords speedy, reliable communication of messages; the digitization of images allows a wider distribution of erotic materials; and so it goes. The Internet, then, is modern in the sense of continuing the tradition of tools as efficient means and in the sense that prevailing modern cultures transfer their characteristics to the new domain. These issues remain to be studied in detail and from a variety of standpoints, but for the time being the above conclusion may be sustained. Other areas of the Internet are less easy to contain within modern points of view. The examination of these cyberspaces raises the issue of a new understanding of technology and finally leads to a reassessment of the political aspects of the Internet. I refer to the bulletin board services that have come to be known as "virtual communities," to the MOO phenomenon, and to the synthesis of virtual reality technology with the Internet.

In these cases what is at stake is the direct solicitation to construct identities in the course of communication practices. Individuals invent themselves and do so repeatedly and differentially in the course of conversing or messaging electronically. Now there is surely nothing new in discursive practices that are so characterized: reading a novel,[8] speaking on CB radio, indeed watching a television advertisement, I contend, all in varying degrees and in different ways encourage the individual to shape an identity in the course of engaging in communication. The case of the limited areas of the Internet I listed above, however, goes considerably beyond, or at least is quite distinct from, the latter examples. The individual's performance of the communication requires linguistic acts of self-positioning that are less explicit in the cases of reading a novel or watching a television advertisement. On the Internet, individuals read and interpret communications to themselves and to others and also respond by shaping sentences and transmitting them. Novels and TV ads are interpreted by individuals who are interpellated by them, but these readers and viewers are not addressed directly, only as a generalized audience, and, of course, they respond in fully articulated linguistic acts. (I avoid framing the distinction I am making here in the binary active/passive, because that couplet is so associated with the modern autonomous agent that it would appear that I am depicting the Internet as the realization of the modern dream of universal, "active" speech. I refuse this resort because it rests upon the notion of identity as a fixed essence, presocial and prelinguistic, whereas I want to argue that Internet discourse constitutes the subject as the subject fashions himor herself. I want to locate subject constitution at a level that is outside the oppositions of freedom/determinism and activity/passivity.) On the Internet individuals construct their identities, doing so in relation to ongoing dialogues, not as acts of pure consciousness. But such activity does not count as freedom in the liberal-Marxist sense because it does not refer back to a foundational subject. Yet it does connote a "democratization" of subject constitution because the acts of discourse are not limited to one-way address and not constrained by the gender and ethnic traces inscribed in face-to-face communications. The magic of the Internet is that it is a technology that puts cultural acts, symbolizations in all forms, in the hands of all participants; it radically decentralizes the positions of speech, publishing, filmmaking, and radio and television broadcasting, in short the apparatuses of cultural production.

Gender and Virtual Communities

Let us examine the case of gender in Internet communication as a way to clarify what is at stake and to remove some likely confusions about what I am arguing. In real-time chat rooms, MOOs, and MUDs, participants must invent identities that consist, as a minimum, of a name and a gender. Gender, unlike age or ethnicity, is thus a general attribute of Internet identities. This gender, however, bears no necessary relation to one's gender in daily life. The gendered body is replaced by the gendered text. Studies have pointed out that the absence of bodily gender cues in bulletin board discussion groups does not eliminate sexism or even the hierarchies of gender that pervade society generally.[9] The disadvantages suffered by women in society carries over into "the virtual communities" on the Internet: women are underrepresented in these electronic places (although this is changing, as in 1998 more women than men went on-line for the first time in the United States), and they are subject to various forms of harassment and sexual abuse. The fact that sexual identities are self-designated does not in itself eliminate the annoyances and the constraints of patriarchy. Yet Internet social relations are often taken seriously by participants, so much so that gender problems in daily life take on new dimensions in cyberspace. There is an articulation of gender on the Internet that goes beyond the reproduction of real-life hierarchies to instantiate new conditions of inscription.

The case of "Joan" is instructive in this regard. A man named Alex presented himself on a bulletin board as a disabled woman, "Joan," in order to experience the "intimacy" he admired in women's conversations. Alex wanted to talk to women as a woman because of the limitations he perceived in real-life masculine identities. Lindsy Van Gelder (1991) reports that when his "ruse" was unveiled, many of the women "Joan" had interacted with were deeply hurt. But Van Gelder also reports that their greatest disappointment was that "Joan" did not exist (373). The construction of gender in this example indicates a level of complexity not accounted for by the supposition that cultural and social forms are or are not transferrable to the Internet. Alex turned to the Internet virtual community to make up for a perceived lack of feminine traits in his masculine sexual identity. The women who suffered his ploy regretted the "death" of the virtual friend "Joan." These are unique uses of virtual communities not easily found in "reality." In cyberspace, one may create and live a gendered identity that differs from one's daily life persona; one may build friendships within this identity and experience joy and sadness as these relations develop, change, and end. Still, in the "worst" cases, one must admit that the mere fact of communicating under the conditions of the new technology does not cancel the marks of power relations constituted under the conditions of face-to-face, print and electronic broadcasting modes of intercourse.

Nonetheless the structural conditions of communicating in Internet communities do introduce resistances to and breaks with these gender determinations, including sexual preferences.[10] The fact of having to decide on one's gender and sexual preference itself raises the issue of individual identity in a novel and compelling manner. If one is to be masculine, one must choose to be so. Further, one must enact one's gender choice in language and in language alone, without any marks and gestures of the body, identifying clothing, or intonations of voice. Presenting one's gender is accomplished solely through textual means, although this does include various iconic markings invented in electronic communities, such as emoticons or smilies—for example, :-) . Also one may experience directly the opposite gender by assuming it and enacting it in conversations.[11] Finally the particular configuration of conversation through computers and modems produces a new relation to one's body as it communicates, a cyborg in cyberspace who is different from all the embodied genders of earlier modes of information. These cyborg genders test and transgress the boundaries of the modern gender system without any necessary inclination in that direction on the part of the participant.[12]

If Internet communication does not completely filter out preexisting technologies of power as it enacts new ones, it reproduces them variably depending on the specific feature of the Internet in question. Some aspects of the Internet, such as electronic mail between individuals who know each other, may introduce no strong disruption of the gender system. In this case, the cyborg individual does not overtake or displace the embodied individual, though even here studies have shown some differences in self-presentation (more spontaneity and less guardedness).[13] From e-mail at one end of the spectrum of modern versus postmodern identity construction, one moves to bulletin board conversations, where identities may be fixed and genders unaltered but where strangers are encountered. The next, still more postmodern example would be the situation where identities are invented but the discourse consists in simple dialogues, as in "virtual communities" like the Well. Further removed still from ordinary speech is the Internet Relay Chat (IRC),[14] in which dialogue occurs in real time with very little hierarchy or structure. Perhaps the full novelty enabled by the Internet are the multiuser domains, object oriented (MOOs), which divide into adventure games and social types. More study needs to be done on the differences between these technologies of subject constitution.

On the MOOs of the social variety, advanced possibilities of postmodern identities are enacted. Here identities are invented and changeable; elaborate self-descriptions are composed; domiciles are depicted in textual form and individuals interact purely for the sake of doing so. MOO inhabitants, however, do not enjoy a democratic utopia. There exist hierarchies specific to this form of cyberspace: the site administrators who initiate and maintain the MOOs have abilities to change rules and procedures that are not available to most regular players. After these "gods" come the players themselves, who, by dint of experience in the electronic space and with the programming language, accumulate certain skills, even privileges, for ease of access to an array of commands. These regular members are distinguished from "guests," who, as a result of their temporary status, have fewer privileges and fewer skills in negotiating the MOO.[15] Another, but far more trivial, criterion of political differentiation is typing skill, since this determines in part who speaks most often, especially as conversations move along with considerable speed. Even in cyberspace, asymmetries emerge that could be termed "political inequalities." Yet the salient characteristic of Internet community is the diminution, in different ways, of prevailing hierarchies of race,[16] class, age, status, and especially gender. What appears in the embodied world as irreducible hierarchy plays a lesser role in the cyberspace of MOOs. And as a result, the relation of cyberspace to material human geography is decidedly one of rupture and challenge to existing identity configurations. In this sense, Internet communities function as places of difference from and resistance to modern society. In a sense, they serve the function of a Habermasian public sphere, however reconfigured, without intentionally or even actually being one. They are places not of the presence of validity claims or the actuality of critical reason, but of the inscription of new assemblages of self-constitution. As audio and video features begin to enhance the current textual mode of conversation, the claims of these virtual realities may become even more exigent.[17] The complaint that these electronic villages are no more than the escapism of white, male undergraduates may then become less convincing.

Cyborg Politics

The example of the deconstruction of gender in Internet MOO communities illustrates the depth of the stakes in theorizing politics in the mode of information. Because the Internet inscribes the new social figure of the cyborg and institutes a communicative practice of self-constitution, the political as we have known it is reconfigured. The wrapping of language on the Internet, its digitized, machine-mediated signifiers in a space without bodies,[18] introduces an unprecedented novelty for political theory. How will electronic beings be governed? How will their experience of self-constitution rebound in the existing political arena? How will the power relations on the Internet combine with or influence power relations that emerge from face-to-face relations, print relations, and broadcast relations? Assuming that the U.S. government and the corporations do not shape the Internet entirely in their own image and that places of cyberdemocracy remain and spread to larger and larger segments of the population, what will emerge as a postmodern politics?

If these conditions are met, one possibility is that authority as we have known it will change drastically. The nature of political authority has shifted from embodiment in lineages in the Middle Ages to instrumentally rational mandates from voters in the modern era. In each case a certain aura becomes fetishistically attached to authority holders. In Internet communities such an aura is more difficult to sustain. The Internet seems to discourage the endowment of individuals with inflated status. The example of scholarly research illustrates the point. The formation of canons and authorities is seriously undermined by the electronic nature of texts. Texts become "hypertexts," which are reconstructed in the act of reading, rendering the reader an author and disrupting the stability of experts or "authorities."[19] Similar arguments have been made by Walter Benjamin regarding film and by Roland Barthes regarding novels.[20] But the material structure of Internet relations instantiates the reversibility of authorial power at a much more fundamental level than that in film and the novel.

If scholarly authority is challenged and reformed by the location and dissemination of texts on the Internet, it is possible that political authorities will be subject to a similar fate. If the term *democracy* refers to the sovereignty of embodied individuals and the system of determining officeholders by them, a new term will be required to indicate a relation of leaders and followers that is mediated by cyberspace and constituted in relation to the mobile identities found therein.

Notes

1. The Culture of Underdetermination

1. *Wired News* reports that twenty nations attempt to keep the Internet out of their borders, that forty-five nations seriously censor it, and that this is an improvement in Internet "freedom" over the recent past (McCabe 1999).

2. For an excellent review of Castells's trilogy see Stalder 1998.

3. Sherry Turkle (1998) argues that children also treat media machines as human.

2. The Being of Technologies

1. For a discussion of Heidegger's politics in relation to the issue of technology (and modernity more generally) see Zimmerman 1990.

2. This criticism is also raised by Coyne 1995 (98), but R. L. Rutsky (1999) finds that Heidegger in places moves toward a recognition of the difference between productive and reproductive or representational machines (2).

3. Here is an example of Heidegger's extravagant evaluation of the Greeks: "In Greece, at the outset of the destining of the West, the arts soared to the supreme height of the revealing granted them. They brought the presence of the gods, brought the dialogue of divine and human destinings, to radiance" (1977, 34).

4. See the critique by Jacques Derrida (1987).

5. This argument is also made by Cooper (1997), but he does not explore the difference between mechanical and information technologies. The literature on Heidegger's view of technology is enormous and I cannot review it in the context of this essay.

6. For an opposite view see Chesher 1997; he writes, "Computers store up the real in digital domains as symbolic standing reserve" (88), thereby equating information and industrial technology as enframing.

7. Samuel Weber has made this argument to me. See his important treatment of Heidegger on technology (1995b).

8. For an exploration of the body/machine interface from the perspective of artists see Stocker and Schöpf 1997. Of course, the work of the Australian artist Stelarc must not be overlooked.

3. Capitalism's Linguistic Turn

1. The extent of capitalist incursion into culture can hardly be underestimated. One late development is that patents are now given not only for material inventions but also for "business models." This means that new ideas about how to do business may be private property. One person has patented the idea of transmitting, for a price, movies over the Internet. The selling of airline tickets on the Net already has a patent, along with countless other commercial practices in cyberspace. See Miller 1999.

2. For a comprehensive examination of the phenomenon of copying see Schwartz 1996.

4. The Digital Subject and Cultural Theory

1. For a discussion and critique of the role of technology in apocalyptic thinking see Quinby 1994 (xix).

2. Case (1996) argues that orally presented academic papers echo "the condition of having written the paper elsewhere ... [and foreground] the stability of print" (24). She suggests that a more improvised performance is more harmonious with poststructuralist theory and digital writing.

3. See also the valuable collection of essays by Jaszi and Woodmansee (1994). For a discussion of the position of writing before the author, see Pease 1995. Pease connects the premodern *auctor* with the European exploration of the New World.

4. The rare moments where Foucault writes of a future alternative are, to my knowledge, only two: in a conversation with Maoists about the possibility of a system of punishment beyond that of incarceration (1980) and at the end of the first volume of his study of sexuality, where he proposes a "different economy of bodies and pleasures" beyond that of the regime of "sexuality" (1978, 159). Foucault also discusses utopias (1986), but these are spaces of the past and present, not the future, especially bordellos and colonies.

5. Derrida is more sensitive to the technological implications for authorship and the question of the speaking subject. In "Psyche: Inventions of the Other" (1989), he relates his theory of deconstruction to copyright and patent law relating to new technologies: "The patent ... is visibly affected by all sorts of disturbances, especially those resulting from new techniques of reproduction and telecommunication" (45). Because of this, "deconstruction must assume the task of calling into question the traditional status of invention itself" (43). Foucault then is not at all alone in calling for a critique of the author function.

6. Others have also recognized the value of Foucault's theory for understanding the Internet. See, for example, Boyle 1997.

7. I wish to thank Donald Pease for pointing out this problem in Foucault. On this question see also the interesting essay by Aycock (1999).

8. Here are two examples: In Smiley 1995, a junior African American professor, Margaret, responds to "recent fashions in literary theory": "She did not think it any coincidence that ideas denigrating literary authorship had taken center stage simultaneously with the emergence of formerly silent voices for whom the act of writing, and publishing, had the deepest and most delicious possible meaning, simultaneously with the emergence of an audience for whom the act of reading and thinking was an act of skeptical anger" (134–35). And in Fox-Genovese 1986: "Surely it is no coincidence...that the Western white male elite proclaimed the death of the subject at precisely the moment at which it might have had to share that status with the women and peoples of other races and classes who were beginning to challenge its supremacy" (121).

9. For a similar argument see also Grosz 1995 (64).

10. There is a lively debate over the value of Butler's theory of performativity, especially in relation to queer theory. See for example Walters 1996.

11. For a more recent formulation of Case's position on this question see "Performing the Cyberbody on the Transnational Stage," in a collection of her essays forthcoming at University of Michigan Press.

5. Authors Analogue and Digital

1. This situation is changing rapidly, I am happy to say. There are numerous recent works that attempt to account for the mediation of information machines. See in particular Aarseth 1997; Masten, Stallybrass, and Vickers 1997; and Ward and Taylor 1998.

2. The first important discussion of the analogue/digital distinction is in Wilden 1972.

3. Marshall McLuhan (1962) sees the innovation of the alphabet in relation to an emphasis on the visual: "For writing is a visual enclosure of non-visual spaces and senses" (43).

4. Ong (1982) argues that Greek is therefore the only true language.

5. *Discourse Networks: 1800/1900* was translated by Michael Metteer (Stanford, Calif.: Stanford University Press 1990). Selections of *Gramophone, Film, Typewriter* and *Dracula's Legacy* are included in Kittler and Johnston 1997, and the complete book is now available (Kittler 1999).

6. Another translation omits the word "sad": see Kittler and Johnston 1997 (147). See also Kittler 1994 (319–34).

7. I thank Anne Balsamo for informing me about this interesting and useful book. See also Levinson 1997 for an overview of the history of writing in relation to the Internet.

8. Mark Rose, in a personal communication (May 1998), tells me that the term *intellectual property* was first used in a mid-nineteenth-century case: *Davoll v. Brown* (Circuit Court, District of Massachusetts, 7 F.cas. 197, 1845). There is, he says, also an early reference to "intellectual property" in a letter entered in evidence in *Mitchell v. Tilghman* (86 US 287, 1873). To my knowledge the term does not come into general usage until the 1990s.

9. The case of technological determinism in film, with the camera serving as the pivot, is magnificently refuted by Comolli (1980, 121–42).

6. Nations, Identities, and Global Technologies

1. What Mowshowitz says about political organization also applies to economic organization.

2. Negroponte (1995) grasps the implications of the digital but perhaps is over-enthusiastic about its implications. Negroponte forgets that digital culture folds into existing relations of force, institutions, and patterns of social life that will affect seriously its realization.

3. Cited in *Wired* 4, no. 10 (October 1996): 48.

4. These examples come from Mattson and Duncombe 1996, in a special issue of the zine *Primary Documents* entitled "The March of Radio."

5. For many examples of telephone anxiety see Marvin 1988.

6. For a classic statement of this position see Renan 1996.

7. Or see this warning of personal danger from communicating on the Internet: "You Could Get Raped" (Foote 1999).

8. Informed discussions of these issues are found in Gordon 1996 and Clough 1996.

9. See Taylor 1994.

10. For a discussion of the technical aspects of the Clipper Chip see Hotz 1993.

11. U.S. politicians of all stripes have publicly voiced great enthusiasm for the Internet, it must be admitted. In addition to Al Gore's advocacy of the National Information Infrastructure and his proposal to provide free access to all schools, Perot supported an electronic town hall to foster participation in politics. Not to be outdone, the neoconservatives, in the person of Newt Gingrich, championed laptop computers for poor people (see "Newt's Notion: Laptops for All," *International Herald Tribune,* January 7–8, 1995, 3). Politicians, I suppose, continue to speak out of both sides of their mouths.

12. Available electronically from *Cybersphere* 9 (March 1996), http://www.uta.edu/english/apt/collab/texts/newtech.html.

13. Jürgen Habermas, "The European Nation-State: On the Past and Future of Sovereignty and Citizenship," trans. Ciaran Cronin, *Public Culture* 10, no. 2 (winter 1998): 397–416. I am grateful to Robyn Wiegman for telling me about this piece.

14. See, for example, Ross 1995. The long tradition of ambivalence about the United States among French intellectuals is evident in writings from de Tocqueville to Baudrillard.

15. For an excellent statement of the historicity of the nation see Gellner 1996.

16. For another excellent argument for the historicity of the state in general see Clastres 1989.

17. See Étienne Balibar's magnificent essay, "Citizen Subject" (1991). Also of great interest is Balibar's "Subjection and Subjectivation" (1994).

18. Jürgen Habermas, "Citizenship and National Identity," cited in Perry 1995 (564).

19. For an insightful evaluation of *Imagined Communities* see Thompson 1996 (62–63).

20. See also Waldstreicher 1995.

21. For a compelling argument for the importance of the photographic image in this context see Flusser 1984.

22. Among the most interesting of these is the special issue *October* 61 (summer 1992), republished as Appiah and Gates 1995; see also Hall and du Gay 1996; Rajchman 1995; and Woodward 1997.

23. Ernesto Laclau (1996) argues that the difference between the universal and the particular is what animates the political and opens the path to democracy (57).

7. Theorizing the Virtual

1. For some treatments of this theme see Saco 2000.

2. See the article "Cybersex Threatens Plain Old Kind: Church, Lay Experts," distributed on the Internet by Agence France Presse (May 13, 1995).

3. See also the discussion of Baudrillard's political analysis in Der Derian 1994.

4. This Hegelian gesture of identifying one's thought with reality is also made by Derrida (1993), albeit more modestly, when he reports that, on a trip to Moscow, his then Soviet hosts defined *perestroika* as deconstruction: "A Soviet colleague said to me, scarcely laughing, 'But deconstruction, that's the USSR today'" (222). He relates this incident anew in Derrida 1994 (89). One is tempted to make a comment about the role of intellectuals in the age of mass media as a condition for this new insistence on the inscription of theory in history.

5. This translation by François Debrix appeared in Baudrillard 1995c and is taken from a pamphlet Baudrillard published (1994a), which appears in revised form in *Le crime parfait*. It has been published in print as Baudrillard 1995d.

6. Baudrillard is not wholly consistent in this regard. *Le crime parfait* contains many passages that read like the Baudrillard of the 1980s, as, for example, "That thought disappeared under the pressure of a gigantic simulation, a technical and mental one, under the pressure of a precession of models to the benefit of an autonomy of the virtual, from now on liberated from the real, and of a simultaneous autonomy of the real that today functions for and by itself—motu propio—in a delirious perspective, infinitely self-referential" (1995a, 141).

7. For a suggestive genealogy of the screen with a differential analysis of screens see Manovich 1994.

8. Baudrillard responds to such critics as follows: "Because of the media, our scientific means, our knowhow, progress all take an uncontrollable, inhuman dimension. Evil, for me is just that form" (Bayard and Knight 1995).

9. See the interesting essay by Krapp (1996).

10. Derrida also refers to the political implications of the Internet in an interview by Thomas Assheuer in *Die Zeit*, no. 11 (April 5, 1998). The original French version of the text may be found at the Derrida Web site, http://www.hydra.umn.edu/derrida.

11. For an important deconstructionist analysis of the screen as a technology of reorganization of space and time see Weber 1995a and 1995b.

8. Virtual Ethnicity

1. For a similar critique of Lowe's position, and the notion of hybridity upon which it rests, see Friedman 1997 (70–89).

2. I am indebted to Michael Lang for drawing my attention to this passage.

3. Weber (1995b, 83) argues persuasively that the translation of Benjamin's essay (1969) as "The Work of Art in the Age of Mechanical Reproduction" does not render the German *technischen* as well as the English *technical.*

4. The term *identity* is widely used in critical theory and cultural studies today, yet it remains a problem. In its psychological version, *identity* entered the discursive scene with Erikson 1968. In the philosophical tradition, identity is a fundamental category of logic and ontology. In social theory, it emerged in Theodor Adorno's work, especially in Adorno 1973, as part of the critique of the cultural figure of the individual as subject. This line of criticism continues, with important changes, in poststructuralist positions as well as in postcolonial writings.

The problem is twofold: first, the category is Western yet appears in discourse as universal, and, second, it presumes what it needs to demonstrate, that the subject has a coherence, unity, foundation. On the first issue see the important essay by Rouse (1995). Also of interest is the special issue of *October* on identity, vol. 61 (summer 1992), with essays by Joan Scott, Homi Bhabha, Jacques Rancière, Ernesto Laclau, and others. Here I wish only to add a serious caution to the use of the term.

5. See, for example, Certeau 1984, chap. 7, "Walking in the City," and chap. 12, "Reading as Poaching."

6. The most interesting statement of this position is Adorno 1972.

7. Warner 1992, chap. 1, is particularly good on this issue in relation to print technology.

8. This interview with Geert Lovink in Linz, Austria, on June 20, 1995, may be found as Lovink 1996.

9. This phrase is used by J. Hillis Miller in an essay on Anthony Trollope's *Ayala's Angel* (Miller and Asensi 1999).

10. The terms "modern" and "postmodern" are mine.

11. Many Jews agree with Nora's assessment of their situation regarding memory. One Joel Rosenberg says, "I marvel at the resilience of the Jewish people. Their best characteristic is their desire to remember. No other people has such an obsession with memory!" (cited in Eshman 1996, 8). I am indebted to Jonathan Judaken for showing me this essay.

12. Lott (1993) shows how drama provides an intermediary example that functions like the media. I thank Linda Williams for calling my attention to this important work.

13. For a generous sample of cultural studies writing see Grossberg and Nelson 1992.

14. See Baudrillard 1995a; Derrida 1995; Heim 1993, 1998; and Virilio 1995.

15. My citations are from the copy of the book on the World Wide Web at http://www.hypermedia.UNIV-PARIS8.FR/PIERRE/VIRTo.htm.

16. See Aarseth 1997 for a good discussion of hypertext.

17. See Poster 1995, chap. 5.

18. For an analysis of ethnicity and race on the Internet see Nakamura 1995; she argues that race is not eliminated in MOOs.

19. The coordinator of the listserve is Moshe Dror, and CyberJew is found at CYBERJEW@bguvm.bgu.ac.il. Dror is a member of World Futures Society, Israel Chapter and World Network of Religious Futurists. There is a sci-fi tone to some of the messages, such as the one by a member who pondered the first synagogue in

space. I began my subscription in April 1996. On the Web, CyberJew is found at http://www.jewishnet.net.

20. A seder is a ritual meal eaten during the Passover holiday that commemorates the exodus of the Israelites from Egyptian captivity.

21. Tefillah are leather straps donned by Jewish males each morning when certain prayers are recited. Yavneh time suggests a period of fundamental political and social reorganization, as in the shift from the synagogue system to the rabbi system.

9. CyberDemocracy

1. For an intelligent review of the battle over encryption see Levy 1994.

2. When I wrote this I had forgotten that Heidegger uses the example of the hammer in his discussion of technology (1962, 69 ff.). I was reminded of this while reading Don Ihde's illuminating work (1990, 31–34). Heidegger does not exactly speak of human beings becoming hammers, as I suggest, but something pretty close: *Dasein* is "absorbed" in equipment (102).

3. See the most suggestive essay by Hayles (1993).

4. For a study of the role of the media in the formation of a public sphere see Hartley 1992 (1). Hartley examines in particular the role of graphic images in newspapers.

5. See especially Fraser 1989, chap. 6, "What's Critical about Critical Theory? The Case of Habermas and Gender." For a critique of Habermas's historical analysis see Landes 1988.

6. The foreword to Negt and Kluge 1993 by Miriam Hansen (ix–xli) is essential and important in its own right.

7. See the discussion of privacy in relation to electronic surveillance in Lyon 1994 (14–17).

8. Ryan 1994 presents a subtle, complex comparison of reading a novel and virtual reality. She does not deal directly with MOOs and Internet virtual communities.

9. Cherny (1994) concludes that men and women have gender-specific communications on MOOs. For an analysis of bulletin board conversations that reaches the same pessimistic conclusions see Herring 1993. Herring wants to argue that the Internet does not foster democracy since sexism continues there, but she fails to measure the degree of sexism on bulletin boards against that in face-to-face situations or even to indicate how this would be done. The essay may be found at http://www.cios.org/www/ejc/V3N293.htm.

10. For a discussion of sexual preference and identity on the Net see Case 1996 and Wakeford 1997. Sadie Plant (1995, 1996) has argued that the Net, far from a haven of masculinity, is suited better to feminine characteristics.

11. One example of education through gender switching is given by K. K. Campbell in an e-mail message entitled "Attack of the Cyber-Weenies." Campbell explains how he was harassed when he assumed a feminine persona on a bulletin board. I wish to thank Debora Halbert for making me aware of this message.

12. For an excellent study of the cultural implications of virtual communities see Reid 1992, also published in a revised version as Reid 1994.

13. Jill Serpentelli (1995) studies the differences in communication patterns on

different types of Internet structures. Kiesler, Siegel, and McGuire (1991) report that spontaneity and egalitarianism are trends of these conversations.

14. For a fascinating study of the IRC see Reid 1992, an electronic essay also published in *Intertek* 3, no. 3 (winter 1992): 7–15.

15. I wish to thank Charles Stivale for pointing this distinction out to me and for providing other helpful comments and suggestions.

16. See Nakamura (1995), who argues that race persists on MOOs but is constructed differently from "real life."

17. For a discussion of these new developments see Curtis and Nichols 1995.

18. On this issue see the important essay by Gumbrecht (1994).

19. Burnett (1991) explores this issue with convincing logic.

20. Benjamin 1969 (232): "The distinction between author and public is about to lose its basic character.... At any moment the reader is ready to turn into a writer." See also Barthes 1974 (4) for the concept of readerly texts *(texte lisibleu)* and writerly texts *(texte scriptible)* and for another way of theorizing the reversibility of positions.

References

Aarseth, Espen. 1997. *Cybertext: Perspectives on Ergodic Literature.* Baltimore, Md.: Johns Hopkins University Press.

Adorno, Theodor. 1972. *Dialectic of Enlightenment.* Trans. John Cumming. New York: Continuum.

———. 1973. *Negative Dialectics.* Trans. E. B. Ashton. New York: Seabury.

———. 1978. "On the Fetish Character in Music and the Regression of Listening." In *The Essential Frankfurt School Reader,* ed. Andrew Arato and Eike Gebhardt, 29. New York: Urizen.

Althusser, Louis. 1970. "Contradiction and Overdetermination." Trans. Ben Brewster. In *For Marx,* 87–128. New York: Vintage.

Anderson, Benedict. 1983. *Imagined Communities: Reflections on the Origin and Spread of Nationalism.* New York: Verso.

Appadurai, Arjun. 1990. "Disjuncture and Difference in the Global Cultural Economy." *Public Culture* 2, no. 2: 1–24.

Appiah, Kwame, and Henry Gates, eds. 1995. *Identities.* Chicago: University of Chicago Press.

Aycock, Alan. 1999. *"Technologies of the Self": Foucault and Internet Discourse.* Available at http://www.ascusc.org/jcmc/vol1/issuez/aycock.html.

Balibar, Étienne. 1991. "Citizen Subject." In *Who Comes after the Subject?* ed. Eduardo Cadava, Peter Connor, and Jean-Luc Nancy, 33–57. New York: Routledge.

———. 1994. "Subjection and Subjectivation." In *Supposing the Subject,* ed. Joan Copject, 1–15. New York: Verso.

Barker, Francis. 1995. *The Tremulous Private Body: Essays on Subjection.* Ann Arbor: University of Michigan Press.

Barthes, Roland. 1974. *S/Z.* Trans. Richard Miller. New York: Hill and Wang.

———. 1977. "Death of an Author." In *Image, Music, Text,* ed. Stephen Heath, 142–48. New York: Hill and Wang.

Baudrillard, Jean. 1983. "What Are You Doing after the Orgy?" Trans. Lisa Liebmann. *Artforum* 22, no. 2 (October): 42–46.

———. 1991a. *La guerre du golfe n'a pas eu lieu.* Paris: Galilée.

———. 1991b. "The Reality Gulf." *Guardian,* January 11.

———. 1993. *The Transparency of Evil: Essays on Extreme Phenomena.* London: Verso.

———. 1994a. *La pensée radicale.* Paris: Sens & Tonka.

———. 1994b. *Simulacra and Simulation: The Body, in Theory.* Ann Arbor: University of Michigan Press.

———. 1995a. *Le crime parfait.* Collection L'espace critique. Paris: Galilée.

———. 1995b. *The Gulf War Did Not Take Place.* Bloomington: Indiana University Press.

———. 1995c. "Radical Thought." *CTheory* 18, nos. 1–2: n.p.

———. 1995d. "Radical Thought." *Parallax* 1 (September): 53–62.

———. 1998. *Paroxysm: Interviews with Philippe Petit.* Trans. Chris Turner. London: Verso.

Bayard, Caroline, and Graham Knight. 1995. "Vivisecting the 90's." *CTheory* 18, nos. 1–2.

Benjamin, Walter. 1969. "The Work of Art in the Age of Mechanical Reproduction." In *Illuminations,* trans. Harry Zohn, 217–51. New York: Schocken.

Bolter, J. David. 1990. *Writing Space: The Computer, Hypertext, and the History of Writing.* Cambridge, Mass.: Eastgate Systems.

Bolter, Jay, and Richard Grusin. 1996. "Remediation." *Configurations* 4, no. 3: 311–58.

Boyle, James. 1997. *Foucault in Cyberspace: Surveillance, Sovereignty, and Hard-Wired Censors.* Available at http://www.wcl.american.edu/pub/faculty/boyle/foucault.html.

Braidotti, Rosi. 1997. "Nomadism, the European Union, and Embedded Identities: An Interview." *Crossings: A Counter-Disciplinary Journal of Philosophical, Cultural, Historical, and Literary Studies* 1, no. 2: 1–18.

Briggs, Charles F., and Augustus Maverick. 1858. *The Story of the Telegraph, and a History of the Great Atlantic Cable.* New York: Rudd & Carleton.

Brown, Wendy. 1998. "Democracy's Lack." *Public Culture* 10, no. 2: 425–29.

Browning, John. 1997. "Africa 1, Hollywood 0." *Wired* 5, no. 3: 61–62, 64, 185–88.

Bryson, Norman. 1988. "The Gaze in the Expanded Field." In *Vision and Visuality,* ed. Hal Foster, 87–108. Seattle: Bay Press.

Bunn, Austin. 1998. "Progress or Piracy? Next-generation Walkman Has Music Industry Howling." *OC Weekly,* November 6–12, pp. 17–18.

Burkhalter, Byron. 1999. "Reading Race Online: Discovering Racial Identity in Usenet Discussions." In *Communities in Cyberspace,* ed. Marc Smith and Peter Kollock, 60–75. New York: Routledge.

Burnett, Kathleen. 1991. "The Scholar's Rhizome: Networked Communication Issues." At http://www.scils.rutgers.edu/~kburnett/burnetth.html.

Bush, Vannevar. 1945. "As We May Think." *Atlantic Monthly,* July, 101–8.

Butler, Judith. 1993. "Endangered/Endangering: Schematic Racism and White Paranoia." In *Reading Rodney King, Reading Urban Uprising,* ed. Robert Gooding-Williams, 15–22. New York: Routledge.

———. 1995. "Contingent Foundations: Feminism and the Question of 'Postmodernism.'" In *Feminist Contentions: A Philosophical Exchange,* ed. Seyla Benhabib, 35–57. New York: Routledge.

———. 1997. *Excitable Speech: A Politics of the Performative.* New York: Routledge.

Case, Sue Ellen. 1996. *The Domain-Matrix: Performing Lesbian at the End of Print Culture.* Bloomington: Indiana University Press.

Castells, Manuel. 1993. "The Informational Economy and the New International Division of Labor." In *The New Global Economy*, ed. Martin Carnoy. University Park: Pennsylvania State University Press.

———. 1997. *The Power of Identity*. Vol. 2 of *Information Age*. Ed. Manuel Castells. Malden, Mass.: Blackwell.

Certeau, Michel de. 1984. *The Practice of Everyday Life*. Trans. Steven Rendall. Berkeley: University of California Press.

Chardin, Teilhard de. 1959. *The Phenomenon of Man*. Trans. Bernard Wall. New York: Harper and Row.

Cheah, Pheng, and Bruce Robbins, eds. 1998. *Cosmopolitics: Thinking and Feeling beyond the Nation*. Minneapolis: University of Minnesota Press.

Cherny, Lynn. 1994. "Gender Differences in Text-Based Virtual Reality." *Proceedings of the Berkeley Conference on Women and Language*, April, n.p.

Chesher, Chris. 1995. "Colonizing Virtual Reality." *Cultronix* 1, no. 1: n.p.

———. 1997. "The Ontology of Digital Domains." In *Virtual Politics: Identity and Community in Cyberspace*, ed. David Holmes, 79–92. London: Sage.

Chow, Rey. 1996. *Primitive Passions: Visuality, Sexuality, Ethnography, and Contemporary Chinese Cinema*. New York: Columbia University Press.

Clastres, Pierre. 1989. *Society against the State*. Trans. Robert Hurley. New York: Zone Books.

Clough, Michael. 1996. "U.S. Business Could Help Undercut China's Internet Controls." *New York Times*, September 15.

Clough, Patricia. 2000. *Autoaffection: Unconscious Thought in the Age of Teletechnology*. Minneapolis: University of Minnesota Press.

Coombe, Rosemary. 1998. *The Cultural Life of Intellectual Property: Authorship, Appropriation, and the Law*. Durham, N.C.: Duke University Press.

Comolli, Jean-Louis. 1980. "Machines of the Visible." In *The Cinematic Apparatus*, ed. Teresa de Lauretis and Stephen Heath, 121–42. New York: St. Martin's Press.

Cooper, Simon. 1997. "Heidegger and a Further Question concerning Technology." *Arena* 9: 23–56.

Coyne, Richard. 1995. *Designing Information Technology in the Postmodern Age: From Method to Metaphor*. Cambridge: MIT Press.

Crary, Jonathan. 1992. *Techniques of the Observer: On Vision and Modernity in the Nineteenth Century*. Cambridge: MIT Press.

Curtis, Pavel, and David Nichols. 1995. "MUDs Grow Up: Social Virtual Reality in the Real World." At ftp.parc.xerox.com in /pub/Moo/Papers (access date February 1995).

Dahlburg, John-Thor. 1996. "Technology Lets Tentacles of Terrorism Extend Reach." *Los Angeles Times*, August 6.

De Landa, Manuel. 1997. *A Thousand Years of Nonlinear History*. New York: Zone Books.

Deibert, Ronald. 1997. *Parchment, Printing, and Hypermedia: Communication in World Order Transformation*. New York: Columbia University Press.

Deleuze, Gilles. 1994. *Difference and Repetition*. Trans. Paul Patton. New York: Columbia University Press.

Deleuze, Gilles, and Félix Guattari. 1987. *A Thousand Plateaus: Capitalism and Schizophrenia*. Trans. Brian Massumi. Minneapolis: University of Minnesota Press.

DeLillo, Don. 1997. *Underworld: A Novel.* New York: Simon and Schuster.

Der Derian, James. 1994. "Simulation: The Highest Stage of Capitalism?" In *Baudrillard: A Critical Reader,* ed. Douglas Kellner, 189–208. London: Blackwell.

Derrida, Jacques. 1978. "Structure, Sign, and Play in the Discourse of the Human Sciences." In *Writing and Difference,* trans. Alan Bass. Chicago: University of Chicago Press.

———. 1987. "Geschlecht II: Heidegger's Hand." Trans. John Leavey. In *Deconstruction and Philosophy,* ed. John Sallis, 161–96. Chicago: University of Chicago Press.

———. 1989. "Psyche: Inventions of the Other." Trans. Catherine Porter. In *Reading de Man Reading,* ed. Lindsay Waters and Wlad Godzich, 25–65. Minneapolis: University of Minnesota Press.

———. 1993. "Back from Moscow in the U.S.S.R." In *Politics, Theory, and Contemporary Culture,* ed. Mark Poster, 197–235. New York: Columbia University Press.

———. 1994. *Specters of Marx: The State of the Debt, the Work of Mourning, and the New International.* Trans. Peggy Kamuf. New York: Routledge.

———. 1995. "Archive Fever: A Freudian Impression." *diacritics* 25, no. 2: 9–63.

———. 1996. *Archive Fever: A Freudian Impression.* Chicago: University of Chicago Press.

Diamond, Irene, and Quinby, Lee, eds. 1988. *Feminism and Foucault: Reflections on Resistance.* Boston: Northeastern University Press.

Diderot, Denis. 1965. *Encyclopedia: Selections.* Trans. Nelly Hoyt and Thomas Cassirer. New York: Bobbs-Merrill.

Dreyfus, Hubert. 1995. "Heidegger on Gaining a Free Relation to Technology." In *Technology and the Politics of Knowledge,* ed. Andrew Feenberg and Alastair Hannay, 97–107. Bloomington: Indiana University Press.

Ducrot, Oswald, and Tzvetan Todorov. 1979. *Encyclopedic Dictionary of the Sciences of Language.* Trans. Catherine Porter. Baltimore, Md.: Johns Hopkins University Press.

Ebo, Bosah, ed. 1998. *Cyberghetto or Cybertopia? Race, Class, and Gender on the Internet.* Westport, Conn.: Praeger.

Ellul, Jacques. 1964. *Technological Society.* Trans. John Wilkinson. New York: Random House.

Erikson, Erik. 1968. *Identity: Youth and Crisis.* New York: Norton.

Eshman, Robert. 1996. "Caught in a Net of Controversy." *Jewish Journal.*

Farley, Maggie. 1999. "China Activists Hack Holes in Wall." *Los Angeles Times,* January 4.

Feenberg, Andrew. 1991. *Critical Theory of Technology.* New York: Oxford University Press.

Felski, Rita. 1989. *Beyond Feminist Aesthetics: Feminist Literature and Social Change.* Cambridge: Harvard University Press.

Flusser, Vilém. 1984. *Towards a Philosophy of Photography.* Göttingen: European Photography.

———. 1992. *Die Schrift: Hat Schreiben Zukunft?* Göttingen: Edition Immatrix.

Foote, Donna. 1999. "You Could Get Raped." *Newsweek,* February 8, 64–65.

Foucault, Michel. 1978. *The History of Sexuality: An Introduction.* Trans. Robert Hurley. Vol. 1. New York: Pantheon.

———. 1980. "On Popular Justice." In *Power/Knowledge,* ed. Colin Gordon, 1–36. New York: Pantheon.

———. 1983. "Réponse aux questions." *Littoral* 9: 28–29.

———. 1984a. "What Is an Author?" Trans. Josue Harari. In *The Foucault Reader*, ed. Paul Rabinow, 101–20. New York: Pantheon.

———. 1984b. "What Is Enlightenment?" In *The Foucault Reader*, ed. Paul Rabinow, 32–50. New York: Pantheon.

———. 1986. "Of Other Spaces." *diacritics* (spring): 22–27.

———. 1991. "Governmentality." In *The Foucault Effect*, ed. Graham Burchell, Colin Gordon, and Peter Miller, 87–104. Chicago: University of Chicago Press.

Fox-Genovese, Elizabeth. 1986. "The Claims of a Common Culture: Gender, Race, Class and the Canon." *Salmagundi* 72 (fall): 131–43.

Fraser, Nancy. 1989. *Unruly Practices*. Minneapolis: University of Minnesota Press.

———. 1990. "Rethinking the Public Sphere." *Social Text*. Minneapolis: University of Minnesota Press.

Friedman, Jonathan. 1997. "Global Crises, the Struggle for Cultural Identity, and Intellectual Porkbarrelling." In *Debating Cultural Hybridity*, ed. Pnina Werbner and Tariq Modood, 70–89. London: Zed Books.

Frissen, Paul. 1997. "The Virtual State: Postmodernisation, Informatisation, and Public Administration." In *The Governance of Cyberspace*, ed. Brian Loader, 111–25. New York: Routledge.

Galbraith, John Kenneth. 1958. *The Affluent Society*. New York: Houghton Mifflin.

Gellner, Ernest. 1996. "The Coming of Nationalism and Its Interpretation." In *Mapping the Nation*, ed. Gopal Balakrishnan, 98–145. New York: Verso.

Goldberg, Jonathan. 1990. *Writing Matter: From the Hands of the English Renaissance*. Stanford, Calif.: Stanford University Press.

Golding, Sue. 1994. "Virtual Derrida." In *Philosophic Fictions*, ed. Jelica Sumic-Riha, 2:61–66. Lubljana, Slovenia: Academy of Philosophy.

Gordon, Joshua. 1996. "Cyber-Censorship Grows in East Asia." *Los Angeles Times*, September 27.

Graham, Philip. 2000. "Hypercapitalism." *New Media and Society* 2, no. 2 (June): 131–56.

Grossberg, Lawrence, and Carey Nelson, eds. 1992. *Cultural Studies*. New York: Routledge.

Grosz, Elizabeth. 1995. *Space, Time, and Perversion: Essays on the Politics of Bodies*. New York: Routledge.

Guattari, Félix. 1995. *Chaosmosis: An Ethico-Aesthetic Paradigm*. Trans. Paul Bains and Julian Pefanis. Bloomington: Indiana University Press.

Guéhenno, Jean-Marie. 1995. *The End of the Nation-State*. Trans. Victoria Elliott. Minneapolis: University of Minnesota Press.

Gumbrecht, Hans Ulrich. 1994. "A Farewell to Interpretation." Trans. William Whobrey. In *Materialities of Communication*, ed. Hans Ulrich Gumbrecht and K. Ludwig Pfeiffer, 389–402. Stanford, Calif.: Stanford University Press.

Gurak, Laura. 1997. *Persuasion and Privacy in Cyberspace: The Online Protests over Lotus Marketplace and the Clipper Chip*. New Haven, Conn.: Yale University Press.

Habermas, Jürgen. 1989. *The Structural Transformation of the Public Sphere*. Trans. Thomas Burger. Cambridge: MIT Press.

Hall, Stuart. 1995. "Stitching Yourself in Place." *xs2cs electronic archive*.

———. 1996. "The Question of Cultural Identity." In *Modernity: An Introduction to Modern Societies*, ed. Stuart Hall et al. London: Blackwell.

Hall, Stuart, and Paul du Gay, eds. 1996. *Questions of Cultural Identity.* London: Sage.

Hamilton, Walter. 1998. "Theglobe.com Sets Record for 1st-Day Trading." *Los Angeles Times,* November 14.

Haraway, Donna. 1991. *Simians, Cyborgs, and Women: The Re-Invention of Nature.* New York: Routledge.

———. 1997. *Modest_Witness@Second_Millennium.FemaleMan©_Meets_Onco-Mouse™: Feminism and Technoscience.* New York: Routledge.

Harmon, Amy. 1996. "Daily Life's Digital Divide." *Los Angeles Times,* July 3.

———. 1997. "Why the French Hate the Internet." *Los Angeles Times,* January 27.

———. 1999. "Protests Held against Windows System." *New York Times,* February 17.

Hartley, John. 1992. *The Politics of Pictures: The Creation of the Public in the Age of Popular Media.* New York: Routledge.

Hartsock, Nancy. 1990a. "Foucault on Power: A Theory for Women?" In *Feminism/Postmodernism,* ed. Linda Nicholson, 157–75. New York: Routledge.

———. 1990b. "Rethinking Modernism: Minority vs. Majority Theories." *Cultural Critique* 6–7: 187–206.

Hayles, N. Katherine. 1993. "Virtual Bodies and Flickering Signifiers." *October* 66 (fall): 69–91.

———. 1997. "Corporeal Anxiety in *Dictionary of the Khazars:* What Books Talk about in the Late Age of Print When They Talk about Losing Their Bodies." *Modern Fiction Studies* 43, no. 3: 800–820.

———. 1999. *How We Became Posthuman: Virtual Bodies in Cybernetics, Literature, and Informatics.* Chicago: University of Chicago Press.

Heidegger, Martin. 1959. *An Introduction to Metaphysics.* Trans. Ralph Manheim. New York: Anchor.

———. 1962. *Being and Time.* Trans. John Macquarrie and Edward Robinson. New York: Harper and Row.

———. 1969. *Identity and Difference.* Trans. Joan Stambaugh. New York: Harper and Row.

———. 1977. *The Question concerning Technology and Other Essays.* Trans. William Lovitt. New York: Harper and Row.

Heim, Michael. 1993. *The Metaphysics of Virtual Reality.* New York: Oxford University Press.

———. 1998. *Virtual Realism.* New York: Oxford University Press.

Herring, Susan C. 1993. "Gender and Democracy in Computer-Mediated Communication." *Electronic Journal of Communications* 3, no. 2.

Hillis, Ken. 1999. *Digital Sensations: Space, Identity, and Embodiment in Virtual Reality.* Minneapolis: University of Minnesota Press.

Hiltzik, Michael. 1999. "Net Effect: Old Media, New Tech." *Los Angeles Times,* April 12.

Hobart, Michael, and Zachary Schiffman. 1998. *Information Ages: Literacy, Numeracy, and the Computer Revolution.* Baltimore, Md.: Johns Hopkins University Press.

Holmes, David. 1993. "The Breaking Down of the Senses: Virtual Reality and Technological Extension." Paper presented at the Australasian Association for the History, Philosophy, and Social Studies of Science Conference, La Trobe University, May, n.p.

Hotz, Robert Lee. 1993. "Computer Code's Security Worries Privacy Watchdogs." *Los Angeles Times,* October 4.

Huffstutter, P. J. 1999. "Studios Fume as Pirates Flood Internet with Films." *Los Angeles Times,* August 14.

Ihde, Don. 1990. *Technology and the Lifeworld: From Garden to Earth.* Bloomington: Indiana University Press.

"Internet Stimulus." 1999. *Herald Tribune,* June 24.

Irigaray, Luce. 1985. *Speculum of the Other Women.* Trans. Gillian Gill. Ithaca, N.Y.: Cornell University Press.

Jameson, Fredric. 1991. *Postmodernism; or, The Cultural Logic of Late Capitalism.* Durham, N.C.: Duke University Press.

————. 1995. "Marx's Purloined Letter." *New Left Review* 209 (January–February): 71–109.

————. 1998. "Notes on Globalization as a Philosophical Issue." In *The Cultures of Globalization,* ed. Fredric Jameson and Masao Miyoshi, 54–77. Durham, N.C.: Duke University Press.

Jaszi, Martha, and Peter Woodmansee, eds. 1994. *The Construction of Authorship: Textual Appropriation in Law and Literature.* Durham, N.C.: Duke University Press.

Jay, Martin. 1982. "Should Intellectual History Take a Linguistic Turn?" In *Modern European Intellectual History,* ed. Dominick LaCapra and Steven Kaplan, 86–110. Ithaca, N.Y.: Cornell University Press.

Johns, Adrian. 1998. *The Nature of the Book: Print and Knowledge in the Making.* Chicago: University of Chicago Press.

Joyce, Michael. 1987. *Afternoon: A Story.* Cambridge, Mass.: Eastgate Systems.

Joyrich, Lynne. 1996. *Re-Viewing Reception: Television, Gender, and Postmodern Culture.* Bloomington: Indiana University Press.

Keep, C. J. 1993. "Knocking on Heaven's Door: Leibniz, Baudrillard, and Virtual Reality." *Ejournal* 3, no. 2.

Kiesler, Sara, Jane Siegel, and Timothy McGuire. 1991. "Social Psychological Aspects of Computer-Mediated Communication." In *Computerization and Controversy,* ed. Charles Dunlop and Rob Kling, 330–49. New York: Academic Press.

Kirshenblatt-Gimblett, Barbara. 1996. "The Electronic Vernacular." In *Connected: Engagements with Media,* ed. George Marcus, 21–65. Chicago: University of Chicago Press.

Kittler, Friedrich. 1990. *Discourse Networks: 1800/1900.* Trans. Michael Metteer. Stanford, Calif.: Stanford University Press.

————. 1993. *Draculas Vermächtnis: Technische Schriften.* Leipzig: Reclam Verlag.

————. 1994. "Unconditional Surrender." In *Materialities of Communication,* ed. Hans Gumbrecht and Ludwig Pfeiffer, 319–34. Stanford, Calif.: Stanford University Press.

————. 1997. "There Is No Software." In *Being on Line, Net, Subjectivity, Lusitania,* ed. Alan Sondheim. Vol. 8.

————. 1999. *Gramophone, Film, Typewriter.* Trans. Geoffrey Winthrop-Young and Michael Wutz. Stanford, Calif.: Stanford University Press.

Kittler, Friedrich A., and John Johnston. 1997. *Literature, Media, Information Systems: Essays.* Critical Voices in Art, Theory, and Culture. Amsterdam: G1B Arts International.

Kollock, Peter. 1999. "The Economies of Online Cooperation." In *Communities in Cyberspace,* ed. Marc Smith and Peter Kollock, 220–39. New York: Routledge.

Krapp, Peter. 1996. "Derrida Online." *Oxford Literary Review* 18, nos. 1–2: 159–73.

Laclau, Ernesto. 1990. *New Reflections on the Revolution of Our Time.* New York: Verso.
———. 1995. "The Time Is out of Joint." *diacritics* 25, no. 2: 92–93.
———. 1996. "The Question of Identity." In *The Politics of Difference: Ethnic Premises in a World of Power,* ed. Edwin Wilmsen and Patrick McAllister, 45–58. Chicago: University of Chicago Press.

Lacoue-Labarthe, Philippe. 1990. *Heidegger, Art, and Politics.* Trans. Chris Turner. New York: Blackwell.

Landes, Joan. 1988. *Women and the Public Sphere in the Age of the French Revolution.* Ithaca, N.Y.: Cornell University Press.

Landow, George. 1992. *Hypertext: The Convergence of Contemporary Critical Theory and Technology.* Baltimore, Md.: John Hopkins University Press.
———. 1997. *Hypertext 2.0. Parallax.* Rev., amplified ed. Baltimore, Md.: Johns Hopkins University Press.

Lanham, Richard. 1989. "The Electronic Word: Literary Study and the Digital Revolution." *New Literary History* 20, no. 2: 265–90.

Lanier, Jaron. 1990. "Life in the Data-Cloud." *Mondo 2000,* 44–54.

Laurel, Brenda. 1991. *Computers as Theatre.* New York: Addison-Wesley.

Lenk, Klaus. 1997. "The Challenge of Cyberspatial Forms of Human Interaction to Territorial Governance and Policing." In *The Governance of Cyberspace,* ed. Brian Loader, 126–35. New York: Routledge.

Levinson, Paul. 1997. *The Soft Edge: From the Alphabet to the Internet and Beyond.* New York: Routledge.

Lévy, Pierre. 1995a. *Qu'est-ce que le virtuel?* Paris: La Decouverte.
———. 1995b. *Toward Superlanguage.* Available at http://www.uiah.fi/bookshop/isea_proc/nextgen/01.html.
———. 1997. *Collective Intelligence.* Trans. Robert Bonomo. New York: Plenum Press.

Levy, Steven. 1994. "The Battle of the Clipper Chip." *New York Times,* June 12, 44–51.

Lott, Eric. 1993. *Love and Theft: Blackface Minstrelsy and the American Working Class.* New York: Oxford.

Lovink, Geert. 1996. "Civil Society, Fanaticism, and Digital Reality: A Conversation with Slavoj Zizek." *CTheory: Theory, Technology, and Culture* 19: 1–2.

Lowe, Lisa. 1996. *Immigrant Acts.* Durham, N.C.: Duke University Press.

Lury, Celia. 1993. *Cultural Rights: Technology, Legality, and Personality.* New York: Routledge.

Lyon, David. 1994. *The Electronic Eye: The Rise of Surveillance Society.* Minneapolis: University of Minnesota Press.

Lyotard, Jean-François. 1984. *The Postmodern Condition: A Report on Knowledge.* Trans. Geoff Bennington and Brian Massumi. Minneapolis: University of Minnesota Press.

Maffésoli, Michel. 1988. *Le temps des tribus: Le déclin de l'individualisme dans les sociétés de masse.* Paris: Meridiens Klincksieck.

Malkki, Liisa. 1995. *Purity and Exile: Violence, Memory, and National Cosmology among Hutu Refugees in Tanzania.* Chicago: University of Chicago Press.

Manovich, Lev. 1994. *An Archeology of a Computer Screen.* Telepolis. Available at http://www-apparitions.ucsd.edu/~manovich/text/digital_nature.html.

Markley, Robert. 1996. "The Metaphysics of Cyberspace." In *Virtual Realities and Their Discontents,* ed. Robert Markley, 55–77. Baltimore, Md.: Johns Hopkins University Press.

Marvin, Carolyn. 1988. *When Old Technologies Were New: Thinking about Electric Communication in the Late Nineteenth Century.* New York: Oxford.

Marx, Karl. 1970. *A Contribution to the Critique of Political Economy: Introduction.* Trans. S. Ryazanskaya. New York: International.

Masten, Jeffrey, Peter Stallybrass, and Nancy Vickers, eds. 1997. *Language Machines: Technologies of Literary and Cultural Production.* New York: Routledge.

Mattson, Andrew, and Stephen Duncombe, eds. 1996. *Primary Documents.* Vol. 5.

McCabe, Heather. 1999. "The Net: Enemy of the State?" *Wired News,* August 12.

McClintock, Anne. 1995. *Imperial Leather: Race, Gender, and Sexuality in the Colonial Contest.* New York: Routledge.

McLuhan, Marshall. 1962. *The Gutenberg Galaxy.* Toronto: University of Toronto Press.

———. 1964. *Understanding Media: The Extensions of Man.* New York: McGraw-Hill.

McRobbie, Angela. 1994. *Postmodernism and Popular Culture.* New York: Routledge.

Meyrowitz, Joshua. 1985. *No Sense of Place: The Impact of Electronic Media on Social Behavior.* New York: Oxford University Press.

Miller, Greg. 1999. "Online Power Gives David a Little Leverage on Goliath." *Los Angeles Times,* February 1.

Miller, Greg, and Davan Maharaj. 1999. "Will Cyber Patents Stymie Hollywood Giants?" *Los Angeles Times,* September 13.

Miller, J. Hillis, and Manuel Asensi. 1999. *Black Holes: Cultural Memory in the Present.* Stanford, Calif.: Stanford University Press.

Miller, Nancy. 1982. "The Text's Heroine: A Feminist Critic and Her Fictions." *Diacritics* 12, no. 2 (May): 48–53.

Mitchell, Timothy. 1998. "Nationalism, Imperialism, Economism: A Comment on Habermas." *Public Culture* 10, no. 2: 417–24.

Mitchell, W. J. T. 1994. *Picture Theory.* Chicago: University of Chicago Press.

Mitchell, William J. 1994. *The Reconfigured Eye: Visual Truth in the Post-Photographic Era.* Boston: MIT Press.

———. 1997. *City of Bits.* Cambridge: MIT Press.

Monmaney, Terence. 1997. "Cult Targeted Web Sites for Abuse." *Los Angeles Times,* March 28.

Morely, David, and Kevin Robins. 1995. *Spaces of Identity: Global Media, Electronic Landscapes, and Cultural Boundaries.* New York: Routledge.

Morse, Margaret. 1998. *Virtualities: Television, Media Art, and Cyberculture.* Bloomington: Indiana University Press.

Moss, Mitchell. 1998. "Technology and Cities." *Cityscape* 3, no. 3: 107–27.

Moulthrop, Stuart. 1991. *Victory Garden: A Fiction.* Computer software. Eastgate Systems.

Mowshowitz, Abbe. 1992. "Virtual Feudalism: A Vision of Political Organization in the Information Age." *Information and the Public Sector* 2: 213–31.

Murray, Janet. 1997. *Hamlet on the Holodeck: The Future of Narrative in Cyberspace.* New York: Free Press.

Nakamura, Lisa. 1995. "Race in/for Cyberspace: Identity Tourism and Racial Passing on the Internet." *Works and Days* 13, no. 1–2: 181–93.

Nancy, Jean-Luc. 1991. *The Inoperative Community.* Trans. Peter Connor. Minneapolis: University of Minnesota Press.

Negroponte, Nicholas. 1995. *Being Digital*. New York: Knopf.

Negt, Oskar, and Alexander Kluge. 1993. *Public Sphere and Experience: Toward an Analysis of the Bourgeois and Proletarian Public Sphere*. Trans. Peter Labanyi, Jamie Owen Daniel, and Assenka Oksiloff. Minneapolis: University of Minnesota Press.

Nietzsche, Friedrich. 1986. *Human, All Too Human*. Trans. R. J. Hollingdale. Cambridge: Cambridge University Press.

Noble, David. 1977. *America by Design: Science, Technology, and the Rise of Corporate Capitalism*. New York: Knopf.

———. 1998. "Digital Diploma Mills: The Automation of Higher Education." *net-Worker: The Craft of Network Computing* 2, no. 2: 9–14.

Nora, Pierre. 1989. "Between Memory and History: Les Lieux de Mémoire." *Representations* 26: 7–25.

———, ed. 1984. *Les lieux de mémoire*. 3 vols. Paris: Gallimard.

Nunes, Mark. 1995. "Baudrillard in Cyberspace: Internet, Virtuality, and Postmodernity." *Styles* 29: 314–27.

Okrent, Daniel. 1999. "Raising Kids Online: What Can Parents Do?" *Time*, May 10, 38–43.

Ong, Walter. 1982. *Orality and Literacy: Technologizing the Word*. New York: Routledge.

Pareles, Jon. 1998. "With a Click, a New Era of Music Dawns." *New York Times*, November 15.

Pavic, Milorad. 1988. *Dictionary of the Khazars: A Lexicon Novel*. New York: Vintage.

Pease, Donald. 1995. "Author." In *Critical Terms for Literary Study*, ed. Frank Lentricchia and Thomas McLaughlin, 106–9. Chicago: University of Chicago Press.

Peraino, Vito. 1999. "The Law of Increasing Returns." *Wired* 7, no. 8 (August): 144–45.

Perrolle, Judith. 1991. "Conversations and Trust in Computer Interfaces." In *Computerization and Controversy*, ed. Charles Dunlop and Rob Kling, 350–63. New York: Academic Press.

Perry, Richard. 1995. "The Logic of the Nation State." *Indiana Law Review* 28, no. 3: 551–74.

Philips, Chuck. 1999. "IBM Aims to Unplug Online Music Pirates." *Los Angeles Times*, February 8.

Plant, Sadie. 1995. "The Future Looms: Weaving Women and Cybernetics." *Body and Society* 1, nos. 3–4: 45–64.

———. 1996. "On the Matrix: Cyberfeminist Simulations." In *Cultures of Internet: Virtual Spaces, Real Histories, Living Bodies*, ed. Rob Shields, 170–83. London: Sage.

Polly, Jean Armour, and Steve Cisler. 1994. "Community Networks on the Internet." *Library*, June 15, 22–23.

Pomfret, John. 1999. "Frank Debate Surges on Internet Sites in China." *International Herald Tribune*, June 24.

Porush, David. 1998. "Telepathy: Alphabetic Consciousness and the Age of Cyborg Literacy." In *Virtual Futures: Cyberotics, Technology, and Post-Human Pragmatism*, ed. Joan Dixon and Eric Cassidy, 45–64. London: Routledge.

Poster, Mark. 1995. *The Second Media Age*. Cambridge: Blackwell.

———, ed. 1988. *Jean Baudrillard: Selected Writings*. Stanford, Calif.: Stanford University Press.

Postman, Neil. 1985. *Amusing Ourselves to Death*. New York: Penguin Books.

Quinby, Lee. 1994. *Anti-Apocalypse: Exercises in Genealogical Criticism.* Minneapolis: University of Minnesota Press.

Rajchman, John, ed. 1995. *The Identity in Question.* New York: Routledge.

Reeves, Byron, and Clifford Nass. 1996. *The Media Equation: How People Treat Computers, Television, and New Media Like Real People and Places.* New York: Cambridge University Press.

Reid, Elizabeth. 1992. "Electropolis: Communication and Community on Internet Relay Chat." *Intertek* 3, no. 3: 7–15.

———. 1994. "Virtual World: Culture and Imagination." In *Cybersociety,* ed. Steve Jones, 164–83. New York: Sage.

Renan, Ernest. 1996. "What Is a Nation?" In *Becoming National: A Reader,* ed. Geoff Eley and Ronald Suny, 42–55. New York: Oxford University Press.

Rorty, Richard. 1967. "Metaphysical Difficulties of Linguistic Philosophy." In *The Linguistic Turn: Recent Essays in Philosophical Method,* ed. Richard Rorty, 1–19. Chicago: University of Chicago Press.

Rose, Mark. 1993. *Authors and Owners: The Invention of Copyright.* Cambridge: Harvard University Press.

Rosenzweig, Roy. 1999. "AQ as Web-Zine: Responses to AQ's Experimental Online Issue." *American Quarterly* 51, no. 2: 237–46.

Ross, Kristin. 1995. *Fast Cars, Clean Bodies: Decolonization and the Reordering of French Culture.* Cambridge: MIT Press.

Rouse, Roger. 1991. "Mexican Migration and the Social Space of Postmodernism." *Diaspora* 1, no. 1: 8–23.

———. 1995. "Questions of Identity: Reflections on the Cultural Politics of Personhood and Collectivity in Transnational Migration to the United States." *Critique of Anthropology* 15, no. 4: 351–80.

Rutsky, R. L. 1999. *High Technē: Art and Technology from the Machine Aesthetic to the Posthuman.* Minneapolis: University of Minnesota Press.

Ryan, Marie-Laure. 1994. "Immersion vs. Interactivity: Virtual Reality and Literary Theory." *Postmodern Culture* 5.

———, ed. 1999. *Cyberspace Textuality: Computer Technology and Literary Theory.* Bloomington: Indiana University Press.

Saco, Diana. 2002. *Cybering Democracy: Public Space and the Internet.* Minneapolis: University of Minnesota Press.

Samuelson, Pamela. 1992. "Some New Kinds of Authorship Made Possible by Computers and Some Intellectual Property Questions They Raise." *University of Pittsburgh Law Review* 53: 685–704.

———. 1997. "Big Media Beaten Back." *Wired* 5, no. 3: 61 ff.

Sassen, Saskia. 1997. "Electronic Space and Power." *Journal of Urban Technology* 4, no. 1: 1–17.

———. 1998. *Globalization and Its Discontents.* New York: New Press.

Schiller, Dan. 1999. *Digital Capitalism: Networking the Global Market System.* Cambridge: MIT Press.

Schwartz, Hillel. 1996. *The Culture of the Copy: Striking Likenesses, Unreasonable Facsimiles.* New York: Zone.

Serpentelli, Jill. 1995. *Conversational Structure and Personality Correlates of Electronic Communication.* Available at ftp.parc.xerox.com in/pub/Moo/Papers.

Silberman, Steve. 1998. "Ex Libris: The Joys of Curling Up with a Good Digital Reading Device." *Wired* 6, no. 7: 98 ff.

Smiley, Jane. 1995. *Moo.* New York: Knopf.

Snider, Mike. 2000. "Media vs. Web in Digital Copyright War." *USA Today,* February 17, A1.

Stalder, Felix. 1998. "The Network Paradigm: Social Formations in the Age of Information." *Information Society* 14, no. 4: 301–8.

Stallabrass, Julian. 1995. "Empowering Technology: The Exploration of Cyberspace." *New Left Review* 211 (May–June): 3–32.

Stocker, Gerfried, and Christine Schöpf, eds. 1997. *Fleshfactor: Informationsmachine Mensch.* Vienna: Springer-Verlag.

Stoler, Ann Laura. 1995. *Race and the Education of Desire: Foucault's History of Sexuality and the Colonial Order of Things.* Durham, N.C.: Duke University Press.

Stone, Allucquere Rosanne. 1995. *The War of Desire and Technology at the Close of the Mechanical Age.* Cambridge: MIT Press.

Streeter, Thomas. 1996. *Selling the Air: A Critique of the Policy of Commercial Broadcasting in the United States.* Chicago: University of Chicago Press.

Tapscott, Don. 1996. *The Digital Economy: Promise and Peril in the Age of Networked Intelligence.* New York: McGraw-Hill.

Taylor, Jon. 1994. *Electronic Frontiers Japan* 1:206.

Thompson, John. 1996. *The Media and Modernity.* London: Polity.

Tocqueville, Alexis de. 1955. *The Old Regime and the French Revolution.* Trans. Stuart Gilbert. Garden City: Doubleday.

Tomlinson, John. 1999. *Globalization and Culture.* Chicago: Chicago University Press.

Turkle, Sherry. 1995. *Life on the Screen: Identity in the Age of the Internet.* New York: Simon and Schuster.

———. 1998. "Cyborg Babies and Cy-Dough-Plasm." In *Cyborg Babies: From Techno-Sex to Techno-Tots,* ed. Robbie Dumit and Joseph Davis-Floyd, 317–29. New York: Routledge.

Van Gelder, Lindsy. 1991. "The Strange Case of the Electronic Lover." In *Computerization and Controversy,* ed. Charles Dunlop and Rob Kling, 364–75. New York: Academic Press.

Vankin, Jonathan. 1999. "Downloading the Future: The MP3 Revolution—the End of the Industry as We Know It." *LA Weekly,* March 26–April 1, 36, 38, 40.

Virilio, Paul. 1986. *Speed and Politics: An Essay on Dromology.* Trans. Mark Polizzotti. New York: Semiotext(e).

———. 1989. *War and Cinema: The Logistics of Perception.* Trans. Patrick Camiller. New York: Verso.

———. 1993. "The Third Interval: A Critical Transition." In *Rethinking Technologies,* ed. Verena Conley. Minneapolis: University of Minnesota Press.

———. 1994. *The Vision Machine.* Trans. Julie Rose. Bloomington: Indiana University Press.

———. 1995. *La vitesse de libération.* Paris: Galilée.

Wakeford, Nina. 1997. "Cyberqueer." In *Lesbian and Gay Studies: A Critical Introduction,* ed. Andy Medhurst and Sally Munt, 20–38. London: Cassell.

Waldstreicher, David. 1995. "Rites of Rebellion, Rites of Assent: Celebrations, Print Culture, and the Origins of American Nationalism." *Journal of American History* 82, no. 1 (June): 37–61.

Wallace, Amy. 1999. "Can Studios Tame the Net?" *Los Angeles Times Calendar*, May 16, 3, 18–22.

Walters, Suzanna Danuta. 1996. "From Here to Queer: Radical Feminism, Postmodernism, and the Lesbian Menace (or, Why Can't a Woman Be More Like a Fag?" *Signs* 21, no. 4: 830–69.

Ward, Todd, and Irene Taylor, eds. 1998. *Literacy Theory in the Age of the Internet.* New York: Columbia University Press.

Warner, Michael. 1992. *The Letters of the Republic: Publication and the Public Sphere in Eighteenth-Century America.* Cambridge: Harvard University Press.

Weber, Samuel. 1995a. "Humanitarian Interventions in the Age of the Media." *suitcase* 1, nos. 1–2: 130–45.

———. 1995b. *Mass Mediauras: Essays on Form, Technics, and Media.* Stanford, Calif.: Stanford University Press.

Weiss, Kenneth. 1998. "Wary Academia Eyes Cyberspace." *Los Angeles Times*, March 31.

Wiener, Norbert. 1950. *The Human Use of Human Beings: Cybernetics and Society.* New York: Doubleday.

Wilden, Anthony. 1972. *System and Structure: Essays in Communication and Exchange.* London: Tavistock.

Woodward, Kathryn, ed. 1997. *Identity and Difference.* London: Sage.

Yúdice, George. 1992. "We Are Not the World." *Social Text* 31/32: 202–16.

Zack, Ian. 1998. "Universities Finding a Sharp Rise in Computer-Aided Cheating." *Los Angeles Times*, September 23.

Zimmerman, Michael. 1990. *Heidegger's Confrontation with Modernity: Technology, Politics, and Art.* Bloomington: Indiana University Press.

Zuboff, Shoshana. 1988. *In the Age of the Smart Machine: The Future of Work and Power.* New York: Basic Books.

Index

Aarseth, Espen, 96, 191, 194
Adorno, Theodor, 14, 90, 194
Alberti, Leon Battista, 99
Allende, Salvador, 113
Althusser, Louis, 17
Anderson, Benedict, 122–23
Appadurai, Arjun, 103
Appiah, Kwame, 193
Assheuer, Thomas, 193
Aycock, Alan, 190

Balibar, Étienne, 120, 192
Balsamo, Anne, 191
Barker, Francis, 142
Barthes, Roland, 66, 99, 188, 196
Baudrillard, Jean, 14, 16, 20, 23–27,
    113–15, 118, 132–37, 140, 161, 192–94
Bayard, Caroline, 193
Benjamin, Walter, 63–64, 93, 153, 188,
    194, 196
Bentham, Jeremy, 155–57
Bhabha, Homi, 194
Bolter, Jay, 55–56, 94
Boyle, James, 190
Braidotti, Rosi, 128
Briggs, Charles F., 151
Brown, Wendy, 116
Browning, John, 62
Bryson, Norman, 98
Bunn, Austin, 52

Burnett, Kathleen, 196
Bush, Vannevar, 95
Butler, Judith, 72–74, 191
Byrne, David, 171

Campbell, K. K., 195
Case, Sue Ellen, 75–76, 190–91, 195
Castells, Manuel, 7–9, 56, 102, 189
Certeau, Michel de, 153, 161, 194
Cheah, Pheng, 103
Cherny, Lynn, 195
Chesher, Chris, 131, 189
Chow, Rey, 149–50
Cisler, Steve, 175
Clastres, Pierre, 192
Clough, Michael, 192
Clough, Patricia, 5
Comolli, Jean-Louis, 191
Condorcet, Marie-Jean-Antoine
    Nicolas de Caritat, 22, 66
Coombe, Rosemary, 90
Cooper, Simon, 189
Coyne, Richard, 189
Crary, Jonathan, 130
Curtis, Pavel, 196

Dahlburg, John-Thor, 111
Debrix, François, 193
Deibert, Ronald, 104
De Landa, Manuel, 37

Deleuze, Gilles, 27, 113, 145, 164
DeLillo, Don, 39, 58
Der Derian, James, 193
Derrida, Jacques, 20, 59, 73, 132, 138–46, 189–90, 193–94
Descartes, René, 6, 13, 36, 120
Diamond, Irene, 71
Diderot, Denis, 22
Dole, Bob, 105
Dreyfus, Hubert, 34
Dror, Moshe, 194
Ducrot, Oswald, 81
Du Gay, Paul, 193
Duncombe, Stephen, 192

Ebo, Bosah, 3
Ellul, Jacques, 22–23
Erikson, Erik, 6–7, 194
Eshman, Robert, 194

Fanning, Shawn, 50
Farley, Maggie, 111
Feenberg, Andrew, 22
Felski, Rita, 179–80
Flusser, Vilém, 83, 85, 192
Foote, Donna, 192
Ford, Henry, 43
Foucault, Michel, 5, 16, 20, 28, 65–73, 87, 93, 99, 118, 145, 165, 190
Fourier, Charles, 162
Fox-Genovese, Elizabeth, 191
Fraser, Nancy, 179, 181, 195
Freud, Sigmund, 142
Friedman, Jonathan, 193
Frissen, Paul, 127

Galbraith, John Kenneth, 41
Gates, Bill, 44
Gates, Henry, 193
Gellner, Ernest, 192
Gibson, William, 99
Gingrich, Newt, 192
Goldberg, Jonathan, 87
Golding, Sue, 143
Goldmann, Lucien, 73
Gordon, Joshua, 192
Gore, Al, 112, 192
Graham, Philip, 56–57

Grossberg, Lawrence, 194
Grosz, Elizabeth, 191
Grusin, David, 55–56
Guattari, Félix, 26–27, 36, 113
Guéhenno, Jean-Marie, 101
Gumbrecht, Hans Ulrich, 196
Gurak, Laura, 173
Gutenberg, Johann, 81, 88

Habermas, Jürgen, 115–16, 121–22, 179–82, 192, 195
Halbert, Debora, 195
Hall, Stuart, 125, 193
Hamilton, Walter, 45
Hansen, Miriam, 179
Haraway, Donna, 10, 95
Harmon, Amy, 46, 110, 117
Harris, David, 50
Hartley, John, 178, 195
Hartsock, Nancy, 70–72
Hayles, Katherine, 74, 82, 94–95, 135, 137, 195
Heidegger, Martin, 19, 25, 27–36, 189, 195
Heim, Michael, 99, 130, 194
Herring, Susan, 195
Hillis, Ken, 131
Hiltzik, Michael, 45
Hobart, Michael, 5
Holmes, David, 130
Hotz, Robert Lee, 192
Huffstutter, P. J., 54

Ihde, Don, 195
Irigaray, Luce, 72

Jackson, Shelly, 94
Jameson, Fredric, 9–10, 117, 135, 144
Jaszi, Martha, 190
Jay, Martin, 40
Johns, Adrian, 87–89
Johnston, John, 83, 191
Joyce, Michael, 94
Joyrich, Lynne, 10–11
Judaken, Jonathan, 194

Keep, C. J., 135
Kiesler, Sara, 196

King, Rodney, 74
Kirshenblatt-Gimblett, Barbara, 168
Kluge, Alexander, 179–80, 195
Knight, Graham, 193
Kollock, Peter, 57
Krapp, Peter, 193
Kutler, Friedrich, 82–85, 191

Lacan, Jacques, 157
Laclau, Ernesto, 145, 174, 193–94
Lacoue-Labarthe, Philippe, 173
Landes, Joan, 195
Landow, George, 94
Lang, Michael, 194
Lanham, Richard, 94
Lanier, Jaron, 130
Laurel, Brenda, 37
Lenk, Klaus, 105
Levinson, Paul, 191
Lévy, Pierre, 18, 26–27, 126, 164, 169, 195
Liebeskind, Daniel, 99
Lott, Eric, 194
Lovink, Geert, 155–56, 194
Lowe, Lisa, 148–49, 193
Lury, Celia, 86, 90
Luther, Martin, 17
Lyon, David, 195
Lyotard, Jean-François, 9–10, 179

Madonna, 135
Maffésoli, Michel, 161–63
Malkki, Liisa, 2
Manovich, Lev, 193
Markley, Robert, 55–56
Marvin, Carolyn, 192
Marx, Karl, 17, 49–50, 66, 78, 116, 124, 134, 139, 143, 181
Masten, Jeffrey, 191
Mattson, Andrew, 192
Maverick, Augustus, 151
McCabe, Heather, 189
McClintock, Anne, 71
McGuire, Timothy, 196
McLuhan, Marshall, 23–24, 91, 116, 126, 136, 151, 161–63, 191
McRobbie, Angela, 4
McVeigh, Timothy, 105
Metter, Michael, 191

Meyrowitz, Joshua, 141
Miller, Greg, 45, 190
Miller, J. Hillis, 194
Miller, Nancy, 70
Mitchell, Timothy, 116
Mitchell, William, 98–99
Monmaney, Terence, 101
Morely, David, 104
Morse, Margaret, 4
Moss, Mitchell, 102
Moulthrop, Stuart, 94
Mowshowitz, Abbe, 102, 192
Murray, Janet, 94

Nancy, Jean-Luc, 173
Nakamura, Lisa, 194, 196
Nass, Clifford, 11
Negroponte, Nicholas, 192
Negt, Oskar, 179–80, 195
Nelson, Carey, 194
Nichols, David, 196
Nietzsche, Friedrich, 5, 13, 66, 87, 144–45, 152
Noble, David, 41, 60–61
Nora, Pierre, 158–62, 166–67
Nunes, Mark, 132

Okrent, Daniel, 110
Ong, Walter, 191

Pareles, Jon, 48
Pascal, Blaise, 22
Pavic, Milorad, 94
Pease, Donald, 190
Peraino, Vito, 52
Perot, Ross, 192
Perrolle, Judith, 182
Philips, Chuck, 52
Plant, Sadie, 195
Polly, Jean Armour, 175
Pomfret, John, 112
Porush, David, 81
Poster, Mark, 133, 194
Postman, Neil, 14
Quinby, Lee, 71, 190

Rajchman, John, 193
Rancière, Jacques, 194

Reagan, Ronald, 1
Reeves, Byron, 11
Reid, Elizabeth, 195–96
Renan, Ernest, 192
Ricardo, David, 181
Robbins, Bruce, 103
Robins, Kevin, 104
Robertson, Pat, 131
Rorty, Richard, 40
Rose, Mark, 65, 191
Rosenberg, Joel, 194
Rosenzweig, Roy, 95
Ross, Kristin, 192
Rouse, Roger, 103, 194
Rutsky, R. L., 189
Ryan, Marie-Laure, 94, 136–37, 195

Saco, Diana, 193
Samuelson, Pamela, 62, 94
Sassen, Saskia, 120
Schiffman, Zachary, 5
Schiller, Dan, 56
Schöpf, Christine, 190
Schwartz, Hillel, 190
Scott, Joan, 194
Serpentelli, Jill, 195
Shakespeare, William, 142
Shelley, Mary, 94
Siegel, Jane, 196
Silberman, Steve, 91
Smiley, Jane, 191
Snider, Mike, 63
Stalder, Felix, 189
Stallabrass, Julian, 131
Stallybrass, Peter, 191
Stern, Lawrence, 99
Stivale, Charles, 196
Stocker, Gerfried, 190
Stoler, Ann Laura, 71
Stone, Sandy, 60, 74, 99
Streeter, Thomas, 62

Tapscott, Don, 41–43
Taylor, Irene, 191

Taylor, Jon, 192
Teilhard de Chardin, Pierre, 126, 150, 169
Thatcher, Margaret, 155
Thibaut, Claude, 113
Thompson, John, 192
Tocqueville, Alexis de, 119, 192
Todorov, Tzvetan, 81
Tomlinson, John, 104
Torvald, Linux, 50
Trollope, Anthony, 194
Turkle, Sherry, 12, 189

Valenti, Jack, 63
Van Gelder, Lindsy, 185
Vankin, Jonathan, 52
Vickers, Nancy, 191
Virilio, Paul, 23–26, 113–15, 161, 178, 182, 194

Wagner, Richard, 143
Wakeford, Nina, 195
Waldstreicher, David, 192
Wallace, Amy, 53
Walters, Suzanna, 191
Ward, Todd, 191
Warhol, Andy, 124, 135
Warner, Michael, 123, 125, 194
Weber, Samuel, 189, 193–94
Weiss, Kenneth, 60
Wiegman, Robyn, 192
Wiener, Norbert, 35
Wilden, Anthony, 191
Williams, Linda, 194
Woodmansee, Peter, 190
Woodward, Kathryn, 193

Yúdice, George, 49

Zack, Ian, 60
Zimmerman, Michael, 189
Žižek, Slavoj, 155–58
Zuboff, Shoshana, 22

Mark Poster holds appointments in the history department and the film studies program at the University of California, Irvine. His most recent book is *Cultural History and Postmodernity.*